The Culture of Criticism
and
the Criticism of Culture

ALSO BY GILES GUNN

F. O. Matthiessen: The Critical Achievement

The Interpretation of Otherness:
Literature, Religion, and the American Imagination

EDITOR

Literature and Religion

Henry James, Senior: A Selection of His Writings

New World Metaphysics:
Readings on the Religious Meaning of the American Experience

The Bible and American Arts and Letters

Church, State, and American Culture

The Culture of Criticism

and

the Criticism of Culture

GILES GUNN

New York   Oxford
OXFORD UNIVERSITY PRESS
1987

Oxford University Press

Oxford New York Toronto
Delhi Bombay Calcutta Madras Karachi
Petaling Jaya Singapore Hong Kong Tokyo
Nairobi Dar es Salaam Cape Town
Melbourne Auckland

and associated companies in
Beirut Berlin Ibadan Nicosia

Copyright © 1987 by Oxford University Press, Inc.

Published by Oxford University Press, Inc.,
200 Madison Avenue, New York, New York 10016

Oxford is a registered trademark of Oxford University Press

Library of Congress Cataloging-in-Publication Data
Gunn, Giles.
The culture of criticism and the criticism of culture.
Includes index.
1. United States—Intellectual life—20th century.
2. Criticism—United States. I. Title.
E169.12.G86 1987   306'.4'0973   86-12365
ISBN 0-19-504161-5 (alk. paper)

9 8 7 6 5 4 3 2 1

Printed in the United States of America
on acid-free paper

For Deborah

[Philosophy ought] to trust rather to the multitude and variety of its arguments than to the conclusiveness of any one. Its reasoning should not form a chain which is no stronger than its weakest link, but a cable whose fibers may be ever so slender, provided they are sufficiently numerous and intimately connected.

CHARLES SANDERS PEIRCE
Collected Papers 5.264

Preface

This book is principally concerned with an issue that cuts across all the disciplines in what the French call "the human sciences" and has insinuated itself into all the cultures of modern and contemporary critical inquiry. This issue is the place and purpose of moral reflection in the analysis and interpretation of discursive, indeed, of all symbolic, forms. The question now being asked is not whether discrimination or judgment remains the goal of critical inquiry, but whether valuational procedures belong in critical discourse at all.

Lest my interest in this issue be mistaken as merely another moral call to arms, let me hasten to add that I am not urging a restoration of ethical standards in criticism, much less, as George Steiner has proposed in his recent Leslie Stephen Memorial Lecture,[1] a recovery of the conception of transcendence on which they were formerly based. Transcendence is no doubt a very fine thing, but the traditional imagi-

1. A partial text of this lecture has been published by George Steiner under the title "Viewpoint: A New Meaning of Meaning" in *Times Literary Supplement,* November 8, 1985, pp. 1262, 1275–76.

nation of it has been theologically as well as culturally intenable for at least several centuries. The severity of the current intellectual crisis is not due to the breakdown of conventional moral prescriptions and interdictions, much less to forgetfulness of the sacred. It derives rather from the collapse of so many inherited procedures of ethical reflection and assessment and the suspicion that the habits of mind historically preoccupied with questions of sacrality, with questions of metaphysical ultimacy or ontological primacy, are largely to blame. The problem, in other words, is not apostasy or indifference but disbelief. By disbelief I mean that the conventional philosophical and religious justifications for moral reasoning in critical thought have been rendered incredible during the last several decades, and by nothing so much as the disingenuousness with which they have been culturally institutionalized in forms that strike many Western intellectuals as but subterfuges for the expression of various kinds of social, cultural, political, and even religious privilege.

Evidence of this crisis of disbelief can be found everywhere. Negative evidence can be discerned in the increasingly shrill and bitter tone adopted by most advocates of what might be called the argument for moral teleology in critical discourse, people who couple their defense of traditional standards and strategies with strong, though often masked, appeals for the protection of conventional disciplines and their hierarchical distinctions and divisions. Positive evidence is reflected in the new permeability of the conventional disciplines themselves: the lines that formerly separated and compartmentalized species of intellectual inquiry are now rapidly dissolving, and critical methods are in many fields of study becoming more heterodox and syncretistic without sacrificing refinement or precision. Still more positive evidence of this crisis can be found, particularly in the United States, in the new willingness to take critical theory seriously and to construe its aim less as the development of conceptual formulations that will provide us with more secure methodological closure than as the discovery and delineation of avenues of intellectual inquiry that will make possible further, and more discriminating, thought.

In the face of this crisis of disbelief, which has challenged so many of our traditional moral senses as well as our traditional ways of making sense morally, it is my conviction that the only way to revive the possibility of moral reflection in critical inquiry is by reconceiving it. However, I do not think we can reconceive this kind of reflection until we are in a better position to comprehend the operative assumptions, ontological as well as aesthetic, of that mode of discourse in which the imagination of moral concerns has been kept most effectively alive in modern culture, especially in modern American culture. I refer in this case to the genre of cultural criticism that ever since the days of Emerson, Thoreau, and Melville has been, as Alfred Kazin says somewhere, "the great American lay philosophy, the intellectual conscience and intellectual carry-all." Going all the way back to the tradition that Sacvan Bercovitch, echoing Perry Miller, has defined as "the American jeremiad," cultural criticism has been produced in America by everyone from theologians like Reinhold Niebuhr (*The Irony of American History*), public philosophers like Walter Lippmann (*A Preface to Politics*), and sociologists like David Riesman (*The Lonely Crowd*) and Philip Rieff (*The Triumph of the Therapeutic*) to art historians like Harold Rosenberg (*The Tradition of the New*), social and cultural historians like Richard Hofstadter (*Anti-Intellectualism in American Life*) and Christopher Lasch (*The Culture of Narcissicism*), and literary critics like Kazin himself (*On Native Grounds*). For this reason, cultural criticism cannot be exclusively identified with any particular field of intellectual endeavor or restricted to a single methodological orientation. But if this kind of criticism resists definition in narrow disciplinary terms, it can still be defined in loosely intellectual terms. Lionel Trilling probably came closest to describing the frame of mind it exhibits when he once referred to his own disposition "to see literary situations as cultural situations and cultural situations as great elaborate fights about moral issues, and moral issues as having something to do with gratuitously chosen images of personal being."[2] All one would have to do is translate "literary situations" into "religious situations" or "political situations" or "social situations" or "cultural situations" or "intellectual situations" to achieve a perfectly satisfactory description of the above-mentioned books by Niebuhr, Lippmann, Riesman, Rieff, or Hofstadter, respectively.

But the legitimacy of this frame of mind has now come under severe intellectual attack from within the precincts of cultural criticism itself, and most effectively from intellectuals who suspect this critical disposition of sponsoring a subtle but irresistible form of ideological prejudice. Believing, with Nelson Goodman, that we never encounter reality "except under a given description," these intellectuals maintain that

---

2. Lionel Trilling, *Beyond Culture, Essays on Literature and Learning* (New York: The Viking Press, 1965), p. 13.

all descriptions tend to be biased in favor of the one who employs them and that all such biases subvert the purposes of discourse to their own ends.[3] While such an observation may be less than wholly original in the history of, as it were, "reflection about reflection," it has never been developed so extensively, or substantiated so rigorously, as it has in the last several decades. Indeed, so exhaustive and incriminating has this substantiation been that it has called into question the very premises of critical inquiry itself. Therefore, though my own investigation of this crisis of belief begins with the ideological history of the term *culture,* particularly in relation to its historical associations with the correlary term *criticism,* and then looks, in three successive chapters (chapters 2, 3, and 4), at the genre of modern American cultural criticism itself, I then extend the investigation by examining aspects of this crisis, and possibilities for its resolution, in areas of critical discourse as diverse as cultural anthropology (chapter 5) and the theory of the humanities (chapter 6), the American Studies movement (chapter 7) and recent literary theory (chapter 8).

I wish to make clear that I have been drawn to these other forms of intellectual inquiry because of the possibilities they also hold out, in their respective ways, for developing a kind of cultural criticism, and that much of their interest and authority for me derives from their ability, again different in each case, to resist, or to formulate strategies for resisting, modes of thought that are susceptible to hypostatization or essentialization. Yet these forms of critical inquiry often accomplish this task, when they accomplish it at all, only at the expense of suppressing the implications their critique possesses for their own methods, or, contrariwise, of evading the complicity of their own methods in their critique. Either way, the challenge they have posed for me, as a cultural critic in my own right, is whether it is possible to subject their work to the same kind of moral pressure they bring to bear upon the work of others, and the great liability in such an undertaking is always the same: the temptation, as an extremely acute anonymous reader at Oxford University Press put it in response to an earlier version of this manuscript, to use an epistemology for interpreting such work that is at odds with the axiological standards employed to assess them.

In the interests of consistency as well as candor, I should admit that

3. Nelson Goodman, quoted in Richard Rorty, *Consequences of Pragmatism* (Minneapolis: Univ. of Minnesota Press, 1982), p. xxxix.

my own hermeneutics and heuristics, if these two terms don't make too awkward a combination, grow out of, and attempt to extend, the legacy of American pragmatism. I am fully aware that this may strike some of my readers as open to dispute. There are various contemporary proponents of pragmatism within the ranks of critical theory who, like many of its former detractors, do not believe that pragmatism, in either its Jamesian or its Deweyan variants, can provide us with any standards for judgment, or with any instruments for knowing, that are less privileged or ideologically colored than those represented by any other philosophical system. Indeed, many of these same theorists hold that pragmatism's chief contribution has been to destroy, once and for all, the illusion that there are any intellectual positions without interest, any theories without prejudice. In short, they maintain that pragmatism has forced us to reformulate the questions we put to culture.

Though I share this last opinion, I do not think that pragmatism entails an abandonment of questioning as such. If all our questions are self-interested, this does not mean that every process of questioning is simply circular and self-centered and finally solipsistic. While all the questions we put to culture, like the answers we are prepared to accept, may carry with them an inevitable prejudice, both epistemological and moral, in our own favor, there may nonetheless be real (i.e., measurable) differences between conceptions of what constitutes our, or anyone else's, best interests. Moreover, there are better and worse methods for persuading people of the difference. Even if pragmatism amounts in the end to no more than a theory of such differences and of the suasive tactics that help disclose them, it still constitutes, as I hope to show in due course, a genuine intellectual and methodological alternative to all of the ethically, epistemologically, and politically more cynical options in contemporary critical inquiry.

My initial interest in attempting to extend the pragmatic legacy into various territories of intellectual culture where it had been noticeably absent grew out of J. Hillis Miller's very helpful review of my last book, *The Interpretation of Otherness*. Miller pointed out that, in attempting to revive the category of experience as a datum of critical as well as literary reflection, I was running the risk of slighting the other major conceptual category in current theoretical discussion, namely, language. As it happens, this is a risk I was prepared to accept. What I was not prepared to accept, or, rather, appreciate, was the strength of my own biases or predilections in favor of experience as opposed to language. Miller's review not only made me aware of this bias but also encouraged me to try to defend it. This book is the belated result, though one that has been altered immeasurably, first, by a more serious exposure to the claims and, most important, the critiques of the "critics of language" from Derrida to de Man, and, second, by extensive reading in the "critics of experience" from Bakhtin to Rorty. Given its genesis and the substance of its arguments about the nature of culture and cultural criticism, I can only hope that in form this book more closely resembles a discussion than a disquisition, or at least constitutes a response rather than a rationalization; at every point it has been written with a conversation in mind.

It should come as no surprise that I have learned at least as much from those to whose ideas I have taken exception as from those with whose thinking I have found myself in general agreement. Their work, at what I hope is minimal cost to its own integrity of meaning, has provided a constant stimulus and challenge to my own reflections and has vastly extended them. This is as it should be if culture is really conversational, if criticism is actually dialogical; but it is one thing to profess such a theory, quite another to practice it. In any event, I have, in addition, received generous encouragement and constructive criticism from a number of individuals, only the most conspicuous of whom I can thank here but none of whom bear responsibility for deficiencies in my book. Chief among them are J. Hillis Miller, Leo Marx, Alfred Kazin, Alan Trachtenberg, R. W. B. Lewis, John Seelye, Joy and John Kasson, Peter Ivor Kaufman, Grant Wacker, Ruel Tyson, Charles Houston Long, Nathan A. Scott, Jr., Alan B. Anderson, Roland Delattre, Donald Mathews, Henry Samuel Levinson, John McDermott, Clifford Geertz, Hayden White, Barbara Herrnstein Smith, Gerald Graff, Thomas Finn, James Livingston, Scott Donaldson, Bertram and Anne Wyatt-Brown, Gregory Ulmer, Robert Darnton, Mark Rose, Paul Hernadi, Richard Comstock, Porter Abbott, Adam B. Gunn, the members of three seminars I have directed for the National Endowment for the Humanities in the summers of 1979, 1981, and 1984, and, above all, my wife, Deborah Rose Sills, to whom this book is lovingly dedicated, and without whose belief and support it would never have been written.

This book first began to take shape when I was asked to deliver the William R. Kenan lectures at the College of William and Mary in the winter of 1983, the substance of which comprised a much abbreviated and cruder version of chapters 2, 3, and 4, but portions have been delivered as parts of lectures at a variety of universities and colleges where my ideas invariably received thoughtful and considerate reception. These institutions include the University of North Carolina at Chapel Hill, Syracuse University, the University of Colorado at Boulder, King's College, Concordia College in Minnesota, the University of California at Santa Barbara, Central Missouri State University, Loma Linda University, West Virginia University, Texas A&M University, and Virginia Commonwealth University.

Portions of chapters 2, 3, and 4 originally appeared in the *Journal of the American Academy of Religion* and were also published in proceedings of a conference on Modern American Cultural Criticism by Central Missouri State University. Portions of chapter 5 were published in *Studies in Literature* and then reprinted in *American Critics at Work,* ed. Victor A. Kramer, by the Whitson Publishing Company. Portions of chapter 6 appeared in the *William and Mary Magazine* as well as the *Journal of the American Academy of Religion.* Portions of chapter 7 appeared in the *Yale Review.* Portions of chapter 8 were published by the Modern Language Association in Interrelations of Literature, ed. Jean-Pierre Barricelli and Joseph Bibaldi. While all of this material has been extensively revised or expanded, grateful acknowledgement is made to these editors, journals, and publications for permisssion to reprint it here.

I also wish to thank my editor at Oxford University Press, William Sisler, for his generous support of this project and shrewd criticisms. Ms. Susan Meigs and Ms. Linda Robbins skillfully steered this manuscript through production at Oxford; Ms. Karen Salsgiver deserves my thanks for her work on the design of the jacket.

Santa Barbara, California   G.G.
April 1986

Contents

I

Irregular Metaphysics

and

the Criticism of Culture

1

Introduction

There is a good deal of talk nowadays about something called cultural criticism. In 1962 or thereabouts Alfred Kazin defined it as a kind of

> *histoire morale,* that sums up the spirit of the age in which we live and then asks us to transcend it, that enables us to see things in the grand perspective, and that, in the way of Marx on Greek philosophy, of Kierkegaard on Mozart, of Nietzsche on the birth of tragedy, of Shaw on Ibsen, of Lawrence on American literature, asks us—in the light not only of man's history but of his whole striving—to create a future in keeping with man's imagination.[1]

Kazin then went on to declare that the "greatest single attribute" of this criticism "is its force, its passionate declaration of the true nature of man and what his proper destiny must be."[2] According to this construction, cultural criticism is no mere complement or supplement to other, more established disciplines of inquiry, but the foundation for that general revaluation and transvaluation "of established values which must go on in every age."[3] Approximately twenty years later, the philosopher Richard Rorty finds himself obliged to describe cultural criticism rather differently, as the discourse of a culture that must not only seek its reasons for being within itself but has now lost faith in all those disciplines of the mind by which, traditionally, such reasons could be authoritatively established.

The disparity between these two views is clearly dramatic—and in much of this book I will be attempting to determine what difference it makes—but in certain respects it is as much a matter of tone and perspective as of conception. Kazin and Rorty both approach cultural criticism in the guise of Emerson's American Scholar, but each appeals to a different side of that image. Kazin evokes a sense of its heroic aspect, of the Scholar as Man Thinking, as a figure for whom the content of thought is inextricably related to the processes by which it is discovered and secured and the energies that are released along the way. The thinker, the intellectual, or the critic is one whose ideas not only mean but, more important, are. Neither the mind nor its realizations can be dissociated from the act of experiencing them, which only serves to demonstrate the seamlessness of thought and action, the integrity of being itself.

Rorty recalls instead the more nostalgic, or at least poignant, side of the Emersonian image, of the American Scholar as Man Seeking, as a figure in search not of truth so much as of a vocation in which to pursue it, or, rather, to pursue whatever has taken its place now that he has defined his former vocation out of existence. Just as Emerson deprived himself of the possibility of remaining a theologian when he announced the arrival of post-Christian culture, so Rorty has deprived himself of the possibility of remaining a metaphysician in the classic Emersonian mold by trumpeting the arrival of what he calls postphilosophical culture. When the American Scholar, or any of his or her other modern intellectual avatars, can no longer be conceived as a kind of cultural metaphysician whose "job of work" is to display and, where necessary or possible, to defend the architectonics of contemporary experience, then on Rorty's reading he or she becomes a kind of cultural critic whose responsibility is to compare and contrast the way other people have said things hang together. Criticism in such a postphilosophical culture becomes at most, as Hegel insisted, the attempt to comprehend its own time in thought, at minimum an effort to figure out, as Robert Frost says of life in "The Oven Bird," "what to make of a diminished thing."

The elegiac mood in all of this, professions to the contrary notwithstanding, is unmistakable, and perhaps, given the subject matter, unavoidable. Philosophy become criticism, like criticism become philosophical, is a precarious and marginal enterprise in the world of multinational corporate capitalism, and the sense of reduced function, of constricted and weakened focus, that pervades Rorty's writing and that of so many other recent "critics of criticism," in contrast with Kazin's, no doubt does accurately reflect the temper of our own time in thought. Ours is not an age of intellectual self-confidence, and among the intellect's modern functions, the criticism of culture is scarcely regarded as one of its most indispensable. That this was not always the case, that as recently as a century ago, in the writings of Thomas Carlyle and Matthew Arnold no less than in those of Emerson or Whitman or William James, cultural criticism assumed the responsibilities once delegated to theology and then to philosophical ethics, to keep alive a sense of the normative and its bearing upon beliefs and practices no longer felt to derive their legitimacy from traditional religious sources—this is nothing to the point. As a discipline devised specifically to determine the meaning and significance of those portions of modern experience that exert an appeal that is independent of conventional religious authority and is assumed to remain free of the sway of its scrutiny, cultural criticism is itself in need of legitimation both for its defenders and detractors alike.

Versions of this history have been written many times in the last decade—by Rorty himself, by Hayden White, by Geoffrey Hartman, and, most recently, by Terry Eagleton in his accounts of the rise of English studies in *Literary Theory*—but virtually all have been told from the perspective of a critical discourse struggling to be cultural rather than that of a cultural discourse aspiring to be critical. Indeed, if one consults a standard work like René Wellek's six-volume *History of Modern Criticism*, one will not even find mention of the work *culture*, let alone any reference to the term *cultural criticism*, until his fourth volume on the late Romantic age. But this omission is not so much incidental as endemic. Conceptions of culture rarely figure in most histories of criticism, although every theory of criticism is implicitly a theory of culture, and modern criticism, as we generally think of it, is not simply one of the products of modern culture, but, equally important, one of its most characteristic practices. Thus to understand the governance of the term *criticism*, it is necessary to determine something of the provenance of the term *culture*. And to comprehend *culture* in its relationship to *criticism* is to fathom at least one dimension of the meaning of the term *modern*.

1

The word *culture*, like the word *criticism*, has a complex history. Part of this complexity is a result of its association with other words, such as *aesthetics, taste, cultivation, discrimination, sensibility,* and *humanity.* Another part derives from its ill-appreciated connection with such major social developments as the Industrial Revolution and the rise of democracy, which brought an alteration not only in the social formations we call classes but also in the status of a practice that differentiated the higher classes from all those below them—namely, art. The term *culture,* in fact, evolved in large measure as a response to these situations, rather than emerging as a simple product of them, and cannot be understood apart from the way it functioned in some instances to contain their influence, in others to extend it, in still others to convert it, and in all instances to comprehend it.

From the beginning, culture has always been associated with processes of nurture. Deriving from the Latin word *cultura* (from the root *colere,* "to protect, cultivate, inhabit, or honor with worship,") the earliest uses of culture always linked it to natural processes of tending and preservation. But by the early sixteenth century, cultural processes of natural preservation had been extended to human nurture, and before long were transferred from the particular domain of individual experience to the more abstract level of general or collective experience. Although it is extremely difficult to pinpoint just when these developments occurred, or when, still later, culture was further associated not only with a specific process but also with its more abstract product or result, it is not difficult to specify the thinker in whom they first became conscious. That individual was Giambattista Vico, whose contribution to the theory of culture actually came by way of his preoccupation with the category of history.

In his *New Science,* published in 1724, Vico thought he had discovered a method for describing and even predicting the recurrent cycles of history as accurately as the physical sciences of his day could account for the regularities and rhythms of nature. Michelet, Vico's great discoverer at the beginning of the nineteenth century, believed instead that he had anticipated the democratic and populist revolution of Michelet's own age by defending the principle that man is the maker of his own destiny and must wrest from nature the means to create a human world. A century and a half later Isaiah Berlin, one of Vico's most eloquent modern interpreters, insists yet again that Vico's originality lay in his discovery that change is the essential attribute of human experience, since change not only stamps man's nature but marks all of man's continuing attempts to understand himself in relation to his world. All of which may only attest the fact that if Vico's theory of culture was imbedded from the outset in ideological assumptions, so it has remained in each attempt to repossess it.

The irony is that Vico would have been the first to understand this process of ideological coloring. Believing that human beings continuously transform themselves and their world in their quest for understanding, he was also potentially in a position to appreciate that everything human beings create reflects their self-interest in shaping the social definition of their world to meet their needs. But Vico didn't put it this way. He asserted instead that the social world we know historically is to be differentiated from the natural world we know scientifically because of its possession of a common style, or way of perceiving and valuing things, that is reflected in all the activities and actualities that make it up. Indeed, this idea of a common style, as Isaiah Berlin has noted, is "tantamount" to Vico's concept of culture,[4] but it was complicated by Vico's recognition that the study of history discloses the existence of many more cultures than one and that the historical understanding of any society or culture necessarily requires comprehension of its successive phases of development and of the relations among their various components. In addition, Vico held that the most revealing expressions of any people's self-understanding are to be found in the actual practices of its cultural perception, such as art, religion, morality, law, language, and so forth, but only when they are interpreted in relation to the standards apropriate to their own time and place. Interpreting them thus required what Vico thought of as a new kind of imagination or insight and yielded a new kind of knowledge:

> This type of knowledge is yielded by "entering" into the mental life of other cultures, into a variety of outlooks and ways of life which only the activity of *fantasia*—imagination—makes possible. *Fantasia* is for Vico a way of conceiving the process of social change and growth by correlating it with, indeed, viewing it as conveyed by, the parallel change or development of the symbolism by which men seek to express it; since the symbolic structures are themselves part and parcel of the reality which they symbolize, and alter with it. This method of discovery which begins with understanding the means of expression, and seeks to reach the vision of reality which they presuppose and articulate, is a kind of transcendental deduction (in the Kantian sense) of historical truth. It is not, as hitherto, a method of arriving at an unchanging reality via its changing appearances but at a changing reality—men's history—through its systematically changing modes of expression.[5]

Vico's achievement was staggering. Not only did he conceptualize culture as a historically distinct mode of being or form of life, he developed a new method for studying it and defined the distinctive kind of knowledge it would produce. Yet it would be more than a century before his ideas were heeded by Victor Cousins and then passed on to Michelet, and not until the middle of the nineteenth century that Jacob Burckhardt would develop a theory of culture and an equally sophisticated method for studying it. In the meantime, however, the concept of culture was to undergo various corollary and sometimes contradictory developments as a result of its increasing associations with such related concepts as "cultivation" and "taste," which brought with them, as a kind of secondary result, the tendency to identify culture with some social classes and to dissociate it completely from others.

2

These developments were hastened by the conjoining of the term *culture* with the term *civilization,* which in the course of time was to secure an ideological bond between the notion of culture as an achieved condition and the rather different views of culture as either the process of evolution toward such a condition or the standards represented by it. Once this bond was forged, the concept of culture could become wholly politicized, though such was far from the intentions of Johann Gottfried Herder, who, in calling it by another name, merely hoped to extend and complete the conception of culture originally sketched out by Vico.

Herder's notion of civilization was developed in reaction to the philosophes' conception of culture. The philosophes viewed culture as the opposite of barbarism. As contrasted with barbarism and the related conditions of savagery and primitivism, culture constituted for the Enlightenment not only an achieved condition but also a standard of refinement that members of the age were more than willing to use as a measure for all civilizational forms. Herder found the arrogance and historical bias of this practice intolerable and proposed his concept of civilization as an alternative. By civilization he meant essentially a way of life rather than a standard or a process, and one that is commonly found among all peoples even though it is individually expressed by each. Herder therefore conceived of civilization as pluralistic rather than monolithic. Almost more important, he located its source of unity in currents of vernacular experience rather than of cultivated excellence, and claimed that poets and other artists are its truest spokesmen.

Herder's aim was in large part to undermine the Enlightenment view that culture merely represents the culminating stage of a long history of intellectual achievement that reached its apogee in the eighteenth century, but even if he succeeded in challenging one kind of prejudice, he managed to encourage another. His notion of civilization was clearly influenced by Lessing's discussion about the possibility of a national cultural consciousness, and by the time Herder's ideas had been reinterpreted in Fichte's *Addresses to the German Nation* to defend the privileged relation between the collective mind of a people and their mother tongue, Herder's concept of civilization was well on its way to becoming converted into the new gospel of cultural nationalism. Suddenly the term *civilization* had become not only ideological but chauvinistic. And if language was the instrument and cultural uniqueness the claim, political imperialism was the later-nineteenth-century result.[6]

Needless to say, such consequences could scarcely have occurred to those Romantic writers and thinkers to whom Herder's ideas made their initial appeal and who employed his ideas in a variety of ways: in some instances to defend the importance of national or traditional cultures; in others to attack what was mechanical and alienating in the new industrial order then emerging on the Continent and elsewhere; in yet others to distinguish the spiritual from the material, the human from the inhuman. The Romantics used the term *culture* as a weapon in the cause of social and political change; the Victorians turned it into an emblem of social and political reaction. Much of the complexity the term acquired in the nineteenth century can be explained by the fact that it lent itself to appropriation by both the Left and the Right and inevitably acquired associations with each. A secondary reason is that when the terms *culture* and *civilization* were not being confused, they were being contrasted. Thus by the end of the century, even when the primary senses of the word could be differentiated, *culture* had indeed become highly politicized. Whether it referred to a general process of intellectual and aesthetic development, to the products and practices that sustain and enrich such a process, or, finally, to an entire way of life and thought centered in the experience of a people, a nation, or an age, the word had become a primary counter in one of the principal debates of the modern era. And it usually found itself paired with the term *civilization,* which, whether viewed as a synonym or as an antonym, was understood to have suffered a similar development in the course of its modern history, changing from the natural reference of "cultivation" to the social reference of "cultivated" to the spiritual reference of "civilized."

To Edmund Burke and other spokesmen of Enlightenment values, civilization was perceived as synonymous with culture and deemed an irremediable as well as indispensable good, like manners, which society exists both to fashion and to further.

> Without . . . civil society man could not by any possibility arrive at the perfection of which his nature is capable, nor even make a remote and faint approach to it. . . . He who gave our nature to be perfected by our virtue, willed also the necessary means of its perfection—He willed therefore the state—He willed its connexion with the source and original archetype of all perfection.[7]

But to the Romantics the civilization that Burke defended was too closely allied with a particular version of society they found repressive and stagnant, and the term they most often used to express their aversion and rebellion was *culture*. Coleridge defined the distinction quite precisely when he wrote in *On the Constitution of Church and State:*

> The permanency of the nation . . . and its progressiveness and personal freedom . . . depend on a continuing and progressive civilization. But civilization is itself but a mixed good, if not far more a corrupting influence, the hectic of disease, not the bloom of health, and a nation so distinguished more fitly to be called a varnished than a polished people, where this civilization is not grounded in cultivation, in the harmonious development of those qualities and faculties that characterize our humanity. We must be men in order to be citizens.[8]

Like other Romantics, Coleridge already viewed civilization as standing for a whole modern process and perceived culture as a social alternative. John Stuart Mill in his essay on Coleridge put the issue more sharply:

> Take for instance the question how far mankind have gained by civilization. One observer is forcibly struck by the multiplication of physical comforts; the advancement and diffusion of knowledge; the decay of superstition; the facilities of mutual intercourse; the softening of manners; the decline of war and personal conflict; the progressive limitation of the tyranny of the strong over the weak; the great works accomplished throughout the globe by the cooperation of multitudes. . . .[9]

But one could easily shift one's attention, as Mill noted, from "the value of these advantages" to "the high price which is paid for them":

> . . . the relaxation of individual energy and courage; the loss of proud and self-relying independence; the slavery of so large a portion of mankind to artificial wants; their effeminate shrinkage from even the shadow of pain; the dull unexciting monotony of their lives, and the passionless insipidity, and absence of any marked individuality, in their characters; the contrast between the narrow mechanical understanding, produced by a life spent in executing by fixed rules a fixed task, and the varied powers of the man of the woods, whose subsistence and safety depend at each instant upon his capacity of extemporarily adapting means to ends; the demoralizing effect of great inequalities in wealth and social rank; and the sufferings of the great mass of the people of civilized countries, whose arts are scarcely better provided for than those of the savage, while they are bound by a thousand fetters in lieu of the freedom and excitement which are his compensations.[10]

Mill thought, or seemed to think, he was here contrasting the virtues of civilization with its attendant vices, when, in point of fact, he was confusing things that belonged to different historical moments. If part of his criticism derives from the transition from an agrarian to an industrial economy and contrasts the freedom of the village laborer with the servitude of the industrial worker, another part refers to the preindustrial era and contrasts the civilized man with Rousseau's Noble Savage.[11] But this only demonstrates how completely the term *civilization* had already achieved social definition, whether as a normative process or a normative state—so normative, in fact, that an observer as astute as Mill could become confused about which values it represented and which it threatened. And if one consequence of its socialization was to permit it by turns to be coupled and contrasted with the term *culture,* another was to encourage culture or civilization to be differentiated into various spheres, the highest of which, it has been assumed since the eighteenth century, is the aesthetic or artistic, and the discourse about which has come to be called criticism.

This elevation of the artistic to a position of primacy within the civilized or the cultured, and the development of criticism as a discourse specifically designed to interpret the artistic, are features of modern cultural thought so fundamental that it is difficult to imagine how they might have been otherwise and essential to understand how they occurred. Much of what currently appears elitist, privatized, and intellectually eviscerated in the arts and overspecialized, socially marginal, and obsolescent in criticism resulted from the fateful alliance of the public discourses of criticism with the privileged strategies of the aesthetic and from the new valorization of the aesthetic as the quintessence of the civilized.

3

These developments occurred in response to broad social dislocations in eighteenth-century Europe. Chief among them was the emergence of a new social class buoyed up by the expansion of wealth and now endowed with enough leisure to begin imitating some activities of the wellborn or aristocratic. One of those activities, rendered more accessible by the expansion and democratization of the marketplace, was the appreciation and cultivation of the arts, from music and painting to poetry, statuary, sculpture, landscape architecture, interior decoration, and theater. And as the audiences and the appetites for such things grew, so did the feeling that, despite their more obvious differences, they must share certain elements to qualify for the same kind of appreciation, to serve as essentially the same source of enjoyment. Nor was it inconsequential that the enjoyment of these things—some of which were fast becoming consumer objects in a market of commodities, others of which were literally being consumed by avid collectors and connoisseurs—seemed to involve considerations far removed from the realm of the practical or the morally imperative. In the just appreciation of artworks, moral and utilitarian considerations could be suspended because these works seemed to draw on other sources of reflection and to lead away from active engagement toward a new kind of passive attention. And once this pleasurable attention had been likened to a kind of taste or appreciative savoring, new appetites were quickened to acquire this educated taste, and new needs were created to satisfy and define it. All of these interests come together by the beginning of the eighteenth century in Joseph Addison's *Spectator Papers,* and before the century was half over they had contributed to the development of a new science, which Alexander Baumgarten named in the title of his two-volume work *Aesthetica.*

The rise of aesthetics had an enormous impact on both the concept of culture and the career of what we now call critical discourse. For the former, as we shall see momentarily, it not only idealized a whole set of activities and objects within culture associated with artistic creation but also established a new hierarchy of value for appreciating them and things like them. For the latter, it established an alliance between artistic appreciation and intellectual judgment that has been all but unbreakable in the Western tradition from the eighteenth century to the present.

Two notable exceptions are the model of criticism developed recently in France under the inspiration of Friedrich Nietzsche, which can be associated most directly with the work of Michel Foucault, and the model developed earlier in the twentieth century by the American pragmatists, which can be associated with the later writings of William James and John Dewey. In both instances, criticism remains a critique of prejudices that have been institutionalized through discourse and as often institutionalized in discourse. These prejudices inscribed within language and hypostatized through language can only be overcome by critical strategies that, far from pretending to be free of ideological prejudice, actively seek to engage it. To be sure, their respective strategies of engagement, not to mention their individual success in accomplishing it, vary considerably, and, in any event, need not occupy us here, since they will be discussed at length in subsequent chapters; suffice it to say, the two theoretical strategies I have mentioned share a view that every form of criticism, like every form of discourse, is a social practice that can only be comprehended satisfactorily in terms of its effects—effects that are cultural insofar as they extend or refine or revise, however slightly, the symbolic formations in which they are embedded and from which they proceed; political insofar as they alter, challenge, or at least influence, however subtly, the structures of relations, both material and social, that surround and support them. Criticism, which even in its earliest usage had been associated with general social faultfinding and later, by the middle of the seventeenth century, was extended to all acts of cultural judgment, then took a curious and fateful turn when it developed its more selective filiations with the notions of "taste" and "discrimination."

The key to this new development, as I have already said, was the emergence of a new science, or discipline as we might be more tempted to call it, concerned with the study and appreciation of beauty. But if the new preoccupation with beauty and its appropriate valuation was more of a discipline than a science, it was more of a general social practice than either, since it both expressed and fulfilled the needs of an emergent social class by formalizing, really institutionalizing, a new way of interrogating and assessing certain kinds of cultural objects that had already become integral to its own self-conception and self-esteem. The result was more than a contraction of the scope of criticism; what was wrought was a decisive conversion of its purpose. These social developments not only contrived to reduce the focus of the word *criticism,* in most of its usages, to the analysis of things of beauty, and preeminently to works of art, but also succeeded, by virtue of the way art was thus reconceived, in "aestheticizing" criticism itself by reducing the scope of its inquiry to a determination of what constitutes the beauty or perfection inherent in works of art and of how that beauty or perfection is to be justly appreciated. Yet this was, in turn, to discount or to dismiss a variety of other issues that critical inquiry might have explored: where these works come from, what they are a response to, what they both do and don't do to those for whom they have some meaning, and why. What, more precisely, the aestheticization of criticism left out of account was the whole range of questions bearing upon the effects of beauty, of the difference it makes in the circumstances of its social significance. But to see how this alliance between criticism and aesthetics occurred, an alliance that was ever after to restrict the scope even of a "cultural" as opposed to a "literary" criticism, we need to look more closely at the evolution of aesthetics itself.

4

The new theory of aesthetics—which simultaneously generated a complementary theory of critical discourse that was to sweep the whole field before it, or, rather, to subsume virtually every alternative theory of critical discourse within itself—developed, as M. H. Abrams has written, in two distinct but parallel directions.[12] In the first, the artist or creator is central; in the second, the artistic or aesthetic experience is central. Where the artist or maker is primary, the thing made becomes a reflection of the creative imagination itself, which is construed as an analogy of the divine act of creating the universe; this expressive act issues in the production of an artistic object which is best understood as a "secondary world," to use W. H. Auden's phrase, easily distinguishable from the world of nature because it operates according to laws intrinsic to itself and exists only to be itself. Where, on the other hand, primacy is given to the aesthetic experience, then the artistic object is as nothing compared to the special aptitude that is required to comprehend it and the special kind of judgment it demands to be fully appreciated.

Both of these divergent conceptions of the aesthetic transaction derive from contemporary theological and metaphysical notions that lend to the theories they influenced an inevitable and permanent religious coloration. According to the first view, as eventually developed by Baumgarten, the poet's creative act is conceived on the model of Leibniz's cosmogony, where God's creation of the universe exemplifies the laws of noncontradiction and "compossibility." The poet or artist, in other words, creates a "heterocosmic" world that is subject not to those criteria of truth or value that apply in the world of ordinary experience but only to the criteria of self-consistency and internal coherence. Hence the purpose of art is not mimesis or moral insight but the satisfaction of its own internal standards, which, when sensuously apprehended, amount to beauty. But beauty, as Karl Philipp Moritz stated in 1788, "has no need to be useful." Since every work of art is a microcosm, beauty

> needs no end, no purpose for its presence outside itself, but has its entire value, and the end of its existence in itself. . . . [The energy of the artist] creates for itself its own world, in which nothing isolated has a place, but everything is after its own fashion a self-sufficient whole."[13]

The second view of the aesthetic is controlled by ethical and religious norms that Shaftesbury and others had developed to combat contemporary theories inherited from Hobbes and his followers, theories that accentuated prudential calculations in moral life and crudely utilitarian considerations in religion. Against those who urged the love of God for reasons of self-interest, Shaftesbury and Hutcheson recommended what they called "the disinterested love of God" because of the intrinsic excellence of the object itself. But it was only a short step from applying the virtue of disinterestedness in matters of belief to applying it in matters pertaining to any other good or beauty. Indeed, as Abrams points out,

> the disinterested concern with God for His internal rather than instrumental excellence became the model for describing both the "moral sense" and artistic "taste"—that is, both the cultivated man's attitude to moral virtue or moral beauty, and the connoisseur's attitude to artistic virtue or sensuous beauty.[14]

These two traditions finally come together with Immanuel Kant. In the third *Critique*, beauty becomes identified with taste, and taste is dissociated both from moral and from practical concerns. Taste is defined as a faculty of judgment that operates "by means of a delight or aversion *apart from any interest*."[15] Kant called the object of that delight "beauty" in that it exists for the sake of revealing and realizing its own perfection in terms wholly divorced from judgments of truth or moral goodness. Beauty exists solely for contemplative enjoyment and can only be assessed critically and evaluated disinterestedly. Thus discourse about art becomes a discourse seemingly without interests, a discourse committed to the service of good taste, which it exercises by rendering judgments indifferent to every consideration other than the intrinsic excellence of the object.

In retrospect, one can only wish that Kant's formalism had not prejudiced him so strongly against the other potential object of aesthetic delight, namely, the sublime. In contrast with beauty, which "conveys a finality in its form making the object appear, as it were, preadapted to our power of judgment, so that it thus forms of itself an object of our delight," the sublime, Kant held, "may appear in point of form to contravene the ends of our power of judgment, to be ill-adapted to our faculty for imagining, and to be, as it were, an outrage on the imagination, yet . . . judged all the more sublime on that account."[16] Not only was the sublime an offense to the imagination—and to reason as well, since it simultaneously excites rational ideas that admit of no possibility for sensuous, formal representation—more to the point, it was an outrage against Kant's idea of an ordered and meaningful universe. The beauty found in nature—and the beauty associated with art had to conform with those conditions beauty exhibited in nature—revealed processes of a well-ordered system of laws whose principle was not to be found in the intellect of man but that nonetheless demonstrated the possibility of a "finality relative to the employment of judgment" in regard to phenomena encountered in the world of nature. Hence Kant could conclude that the concept of beauty "gives a veritable extension, not of course to our knowledge of objects of nature, but to our concept of nature itself. . . . " But in relation to the sublime, Kant insisted,

> there is such an absence of anything leading to particular objective principles and corresponding forms of nature, that it is rather in its chaos, or in its wildest and most irregular disorder and desolation, provided it gives signs of magnitude and power, that nature chiefly excites the ideas of the sublime."[17]

Kant was right in thinking that the notion of the sublime is called to mind by the very inadequacy of the intellect to conceive it sensuously, that it represents a form of affective apprehension beyond pleasure involving admiration and respect, perhaps, but never comprehension precisely because it transcends our categories for grasping it critically, but he drew the wrong conclusion from this. Seeing in the concept of the sublime no indication of what he took to be a sense of final purpose in nature but only an idea which confounds all categorical efforts to make sense rationally, he decided that the sublime is a deficient notion that refers merely to those incomprehensible, or at least rationally ungraspable, experiences that shatter all our natural models of order and evoke, as the only possible response to them, feelings of awe and wonder. Beauty was the preferable concept on which to base aesthetic inquiry because it refers to those objects of experience whose laws correspond on some deep level to the substratum of principles, of regulated order, underlying a rational, or rationally comprehensible, model of the universe. But there was a price to be paid for this choice. Not only would aesthetics subsequently confine itself to objects and experiences which generally if subtly confirm sense rather than confuse it; in Kant, and largely because of Kant, aesthetics was now in a position to become the new intellectual handmaiden of ontological essentialism, or rather its new philosophical guarantor, and the critical discourse it generated, so long as that discourse remained sufficiently "disinterested" and "objective," was strategically situated to take over much of the conversation that comprised, or at least controlled, culture as a whole.

5

We now know, of course, that the science of aesthetics and its attendant redefinition of criticism as judgment in the service of taste were no more "disinterested" than any other social development. Far from defining a sphere of experience that was free of interest, it defined a new field of experience in which interests of a very specific character—social, economic, religious, political, and moral—could express themselves. More to the point, it solidified deep-rooted historical connections between the strategies of criticism and the concerns of aesthetics that would affect much of the future discourse about culture in the West. From this point on, the dominant meaning of the word *criticism,* even *cultural criticism,* at least where art was tacitly assumed to represent the epitome of cultural experience, was to become a kind of discourse concerned principally with understanding the intrinsic qualities of any objects that can be construed as ends in themselves, rather than a discourse devoted to exploring why, for example, objects are sometimes so conceived, and how, when they are, they acquire the kind of power they do. Instead of asking what kinds of practice such objects presuppose or encourage, given the effects they have, criticism directed upon art, or upon any other facet of culture conceptualized as analogous to art, increasingly restricted itself to determining the kinds of formal elements needed to guarantee their integrity and autonomy and self-reflexivity, and the sorts of pleasure to be derived from such qualities.

There were, of course, exceptions even in the nineteenth century. Charles Augustin Sainte-Beuve, Hippolyte Taine, and Vassarion Belinsky, among others, continued to share the view, first popularized by Madame de Staël, that the central business of criticism is to understand the influences of life upon literature and of literature and the other arts upon life. But the main branch of modern criticism took an opposing direction, toward the view first expressed definitively by Paul Valéry and later canonized by T. S. Eliot, that criticism lives, or should live, in the service of art, and that art exists either to create a realm of experience that is indifferent to life, as one side of modernism supposes, or to create a realm of experience that is a substitute for life, as another side contends.

Within modernism itself, the chief opposition to this dominant view of criticism, even cultural criticism, has come primarily from those writers and thinkers who believe criticism represents a mode of discourse that should be subservient to nothing but its own responsibility to remain culturally self-conscious, which is to say, self-conscious not only about its own place within the economy of discursive practices but also about the difference that any other discursive or symbolic practices make to the economy of human affairs in general. To those of this persuasion, what differentiates critical discourse from any other kind of cultural discourse is simply the single-mindedness of its commitment to what might be termed the moral imagination. For these critics, criticism exists neither to explain what things are nor to legitimate what they do but to determine why and how they matter, or do not matter. But criticism of this sort and the imagination that once served as a gauge of its ethical seriousness have now been called deeply into question during the last several decades, and not only within those social institutions that characteristically find such considerations contemptible or irrelevant; the crisis this has created for modern culture as a whole, and for modern American culture in particular, must now be examined.

2

The Moral Imagination
in Modern American Criticism

One of the most vexing issues for contemporary intellectuals concerns the place of moral reflection in the life of culture. A crisis seems to have overtaken moral thought in our time, a crisis not so much of will as of imagination, that can be seen with unusual clarity in the field of arts and letters, and particularly within that aspect of it that is concerned with interpretation and assessment, the branch we call "criticism." Yet the moment one mentions the possibility of a moral crisis in contemporary culture, one raises the specter of New Right diatribes and neoconservative jeremiads. Therefore I should hasten to add that by moral crisis I do not mean the erosion of traditional—in most cases Protestant Victorian—values so widely lamented by the Right-to-Life movement, the anti-ERA faction, the PTL Club, and other elements of the new Moral Majority. Nor do I refer to perceived threats to the creed of democratic individualism that have been decried so shrilly by defenders of American free enterprise and the system of corporate capitalism. These crises are construed by their respondents as crises of will that can be remedied through right thinking and virtuous exertion. I refer instead to a crisis of conception and comprehension that derives not only from the collapse of so many inherited categories of ethical inquiry but also from the progressive discrediting and displacement of so many traditional norms of evaluation.

One symptom of this general breakdown in moral imagination is the intellectual confusion that so often attends any publicly self-conscious attempt to bring cultural forms under moral scrutiny. "The best lack all conviction," as Yeats said, "while the worst are full of passionate intensity." But this debility is even more vividly apparent in the more limited sphere of literary criticism, where the traditional obligation to make sense morally has yielded to very nearly the opposite tendency to evade such sense on moral grounds. Rather than grapple with the moral issues raised by works of literature, critics have developed one or another argument for the necessity of banishing such discussions from criticism altogether. By and large, therefore, one would have to conclude that the relations between art and morality, between interpretation and ethics, have not proved of interest to most modern literary critics, and that where they have aroused any curiosity or excitement at all, they have generally not engaged the best critical minds.

There are, of course, important exceptions to this general rule. For critics like F. R. Leavis, Georg Lukács, Walter Benjamin, Lionel Trilling, F. O. Matthiessen, Edmund Wilson, Philip Rahv, Perry Miller, and even T. S. Eliot, moral questions were scarcely a matter of indifference. Though comprising no school and associated with no particular method of approach, these critics, and others like them from a younger generation—Alfrèd Kazin, Erich Heller, Isaiah Berlin, Stuart Hampshire, John Bayley, Dorothea Krook, Harry Levin, M. H. Abrams, R. W. B. Lewis, and others—have formulated for most of us the terms by which art, and most especially literature, lays claim to our sense of values and bears directly or indirectly on what we want or think we want, on how we live our lives, on whom we wish to emulate, on whether we care or do not care. But these critics, as I shall presently attempt to show, represent something of a special case. The preponderance of critical schools and emphases in modern American criticism, as in modern Western criticism generally, from the New Critics and the neo-Aristotelians to the newest rhetoricians and poststructuralists, have been curiously deaf to the moral claims of art and strangely insensible of the moral imperatives of criticism. Furthermore, in recent years the whole cultural climate in the West, particularly as it affects the arts and disciplines of thought, has changed drastically, placing the presiding assumptions of these moral critics, as I will call them, under severe pressure.

Among the many developments altering the cultural climate in the West, critics and writers have in effect exchanged places, with critics taking upon themselves the imaginative license and moral subversiveness of the artist, and writers turning their art into a ritual demonstration of the treachery and impotence of their own medium. Not that there aren't ethical discoveries to be made as a result of such maneuvers; only that the interest of artists and critics alike seems to be elsewhere. Writers like Vladimir Nabokov, Thomas Pynchon, and Jorge Luis Borges, as well as critics like Maurice Blanchot and Roland Barthes, have given themselves over with increasing frequency to ironic expressions of self-parody in which all the products of individual and collective consciousness, from advertising slogans to received classics, are suffused with the light of bad faith, or worse, of complete self-delusion. Therefore in much contemporary art and thought we find ourselves confronted with a skepticism not only about the values of human expression but also about the epistemological privileges assumed by the individual self. According to the newest wave of cultural commentators, from E. M. Cioran to Michel Foucault, the very channels of verbal communication are diseased and can only be cured by a surgical procedure so radical as to reduce the self to a cipher for the sign and to restrict all signs to the representation of their own meaninglessness. In this new cultural dispensation, the human self is no longer seen as earning its right to moral respect through its resistance to the interventions of culture; instead, it is conceived as but the last in a long line of metaphysical self-deceptions, or "fictions," as they are called, by which human beings in the West have attempted to evade what Wallace Stevens, in his poem "The Snow Man," calls the "Nothing that is not there and the nothing that is."

1

It is tempting to dismiss this kind of talk as so much metacritical nonsense. Where before the discussion of literature, at least in America and Great Britain, confined itself to noting the seven types of ambiguity, or gauging the difference between tenor and vehicle, or hunting for objective correlatives, or asserting the fallacies of intentionality, affectivity, and imitative form, or decrying the heresy of paraphrase, and otherwise seeing the literary object, as Matthew Arnold put it so memorably, "as in itself it really is," now the air is filled with talk about the anxiety of influence, the hermeneutical circularity of understanding, the deconstruction of metaphors, the semiotics of discourse, the intertextuality of experience, and the demystification of signs. For one thing, this new kind of talk seems so remote from the less turbulent precincts of critical exegesis and literary history. For another, its often scientistic tone sounds so alien to artistic sensibility. But if the present perturbations of contemporary critical discussion in America seem to have taken on a life of their own, and one that strikes many observers as utterly removed from the life of literature, they are still close to the center of some important cultural vexations of the age. Indeed, there are important parallels, as I shall later note, between the "new New Criticism" and postmodern developments in many of the departments of art.

Underlying these shared discontents is an awareness that the genres of thought and discourse have, as the social anthropologist Clifford Geertz has recently put it, become "blurred."[1] The metaphors that undergird the disciplines of the mind and help us differentiate among them are now mixed, confused, and unstable. Critics are turning to philosophy, philosophers to ritual theory and linguistics, social scientists to the study of symbols, and iconographers to the methods of psychology or semiotics. One can deplore this situation as intellectually untidy, but one can scarcely deny that it has raised new and perplexing questions affecting our understanding not only of the provenance of art and literature but also of the needs to which they minister. If the current critical situation in America is less intelligible than it once was, it is also decidedly more challenging and fateful. The difference now is that the stakes have been raised. What is currently at issue is no longer the right to have a say about literature or art but the rites of saying as such.

It is in this new context that the tradition of moral imagination in modern American criticism has come under fresh suspicion. This suspicion is fueled by a profound sense of misgiving concerning the grounds on which the critical imagination has traditionally gone about its work in most fields of cultural inquiry. The intellectual bias of this new suspicion is Nietzschean, by which I mean that it is less interested in suspending moral questions than in transvaluing them. Where the moral issue for criticism in the past turned on how literature and the other arts constitute some sort of criticism of life, the issues of utmost urgency at present have to do with determining what criticism really wants, whether there are any methods or techniques for protecting criticism from its own desires, how systemic the institutional pressures and controls are to which criticism is vulnerable, and why criticism should have to sacrifice the fullness of its own life to preserve the life of its putative object.

But who, more precisely, are those critics against whom this contemporary suspicion is directed? How have they defined the moral importance of art and the ethical obligations of criticism? In what ways have their presiding assumptions been brought into question by the newer critical techniques and disciplines? How seriously should we take the new challenges to which they have been submitted? And what sort of defense can be made against these challenges in an effort to reconstitute the relation between literature and values, between art and morality, on different grounds?

2

If we confine ourselves for the present to literary criticism and the American tradition, it is possible to differentiate between two rather different kinds of moral interest exhibited by modern critics. The first, and from my point of view the less important, is represented by critics like Irving Babbitt, Paul Elmer More, and the Southern Agrarians from an earlier generation, or like Yvor Winters, Prosser Hall Frye, and even William K. Wimsatt from a later. These figures could be described as critical moralists who were interested essentially in measuring all symbolic forms against a prescribed set of values and in maintaining something like an inherited cultural ideal. But where Babbitt, More, and the Southern Agrarians strove in a more general way to adjust the criticism of letters and life to ethical actuality as they conceived it, Winters, Frye, and Wimsatt confined themselves to the more specific formal task of evaluating works of literature against a more or less secure moral standard.

The second kind of moral interest in American literary criticism is represented by all those descendants of Matthew Arnold who have accepted his view of literature as a criticism of life but have sided, whether consciously or not, with John Dewey's rather different conception of the way literature does this. To writers like Wilson, Trilling, and Kenneth Burke, literature does not criticize life overtly, as Arnold, Babbitt, and Winters believed, by appealing to set judgment; rather, it works covertly, as Dewey suggested, by disclosing to the imagination specific possibilities that contrast with actual conditions. Dewey captured their own more radical understanding of literature's bearing upon experience when he wrote that "A sense of possibilities that are unrealized and that might be realized are, when they are put in contrast with actual conditions, the most penetrating 'criticism' of the latter that can be made."[2]

The work of this second group of critics is moral, then, not simply because it is preoccupied with values but because it is preoccupied with values in a particular way. Reflecting Henry James's conviction that the greatest art effects a reconciliation of the aesthetic sense with the moral, they have assumed that literature, and for that matter all art, performs this function less by preserving or repossessing received traditions than by challenging their official sanctions and by showing how they might be revised. It does so by exploring what might be the case, or what might be plausibly adumbrated as the case, if the premises sanctioning more conventional or inherited ways of assessing things were changed. Like any art, then, literature is central to culture for this second group of moral critics just insofar as it constitutes that culture's commentary on itself. Its function, as E. H. Gombrich might have said, is to disturb, and even to violate, moral sets. Indeed, to continue the Gombrich echo, the history of literature for these critics largely amounts to a history of the displacement of such sets. Hence their tendency to value art particularly for its insight into the way the moral life undergoes transformation, either by rearranging the hierarchies of significance into which experience is presently organized or by discovering some new quality hitherto neglected but still considered essential to virtue.

In modern America this critical orientation—it can scarcely be called a tradition—has its roots in the work of John Jay Chapman, Randolph Bourne, the early Van Wyck Brooks, and the H. L. Mencken of the *First Book of Prejudices* (though many other critics and thinkers played a part in its development, from George Santayana and Henry James to Harvey Robinson, Lewis Mumford, and V. L. Parrington), and it extends to such contemporaries as Elizabeth Hardwick, Helen Vendler, Steven Marcus, Richard Poirier, Stanley Cavell, Irving Howe, and Leo Marx. Each of these critics, even if in strikingly different ways, is disposed to view literary criticism as a form of cultural criticism and cultural criticism as a branch of moral philosophy, or at least as part of the history of the moral life of humankind. The critic, they believe, is necessarily involved in what Alfred Kazin once described as that debate about the meaning and purpose of life that goes on in every age, but is always asking us at the same time to transcend it by creating a future commensurate not only with our whole history but with our whole striving, a future commensurate with the human imagination itself.

The single most important category of their criticism has been the category of experience. Literature for them is something felt as well as formed, and formed for the sake of effecting an alteration in the life of feeling, the history of the affections. Setting themselves in firm opposition to any critical procedures that, to adapt Max Frisch's witticism about technology, so manage our relations with literature that we don't have to experience it, they have continually asked themselves what is involved in undergoing, and not just comprehending, the experience associated with any particular work of art. They have not turned their criticism into a reproduction of the experiences provided by works of art, but they have felt obliged, even at the expense of personal and intellectual disruption, to convert the formal properties of any work of art into the elements of ordinary experience to which these properties bear a structural equivalence, and hence to transform the act of criticism from a measurement of the work's fulfillment of its own conditions for being into an exploration of the possibilities and limitations life reveals when viewed from within the work's own felt scheme of values.

In this they have been best served not by specific techniques so much as by their personal authority. Writing frequently from as deep within themselves as they know how to reach, they have struggled to achieve the requisite combination of perplexity and engagement before their material. Convinced in matters of thought as of art that a divided mind is often far more illuminating than a settled one, they have attempted to discern the moral difference that art makes when its moral makings are placed within the circumstances of its personal, social, and cultural significance.

Yet this is already to risk becoming more specific about their assumptions and practice than most of these critics have been willing to be. Suspicious of the generalizations of theory because they seem inimical to the concreteness of art, and impatient with the ingenuities of method because they threaten to reduce interpretation to a formula, critics like Wilson, Blackmur, Kazin, and Trilling have preferred to work at considerable distance from contemporary critical wars, reserving their energies for defining the internecine struggles within art itself. Only when theoretical disputes have insinuated themselves into the general life of cultural discourse have they felt compelled to take up arms, and then most often not to champion one cause against another but rather to explain what the debate really amounts to.

The only exceptions to this general rule have been precipitated by what these critics have perceived as threats to the basis of their own modernist humanism. That humanism is based on the notion that the sum of our potentialities as human beings can never be defined solely in relation to our actual circumstances—biological, psychological, economic, social, or historical—but only in relation to our effort to encompass them. In saying "No" to all that limits or restricts, they have implicitly maintained, we say "Yes" to the spiritual freedom that permits us to imagine otherwise. Hence the centrality in their humanism of the experience of art itself, whose moral function is for them identical with its imaginative function: to express the measure of our independence from those very systems of meaning we have created in culture—indeed, *as* culture—to define and enact ourselves.

Assuming, then, that human beings can, through the imagination, transcend themselves, or at least transcend the meanings by which they have defined themselves, these critics have generally assumed that we live both within culture and, in Lionel Trilling's felicitous phrase, "beyond culture."[3] Not that they have supposed that human beings actually exist outside of culture; only that they believe we human beings can, in a manner of speaking, achieve a standpoint independent of, or at least dissociated from, its official versions. Put more directly, they have maintained that some irreducible element within the self, however base or sublime, exists beyond the reach of cultural control. And it is this elemental ingredient within the self, yet capable of propelling the self beyond its own cultural versions, that enables the critic, the intellectual, to place the versions of his or her culture under scrutiny. More important, it is also this capacity for cultural transcendence that serves as the source of these critics' belief that the noblest or most significant expressions of any culture are those that contain the culture's most searching assessment of itself. In criticizing its own potentialities and problems, these critics insist, culture performs its central moral function.

3

The modern American critic who most clearly epitomized this position was Edmund Wilson. The critic who most compellingly enunciated its presiding assumptions was Lionel Trilling. The two furnish an interesting contrast. Among others equally sensitive to the life within literature as well as to the life beyond it, they really had no critical peers—though it becomes increasingly apparent that in certain respects Alfred Kazin, who belongs to a slightly younger generation, has come to exert an intellectual and critical presence within the world of letters similar to Wilson's, and that R. P. Blackmur, who started his career in a somewhat different tradition, attained a philosophical capaciousness and ethical discrimination, at least in his later criticism, not unlike Trilling's.

Wilson and Trilling present the notable but not unrepresentative spectacle of critics who began their careers as liberals, owing major intellectual allegiance to the Enlightenment, but who developed, over the course of time, greater appreciation for sentiments usually associated with conservatism as they came more fully under the sway of Romantic challenges to eighteenth-century optimism. Yet even where their view of human nature darkened under the influence of the modern Romantic legacy, they never lost faith in the crucial centrality of mind in cultural experience or relinquished the belief that their own minds constituted their chief critical instruments.

Wilson and Trilling were united in their desire to explore, in Wilson's well-known words from *Axel's Castle,* "the history of man's ideas and imaginings in the setting of the conditions which shaped them."[4] They were also of one mind in viewing this history as essentially moral, one in which the value of "man's ideas and imaginings" is directly proportionate to the amount of resistance they offer to their shaping conditions.[5] As time passed, however, Wilson and Trilling were to differ more and more over what sorts of obstacles the intellect and imagination must overcome in expressing themselves historically and over how they have generally succeeded in doing so in the modern period, when they have succeeded at all. Trilling, because of his deeper affinities with the tradition of tragic realism, typically located such obstacles within man himself, in some fissure that divided man from his very essence; Wilson, despite his interest in the Philoctetes legend and his subsequent development of the theory of "the wound and the bow" (as he called it in his book by that title), characteristically located such obstacles instead outside of man, in some deficiency of the environment that should have furnished human existence some support. And while both critics situated the scene of this moral drama against a social background, Trilling took this to be a drama that realizes itself in broadly political terms, while Wilson assumed that it realizes itself in more narrowly personal or biographical terms.

Needless to say, these marked divergences of emphasis in critics whose interests were otherwise so congruent sprang from sharp differences of temperament and background that went all the way to the center of their work. Wilson's secularized Protestantism, for example, gave to his thinking an insistent strain of independence and an almost defensive sense of detached superiority, while Trilling's Jewish cosmopolitanism, equally secular only up to a point, fostered an attitude at once more perplexed and yet involved. Despite his immense range of interests, Wilson appeared, especially in his later years, to write from a position somewhat above the social and political fray, or at least off to one side of it, and to follow the promptings mainly of his own tastes; his special talent always remained the ability to convert his private preoccupations and obsessions into subjects of absorbing public interest. Trilling, by contrast, kept being pulled back into the fray even when he preferred to disengage himself from it, and to follow something closer to the dictates of his own conscience, though, again, with an extraordinary ability to make others feel its force. While Wilson was more intent on telling others what he thought, in a prose that was often matchlessly limpid and trenchant, Trilling was preoccupied, in his winding, recursive essays, with showing others how to think. Thus if Trilling's best criticism reveals an intelligence that was always troubled as well as probing, engaged as well as wary, ironic as well as critical, Wilson's best criticism displayed a mind that was open but also self-possessed, freethinking and yet deeply opinionated, diverse in its sympathies but emphatic, not to say narrow, in some of its judgments.

Instructive as these differences are, however, Trilling and Wilson still practiced a kind of criticism that deserves to be called cultural, and defined its aims in relation to the now somewhat old-fashioned ideal of the man of letters. Respectful of learning but suspicious of expertise, they were emphatically less interested, particularly in an age of increasing specialization such as our own, in treating the objects of knowledge as a subject of scholarship than as a potential source of intelligence. By intelligence they meant the cultivation of a circumstantial understanding of "man's ideas and imaginings" not for their own sake alone but because of their practical—or better, their practicable—bearing on the wider life around them, and not just the life implicated in their first expression but the life they have led from then until now.

Intelligence, then, was not reducible to any single or simple formula. Its possession required something like the historical sense—or the ability not only to bring the present to bear upon the past but also to see the past as ingredient in the present, as part of the present's own historicity—but its orientation was noticeably contemporary. It looked to the past for images and conceptions that might provide an alternative, or at any rate a corrective, to experience in the present. Thus its purpose was never, in the academic sense, to strive for complete mastery of ideas, texts, or meanings so much as to clarify the relations among them and to draw out their consequences for present experience.

In conceiving of art and thought together, Wilson and Trilling wrote against the developing tide of critical fashion in their own time, a fashion that, then as now, increasingly preferred patterns to persons, structures to stories, images and symbols to actions. Indeed, Wilson's and Trilling's concern for intelligence pushed their criticism in an opposite direction, toward viewing works of both the imagination and the intellect in terms of the physics rather than the chemistry or the anatomy of their forms, toward an appreciation of intellectual and artistic expressions as energies to be encountered, forces to be reckoned with. The assumption common to Trilling and Wilson alike was that great works of art and thought play a decisive role not only in shaping the experience of the "educated classes," as Trilling was fond of calling "those people who value their ability to live some part of their lives with serious ideas," but also in shaping the very life of the polity as such.[6] This followed from their mutual conviction that politics in the modern era cannot be understood as anything other than what Trilling termed "the politics of culture, the organization of human life toward some end or other, toward the modification of sentiments, which is to say the quality of human life."[7] But if politics was to be defined chiefly in aesthetic terms—"by the quality of life it envisages, by the sentiments it desires to affirm"—then literature and the other arts of mind could once again be seen to possess an indisputable political provenience and governance. The central unanswered question among liberals and conservatives alike was how to construe them. For the man of letters who was committed before everything else to something called mind, it all seemed to boil down to the question of how, as Denis Donoghue has recently rephrased it, "to keep open the area in which intelligent communication is still possible."[8] Thus the critic's chief tasks were to prevent political discussion from falling into the hands of either the sociological statisticians or the bureaucratic crisis managers and to prevent literary discussion from falling victim to the techniques of the academic specialists.

These tasks were the more difficult to accomplish because the cultural critic, as Wilson and Trilling epitomized him, refused to be assisted by a method any more precise or explicit than what Jacques Barzun once described, thinking specifically of Trilling, as "controlled divination."[9] But if the method of the modern man of letters and cultural critic was idiosyncratic and diffuse, the purpose it served was very nearly the opposite. When directed at "the history of man's ideas and imaginings in the setting of the conditions which shaped them," the goal of this method was to comprehend that subtle interplay of factors which determines the relations that art and thought each bear both to the worlds that help create them (the worlds that, as we say, they reflect or refract) and to the worlds they help in turn to create (the worlds they, as it were, presuppose for their existence and thus project). By bringing to light the always complex, often puzzling, and frequently astonishing connections among these different worlds, Wilson and Trilling hoped, as men of letters, to clarify the way human beings are simultaneously created by their culture and yet capable of imaginatively conceiving, and even sympathetically inhabiting, a position outside the sphere of its governing axioms and postulates.

4

It was Wilson who first brought this issue into the center of his writing, even though it was Trilling who would give its operation clearest conceptual expression. Wilson was already absorbed with the issue of cultural transcendence in his first book, *Axel's Castle*, where he explained his admiration for a modern writer like Proust in relation to Proust's ability to surmount the debilitating conditions of his personal experience through the formal realizations of his art. By attempting to retrieve those moments from his past otherwise lost to the flux of time and fashion them into an enduring work of art, Proust not only overcame his paralysis of will, according to Wilson, but mastered his experience in the very act of creating something transcending it, something invulnerable to time itself. But Wilson was prepared to attribute the same accomplishment, or something very like it, to the symbolists as a whole: their achievement, Wilson could argue, without discounting the increasing social and political irrelevance of their artistic values, lay in the way they awakened their readers, through their extreme repudiation of all materialist and mechanical modes of intellection, "to the untried, unsuspected possibilities of human thought and art."[10]

The emphasis here, as elsewhere in Wilson's work, is on what Trilling was to describe, in one of his later books, as possibly the central paradigm of modernism: the energies of the individual self opposing the exigencies of its culture. The opposition of self to culture, or rather of "the opposing self" to collective culture, was, in fact, to become the central theme of *To the Finland Station*, Wilson's best book. *To the Finland Station* is Wilson's study not of modern history itself but of the revolutionary theory that helped give history its modern shape, the theory we associate somewhat misleadingly with its foremost modern proponent, Karl Marx. Indeed, what aroused Wilson's greatest excitement and admiration for what he preferred to call "the Revolutionary tradition" in social thought from Vico to Lenin was its affirmation that the social world is a creation of human beings themselves and that the historical imagination can, as Marx and Engels proved, intervene in human affairs as a constructive force. The first person to have perceived this truth after Vico himself was the great French historian Michelet. Wilson regarded Michelet's *History of France* as one of the supreme achievements of its age, because it managed to enter into and comprehend the evolution of man's ability to make as well as enact his own history. In this sense, Michelet accomplished the almost unprecedented feat of depicting human beings transcending themselves in the process of creating themselves, but he then surpassed his own achievement: he actually projected his work beyond the present and into the future by leaving his readers with the feeling, as Wilson put it, "that we ourselves are the last chapter of the story and that the next chapter is for us to create."[11]

Yet Michelet's great work was but the prelude to the still more awesome accomplishments of Engels and particularly of Marx. Indeed, it is Marx who actually dominates the central pages of *To the Finland Station* because it was Marx who provided the most compelling vision in that era of how human beings might resist the impositions of circumstance and regain a measure of dominion over their own fate. In pursuing this theme, Wilson very nearly situates Marx outside of history altogether. For if Marx's Jewishness afforded him a perspective independent of nineteenth-century culture and society, his intellectual genius, Wilson implies, gave him a position above it. And from this position, Wilson goes on to argue, once we separate Marx's thought from the coils of metaphysical abstraction in which it was so often bound and allow for errors of distortion and ignorance, Marx was then able to envision how the human spirit, through the use of moral reason, might overcome its animal nature and establish a new social world. Wilson could give his complete assent to the principle on which this new social world was to be founded, namely, the belief that human beings need no longer remain the passive victims of material conditions but can, if they act on the basis of their solidarity with their kind, reshape those conditions in conformity with human need and creative desire. If this would never produce a society in which all were equal, it would at least ensure the creation of a society in which the achievement of some was not purchased at the cost of the victimization of others.

Wilson was not defending Marxism per se but rather the vision he thought he could discern behind or within it. This vision was expressed for him most forcefully in *Das Kapital,* which Wilson interprets so brilliantly as a major work of art. Believing as he did that all great works of art "render articulate the results of fundamental new experiences to which human beings have had to adjust themselves," Wilson found Marx's book, like the vision contained within it, a triumph of spirit over circumstances because it mounted a historical theory designed not merely to account for human misery but to furnish human beings with some of the interpretive instruments necessary to relieve themselves of its burden. And when Wilson later reached that proleptic moment in his own narrative, where the vision of Marx had passed into the revolutionary politics of Bolshevism and finally brought Lenin to the Finland Station, Wilson could discern the same point now being made by history itself:

> Lenin in 1919, with a remnant of Vico's God still disguised in the Dialectic, but with no fear of Roman pope or Protestant Synod, not so sure of the controls of society as the engineer was of the engine that was taking him to Petrograd, yet in a position to calculate the chances with closer accuracy than a hundred to one, stood on the eve of the moment when for the first time in the human exploit the key of a philosophy of history was to fit an historical lock.[13]

Wilson was never again to exhibit such confidence that human beings can resist the tide of events and make history, however temporarily, conform to the shape of the moral imagination—in fact, by the time he wrote *Patriotic Gore* he would be prepared to describe the historical interaction of nations in the imagery of voracious sea slugs motivated not by an imagination of virtue but solely by irrational instinct—but he continued to insist upon, as well as to exemplify, the capacity of the intellect to preserve for itself, through all its inevitable shifts and accommodations within human experience, a margin of moral independence.

This is the real subject of *Patriotic Gore,* Wilson's last major critical study. Even as Wilson himself countered current critical estimates of the likes of Harriet Beecher Stowe, Abraham Lincoln, Alexander H. Stephens, and Oliver Wendell Holmes, so he discussed them all chiefly from the perspective of their efforts to prevail against, and frequently to transcend, the conditions of their cultural and social environment. Harriet Beecher Stowe was not the victim of a narrow moralistic Calvinism but wrote with a moral passion whose judgments were surprisingly balanced and whose interpretations were basically sound. Abraham Lincoln did not become captive to the mythology that grew up surrounding the Civil War but helped to adapt the myth to suit his own purposes, thus revealing a character that, contrary to popular legend, was cold, aloof, shrewd, ambitious, intellectual, and exalted with a sense of its own superiority. Alexander Stephens, the Vice-President of the Confederacy, whom Wilson treats as in some sense Lincoln's opposite in the book, deserves this comparison precisely because, in the very extremism of his loyalty to the South, he was willing to raise tough questions about the rightful exercise of power by force and the claims of government against the individual that were evaded by less courageous leaders of his cause.

But Wilson reserves the longest section of his book and his warmest praise for Justice Holmes. Here is the signal instance of a man who managed to come through the war uncorrupted and to develop a first-rate intellect. In asking himself how Holmes accomplished this feat of social and cultural transcendence, Wilson defined many of the qualities he had eventually come, toward the end of his life, to respect most: an unshakable self-confidence, a studied indifference to current fashions and affairs, high standards of excellence, a jobbist's devotion to work, and a Brahmin sense of election that permits one to act in behalf of ideals in whose ultimate victory or absolute truth one need not necessarily believe. All one need be convinced of is their ultimate rectitude, which enabled Wilson to conclude that in Justice Holmes we essentially confront the legacy of an American Calvinism whose theology has long since died but whose habits of mind still persist.

Trilling would not, I think, have been able to accept Wilson's estimate of Justice Holmes. Far from perceiving some kind of admirable opposition to, or at least independence of, his culture in Holmes' elitist indifference to the world around him, Trilling would have found disturbing signs of cultural accommodation, even capitulation. Holmes's cynicism about ideals, which to Wilson appeared tough-minded and historically consistent with Holmes's war experience, would have struck Trilling as potentially shallow. Holmes's social Darwinism, which earned Wilson's respect for its candid realization that might often makes right, would have impressed Trilling as dangerously reactionary. And Holmes's cult of the "jobbist" who aims to "touch the superlative" would have seemed to Trilling less a defense of standards in a society that continuously contributes to their erosion than a plea for intellectual withdrawal from a world with which one disdains to compromise. The most revealing difference, however, would have been over the question of truth. While Holmes was prepared to equate the validity of ideas with their ability to get themselves accepted in the marketplace, Trilling would have insisted that the question of truth has nothing to do with the competitive appeal of ideas but can only be settled by comprehending more profoundly the dialectical relation between the human spirit and the social and cultural actualities in which it must realize itself.

5

Trilling did not finally get around to defining explicitly the dialectical relationship between self and society, between the human spirit and the conditions of its actualization, until he composed the preface to *Beyond Culture*, though he was then quick to note that his title could easily be misunderstood. Assuming the word *culture* to signify the whole system of morals, manners, and meanings by which human beings are formed, in which they function, and with which they interact, Trilling did not believe that the reach of culture's institutions or influences could ultimately be overcome or escaped even by those who wished to repudiate them. All forms of cultural rebellion are inevitably determined, he insisted, both substantively and stylistically, by the cultural formations against which they are directed. Yet it was equally apparent to Trilling that human beings can detach themselves sufficiently from culture in this largest sense to construct a position that is measurably independent of its official prescriptions and norms. This possibility of developing a critical standpoint "beyond culture" was, in fact, a major presupposition of modern culture itself, according to Trilling, and so powerful were its effects that it had succeeded in generating an "adversary culture" that now possessed as its chief aim the subversion of the premises of the dominant culture itself. This curious cultural dialectic left Trilling wondering if the criticism of culture in our own time might not require a double rather than a single transcendence: a transcendence not only of the premises and prescriptions of the dominant culture but also of the presuppositions and postulates of its chief adversarial tradition.

Trilling's thinking about the process of dissociating oneself from culture sufficiently to bring culture itself under scrutiny derived from many sources, most of them literary, but it was Sigmund Freud who provided him with the most compelling arguments for this possibility. Trilling was convinced that if no modern thinker had seen more clearly than Freud just how completely human beings are implicated within culture, neither had any modern thinker perceived just how inimical culture actually is to the interests of the individual self, or how essential it is, from time to time, for the individual self to break free of culture's control. Freud grounded the possibility of achieving some modicum of individual autonomy from culture in the fact that human beings are both cultural and biological, a complex of acquired sense or learned meaning and instinctual necessity; this "hard, irreducible, stubborn core of biological urgency" within the self, as Trilling called it, enables the self to elude, or at least to frustrate, culture's claims and may eventually, as the self evolves toward maturity, challenge culture's quest for, as it were, absolute dominion over the self.[14]

By accepting the Freudian model of the self as "a tangle of culture and biology" and supporting Freud's contention that the element of the biologically "given" in man's makeup plays a more decisive role in shaping his spiritual independence than any culturally "conditioned" factors, Trilling knew that he was reversing the conventional way of conceptualizing such matters and also taking some liberty with Freud's formulations.[15] But it was Freud, after all, who had authorized such license not only by demonstrating how, as Trilling put it elsewhere, "in a scientific age, we still think and feel in figurative formations," but also by creating, in psychoanalysis itself, what Trilling described as essentially "a science of tropes, of metaphor and its variants, synecdoche and metonomy."[16] Allowing, then, for some freedom of interpretation, Trilling concluded that the Freudian model of the self's relation to culture suggests that "there is a residue of human quality, beyond the reach of cultural control, and that this residue of human quality, elemental as it may be, serves to bring culture itself under criticism and keeps it from being absolute."[17]

Trilling's difficulty with Freud arose precisely at the point where Freud tried to explain how this process occurs. Freud's biological metaphor did not enable him to account for the way that art, and even thought itself, plays a part in this transcendence of culture by self; or, to state it more directly, Freud's biological frame of thinking did not permit a sufficiently positive view of the imagination. Even though, on Trilling's account, Freud had made poetry, or the poetry-making faculty, indigenous to the constitution of the human mind, Freud misconstrued the place of art in life because he could rarely conceive of the role of the aesthetic in any other terms than those of psychic—which is to say, moral—aberration. More to the point, Freud failed to comprehend what Hegel as well as Schiller had perceived so clearly—that in the relationship between the aesthetic and the moral, the order of priority must be reversed. As the Romantics had understood but their eighteenth-century predecessors had not, aesthetics should provide the criteria for morality, not vice versa. Yet in this instance Freud remained a disciple of the eighteenth century and was therefore unable to explain, to Trilling's satisfaction at least, how art, indeed all works of imaginative intellect, could assist in the criticism of culture, or, to put it differently, how the imagination, by enabling the transcendence of cultural forms, could perform a moral function.

The classic explanation of this process had been made in the nineteenth century by Matthew Arnold, the subject of Trilling's first book, when he defined literature, and by implication all art, as life's foremost criticism of itself. But when Trilling attempted to formulate his own understanding of the relation between the moral function of the imagination and the critical purpose of culture, he turned to two other nineteenth-century figures, Friedrich Nietzsche and Henry James. Nietzsche's understanding of the historical sense provided him with the terms to explain how culture operates, at least in its most serious expressions, as a criticism of life; James's understanding of romance enabled him to specify the role that the imagination plays in effecting this operation of critical transcendence.

Nietzsche brought the historical sense into conjunction with the critical sense, and then coupled the critical sense with the moral sense, when he defined the historical sense as "the capacity for divining quickly the order of the rank of the valuation according to which a people, a community, or an individual has lived."[18] Trilling found this definition compelling for several reasons. For one, it confirmed his own belief that cultures are composed of implicit as well as explicit systems of valuation, many of which are in direct competition with one another, and that an essential job of culture is to adjust or manage the conflict among them. For another, it supported his assumption that these valuations often operate far below the level of manifest statement in culture, constituting rather the latent context of implication that gives those more manifest statements their cultural meaning and can only be guessed at or intuited rather than empirically verified. For still another, it buttressed his conviction that such valuations are revealed not only in the larger institutional formations of culture, what Nietzsche called "the operating forces," but also in symbolic or figurative cultural forms such as art and thought, manners and morals.[19]

Nietzsche's main point, and the source of Trilling's greatest interest, was that the historical sense deserves to be called the critical and moral sense only because its overriding aim is to divine the relationship between and among the cultural valuations themselves and then to determine their relation to "the operating forces." But Trilling made his most characteristic move only when he deduced from this that the historical sense, as Nietzsche's entire career attested, is really no different from the artistic sense. In point of fact, Trilling reasoned they are "not two senses but one," for both depend on the power of the moral imagination not only to discern the order of rank among the cultural expressions themselves but also to see all cultural expression as implicit, even complicit, forms of valuation.[20]

In saying this Trilling came perilously close to a kind of aesthetic reductionism in which, as he nearly proposed in the preface to *The Liberal Imagination,* all cultural issues are convertible into questions of sentiment and style. But he could also be interpreted as flirting here with the more radical proposition that all cultural formations, including historical ones, are finally figurative, being the product, as a more recent generation of cultural critics has contended, of wholly fictive constructions. In actuality, Trilling's intention seems to have been less restrictive than the first alternative and more moderate than the second. To perceive the unity of the historical and the aesthetic as these senses were embodied in Nietzsche's own person was to realize that culture should "be studied and judged as life's continuous evaluation of itself, the evaluation being understood as never finding full expression in the 'operating forces' of a culture, but as never finding expression at all without reference to these gross, institutional facts."[21]

Trilling was here exploring a dialectic that James had put more precisely, or, at any rate, more suggestively, in his contrast between the terms *reality* and *romance.* When Trilling turned to a discussion of this contrast, his object was to explain how the novel might contribute to a reconstitution of the moral will, which seemed to be dying in our time of its own excesses. Trilling realized, of course, that many intellectuals had long since abandoned any hope of reconstituting "the great former will of humanism," as he called it, because of their conviction that it was this will that had brought modern civilization to this new Dark Ages.[22] Trilling could in fact sympathize with their modern sense of apocalypticism and its attendant dream of cultural renovation, especially when, as in a D. H. Lawrence or a Franz Kafka, it was voiced by that kind of moral genius whose attachment to life itself goes beyond attachment to any of its individual forms. But Trilling also knew that a similar political radicalism characterized people with no attachment to life in any form and that most of us, being neither the one nor the other, dream, when we dream at all, for a change less cataclysmic or final. For those more moderate souls like himself whose notions of reformation remained, as he admitted, "in the literal sense of the word conservative," Trilling accounted the novelistic intelligence "most apt" and Henry James's delineation of its central moral preoccupations most constructive.

James attributed the power exerted over us by all the great novelists from Cervantes to Zola to their dual commitment to "reality" on the one side and "romance" on the other. By *reality* James meant quite simply "the things we cannot possibly not know"; by *romance* he intended to suggest "the things that, with all the facilities in the world, all the wealth and all the courage and all the wit and all the adventure, we never *can* directly know; the things that can reach us only through the beautiful circuit of belief and desire."[23] By *reality,* then, James (and after him, Trilling) meant Nietzsche's world of operant forces, by *romance* the world not of ideality or the unknown but "of unfolding possibility."[24] The notion of "romance" represented the world of the will, as Trilling termed it, "in its creative aspect," the world of the will as a moral instrument that "submits itself to criticism and conceives for itself new states of being."[25] Created by the imaginative unification of aspiration and idea, the world of "romance," when brought into contact with the world of "reality," constituted the most profound criticism of the latter that could be made. For by rendering as actual, or rather as virtual, modes of experience that before were imagined, if at all, merely as potential, the novel showed us how life, acting under the impulse of the will in its moral creativity, goes about testing itself.

It is just here, however, where we reach the outer limits of Trilling's conceptualization of the relation between moral creativity and cultural criticism, that we confront its limitations as well. Those limitations have to do with the terms in which Trilling defines that relationship and the responsibility he reserves for it. Trilling's recourse is consistently to the will as it is actualized in the imagination, or to the will, if in its morally creative aspect, also in its conscious and more or less rational aspect. In other words, it is with the will as an element of mind that Trilling was ultimately concerned, and he indicated the moral, not to say mental or cognitive, ambition he envisaged for this rationalized will when he described the novel's "long dream of virtue" as a moral fantasy "in which the will, while never abating its strength and activity, learns to refuse to exercise itself upon the unworthy objects with which the social world tempts it, and either conceives its own right objects or becomes content with its own sense of its potential force. . . ."[26] This is the will as it constitutes what, in another essay, Trilling was to call "the ground of man's dream of his transcendence, of his projection of his being into the permanence of the future, into what he calls " 'immortality' and 'glory' or at least 'dignity,' which is to say 'worth.' "[27] Trilling was at this point thinking of how one of Keats's letters distinguishes the will from all other faculties of the mind and thereby establishes its authority as perhaps the highest expression of humanistic culture, by affirming "that a chief value of life lies in [life's] ability to make itself, and especially its various forms of aggressivity, the object of its own admiring contemplation."[28]

What is missing from this remarkable series of statements about the will, even where the terms *imagination* and *transcendence* come into play, is any acknowledgment of the kind of service that imaginative transcendence might render the moral will. Trilling never seems to have allowed for the fact that the moral function of the imagination might consist precisely in its ability to transcend the will and its own dream of virtue. Or if he allowed for this fact, he never let it reshape his own conception of the will. To put this point in the form of a question: What if the image of life selected by the will as the object of its own contemplation were too narrow and self-serving? What is to prevent the will from being seduced by the admiration of its own objects? Trilling never quite managed to find an answer even when he entertained the question. Indeed, by here and elsewhere subordinating the imagination to the will instead of subordinating the will, as he had earlier proposed, to the imagination, Trilling risked depriving the will of any capacity for self-criticism.

There is considerable irony in this inversion, because no critic of Trilling's generation, and certainly not Edmund Wilson, possessed a clearer understanding of the corruptions to which the moral will is always and everywhere susceptible. No one, that is, perceived more clearly than Trilling how the moral will, through its very ability to resist the coercions of culture, can become a cultural agent of coercion itself. Moralist that he was, Trilling recognized almost instinctively that the greatest moral danger represented by the will lay not in the direction of its most selfish motives but of its most selfless: "Some paradox of our nature leads us, when once we have made our fellow men the objects of our enlightened interest, to go on to make them the objects of our pity, then of our wisdom, ultimately of our coercion."[29] Trilling thought of this paradox as a form of Kant's "Radical Evil" and assumed that it could be contained only by the most extraordinary vigilance of the critical intellect. Yet when push came to shove, Trilling so clearly associated morality with mind rather than with imagination that he deprived the will of some of its moral credibility. By imputing to the will the ability to choose its own objects and to find satisfaction in the expression of its own energies, Trilling overlooked or discounted the possibility that the moral will might itself be in need of radical revision, that the will to morality might simply be a screen for the expression of self-love or, in other terms, might be an expression of the love of one's own moral screens.

As it happens, this possibility was lost neither on Nietzsche nor on James, because they both tended to vest greater moral authority in the imagination itself, viewing the imagination as the one human faculty capable of challenging the will with a revelation of what lies beyond its mental frames. Nor has this possibility been lost on the generation of cultural critics that has succeeded Wilson and Trilling, because of its greater suspicion of mental frames as such and its more radical skepticism about the category of morality. But to Trilling and Wilson, as to the great majority of American critics who shared with them an essentially modernist outlook, the office of the moral will or imagination remained clear: it was to show us that culture should be studied and judged "as life's continuous evaluation of itself"; therefore its service is in behalf of those irreducible—or, better, indispensable—elements of the self, of the human, that resist complete conditioning by all that culture does both to shape the experience of the self and to stabilize and control that experience in socially approved forms.

tion can, in principle at least, be reduced to a few simple laws. For structuralists and poststructuralists alike, this search for the laws that underpin cultural orders transforms all literary and art criticism into cultural criticism and cultural criticism into a kind of metaphysical deontology.

Derrida begins where the structuralists leave off, from the assumption that all human experience can be conceived on the model of a text and that all human activity can be regarded as a form of reading and writing, or deciphering and inscribing. But poststructuralists carry this line of reasoning one step further by challenging the ontological integrity of those elemental grammars of signification with which texts, according to traditional structuralists, are supposedly inscribed. To the structuralists, such grammars represent what was once conceived as the historically and culturally, if not quite the metaphysically, given, or rather the closest we can come to it in a world where all experience is mediated through signs. To the poststructuralists, on the other hand, these grammars are not only mere fictions that can be shown to be essentially unstable but purposeful deceptions that need to be perceived as inherently hegemonic.

What results from these conclusions is a literary method—or, better, a critical cast of mind—that purports, at least on the face of it, to question, indeed to subvert, the cognitive and moral pretensions of all cultural forms by exposing their false claims to epistemic and ontological privilege. The technique for doing so involves some method of "decentering" by means of which the linguistic axis of any text is isolated in order to show how referentially and even reflexively unstable it is. At the minimum, this critical method of decentering aims to show us how arbitrary and subjective and, notably, self-serving are all acts of intellectual closure; at the maximum, it seeks to vouchsafe some glimpse of whatever it is (or isn't) that underlies the significative material in all texts. In either case, poststructural criticism tends to carry what has sometimes been called the "hermeneutics of suspicion" to the point of converting disbelief into the only operative intellectual category and playful cynicism into the only viable critical stance.

Little wonder, then, that this critical movement—which cuts across all the conventional academic specialties within the human sciences and which violates so much of the disciplinary protocol these specialties were created, at least in part, to protect and preserve—has produced reactions varying from militant indifference to hysterical militance. Except in the minds of its votaries, poststructuralism seems to undercut the very possibility of cultural criticism by displacing the assumptions that once legitimated it. Put simply, poststructuralism, according to its own testimony, and despite the prolixity of its own practitioners, leaves the cultural critic with so little left to do. And what it does warrant doing—endless acts of deconstruction—seems so repetitious and, again on its own testimony, self-defeating.

Yet in the hands of its master practitioners—in, for example, the Rabbinic deconstructions of Derrida, the mandarin demystifications of the later Barthes, or the Viconian dismantlings of Foucault—poststructuralism has yielded a brilliance of critical analysis that only the intellectually prejudiced can discount and has generated an appeal, particularly among some of the brighter, younger scholars in humanistic study, that only the professionally indifferent can deny. Derrida's *Of Grammatology* and *Glas,* Barthes's *S/Z* and *Camera Lucida,* and Foucault's *The Archeology of Knowledge* and *Discipline and Punish,* no matter how strange or alienating their critical idioms may strike us on first exposure, display an imaginative daring and critical severity that illumine whole territories of intellectual and social experience even, as so often, in the process of exposing their false premises or self-canceling oppositions. It may thus be that poststructuralism leaves one sometimes feeling, as Marianne Moore said about poetry, that "there are things important beyond all this fiddle," but it also brings to mind the lines that follow: "Reading it, however, with a perfect contempt for it, one discovers in it, after all, / a place for the genuine." The difficulty comes in defining just what one means by "the genuine" and in determining how one can presume to apply a category so benign to a critical method so radically suspicious.

1

One could, I suppose, associate "the genuine" in poststructuralist criticism with the very radicality of the suspicion, a radicality so extreme that it has brought Derrida and others to the point of asserting that all verbal texts are composed of no more than black marks on a page, marks that can be distinguished from one another not by virtue of any intrinsic meaning they may possess, or intention they may convey, or presumed effect they may produce, but solely because of their difference from one another. This *différance,* as Derrida calls it, is constituted exclusively by the size of the marks, the spaces between them, their degree of blackness, and their shape. According to Derrida, this *différance* allows us to attach any number of significations to them but prevents these significations from possessing any inherent relation either to the marks to which they are attached or to the objects to which they are meant to refer. There is no meaning or significance implicit within or secreted behind any marks or signs as part of their nature, and thus there is nothing sedimented underneath or projected around or in front of any particular text. For the poststructuralist, there is only the infinite elaboration of significations opened out by the signs of the text in whose semiotic activity we may participate once we realize that its inevitable movement is in the direction of dismantling the text's own meanings. No text has any core of stable or determinate meaning for most poststructuralists, only a potentially infinite number of unrestricted and possible meanings. The critic's task is to enter into their play without coming under their sway. The trick is to keep from being "taken in," and this requires an almost superhuman critical vigilance. In this radically skeptical hermeneutics, the motive force behind all interpretive activity is not to understand the innerness of other minds but to resist their domination, and criticism is reduced in whole—rather than, as surely it is, in part—to a science of the semantics and semiotics of discourse, which not only delimit but essentially control all forms of expressive interchange.

Instead of associating the word *genuine* with this radical interpretive suspiciousness, however, one could also identify it with the symptomatic accuracy with which poststructuralism has identified and diagnosed our contemporary metaphysical malady. According to poststructuralists, the freight of our expressive life, particularly in the West, has been carried since the time of Plato by a metaphysics of substance— Derrida calls it a metaphysics of presence—that has now collapsed under the weight of three centuries of philosophical criticism. This means that the essentialist notion that our assertions, like our actions, are supported, if we could but dig beneath them deep enough, by an ontological bedrock called reality whose structure they must ultimately reflect or mirror in order to be true has given way to the realization that our conceptions of the thing called reality, no less than the statements we make in an effort to define it, are cultural constructs whose veracity or validity is wholly restricted to what our linguistic equipment permits us to know and say about it. But since we are now unable to get beyond the linguistic signs by which we name the features of our experience, we must be prepared to accept that all we have ever experienced is, in fine, a creation of those signs and, as such, is subject to the same rules or conventions that affect any other semiotic system.

This radically revisionist view of experience has destroyed the theory of language by which we attempted in the West to think of reality otherwise, as a formation whose substance or essence existed independent of our language about it. This "logocentric theory of language," as Derrida has named it, simply confirmed an essentialist or substantialist metaphysic by allowing us to think that words possess a determinate relation to their referents because language possesses a congruent relation with Being. But when Saussurean linguistics successfully challenged the first proposition, it opened up the possibility of undermining the second as well. However, the full ramifications of this "linguistic turn" in criticial theory were not registered until thinkers in other respects as different as Derrida, Lacan, and Foucault fathomed its metaphysical implications. But once "the sovereignty of the signifier," as Foucault calls it, was recognized as an arbitrary logocentric construct, then a new, and for some very daunting, interpretive environment suddenly opened up, in which disinherited subjects float free of their putative objects and minds now liberated from the usual institutional constraints of what Thomas Kuhn calls the "disciplinary matrix" contemplate anew the Nietzschean ethic that, at least within hermeneutics, everything is permissible.

In this second version, which is no less selective and angular than the first, poststructuralism seems to comprise instead an ultimate critical iconoclasm, all the more radical and subversive for having hunted out and destroyed the last metaphysical refuge of Western consciousness. With the death of logocentricity, the authority it once conferred, (and still does, upon its adherents) the authority to speak of, if not for, the Being present in words, can not be seen for what it always was: a disguised expression of the will to power. Therefore in this variant reading, poststructuralism becomes a radical critique not of language per se but of the politics of culture. This critique is, to be sure, much more readily apparent in the writings of Foucault or even Lacan than it is in those of Derrida, but only because of what Derrida sees, in his essay "The Conflict of Faculties," as the narrowness of our conception of deconstruction. Derrida decries the tendency to limit deconstruction to a set of specialized discursive procedures, and still more the disposition, so evident in America, to reduce it to a critical method or hermeneutic designed strictly for the interpretation of literary texts "in the shelter of a given and stable institution."

> It is also, at the very least, a way of taking a position, in its work of analysis, concerning the political and institutional structures that make

possible and govern our practices, our competencies, our performances. Precisely because it is never concerned only with signified content, deconstruction should not be separable from this politico-institutional problematic and should seek a new investigation of responsibility, an investigation which questions the codes inherited from ethics and politics. This means that, too political for some, it will seem paralyzing to those who only recognize politics by the most familiar road signs. Deconstruction is neither a methodological reform that should reassure the organization in place nor a flourish of irresponsible and irresponsible-making destruction, whose most certain effect would be to leave everything as it is and to consolidate the most immobile forces within the university.[1]

That most of these meanings of deconstruction have been lost on Derrida's disciples and detractors alike is evidence of just how apolitical criticism tends to remain in the United States among everyone but feminists and committed Marxists. Derrida has been appropriated or rejected, as the case may be, primarily on formalist grounds that have restricted deconstruction to a critical technique and associated it with, at best, a politics of indifference and reaction, at worst, a politics of anarchy and hedonism. Not that there aren't grounds for associating such motifs with much deconstructionist criticism, but the central thrust of the poststructuralist critique, of which Derrida's work is one variant, is all of a different order.

There are, in any event, many things that one might say in response to the two fundamentally different challenges posed by this critique, but I will have to confine myself to those directly related to our understanding of the moral imagination and the possibilities for its reconstitution, or, at any rate, reconception, in the present state of cultural crisis. I wish to show, first, that poststructuralism, particularly in its deconstructive form, is not an isolated phenomenon of concern only to literary theorists and philosophical ontologists, but that it reflects a profound shift in values and worldview that is now occurring throughout Western culture and especially in the literary arts. Second, I hope to demonstrate that the cogency of the cultural critique mounted by the deconstructionists, despite the brilliance of many of its insights, finally undermines its own premises and thereby forces us back on an intellectual procedure in all forms of cultural criticism that accepts the prejudices inherent in thinking but according proposes a radically different model for thought. Third and finally, I intend to suggest that the only model of thought that may open the way for a renewed understanding of the place of moral reflection in all acts of critical interpretation is a pragmatic and loosely hermeneutic one.

2

Like the structuralists before them (and the existentialists before them), the poststructuralists and their literary fellow travelers, from Donald Barthelme to John Barth, have in many respects only carried to an extreme that radical skepticism toward Western values which constitutes much of the modern legacy in all the arts and disciplines of thought. Belonging to a tradition whose intellectual roots go back at least as far as the philosophical work of Kierkegaard, Marx, and Nietzsche, structuralism and the deconstructive phase of poststructuralism have their origin in the Romantic and post-Romantic attempt to challenge, and where possible to subvert, all the privileged forms of Western consciousness by getting back, as Melville once put it, to "what remains primeval in our formalized humanity." From this point of view, they have in considerable measure only continued and extended the decreative impulse of cultural modernism itself.

The word *decreation* was first used by Simone Weil and then picked up by Wallace Stevens to define a particular kind of change—not from created to nothingness but from the created to the uncreated. *Decreation* refers to the process of clearing the world of what Stevens terms "its stiff and stubborn, man-locked set," of getting back to that in experience which remains uncontaminated by the imperial designs of the self. The object of such strategies is to reach a point where one can comprehend what Stevens meant by saying, in his poem on Santayana, that "It is poverty's speech that seeks us out the most." This condition of unmediated, unaccommodated simplicity can only be attained in most modern art and thought through a radical process of relinquishment and divestiture. Nonetheless, its aim is not so much repudiation as recovery. Experience is purged of its false overlay of indurated habit and inherited form so that what is perceived or, better, felt to be its essential ground or particular integrity can once again reveal itself. The art and thought reflective of such strategies therefore exhibit a double and not a single movement: they criticize only that they may conserve; they relinquish, even renounce and reject, only so that they may reconstitute.

There is thus in modern literature a remarkable convergence between Eliot's "moment in the rose garden" and Kurtz's confession of horror from the depths of Conrad's *Heart of Darkness,* or between Yeats's devious and sometimes tortuous journey back to "the foul rag-and-bone shop of the heart . . . where all the ladders start" and Ivan Ilych's discovery of the suffocating darkness of death that can sometimes inexplicably provide a tentative opening to the light. All such moments culminate in an intuition that is essentially numinous, not because they appeal to orthodox traditions of faith or heterodox forms of religion but because, in response to the increasing profanation of modern experience, they represent an almost heroic effort to resacralize life by locating and defining its chthonic source, its *point d'appui*. These moments are the result of an often excruciating attempt to strip nature, life, and history of the false accretions of ego so that in the new world of the modern poem, novel, or painting we may be chastened, if not renewed, by that irreducible sense of strangeness, of otherness, which, however terrifying or sublime, will not play us false.

But like postmodern writing in general, poststructuralism, especially in the speculations of Derrida, Barthes, and de Man, dismisses this counterthrust of modern decreative art and thought in favor of carrying its critical impulse to the absurd but logical extreme. This point is reached as soon as one is prepared to argue that the decreated core of experience sought in so much modern art and literature is itself only another privileged perspective by which to assert the superiority of one form of consciousness over another. Hence to posit, as traditional moral critics do, the existence of some elemental self, or primordial element within the self, that is somehow transcendent to, as well as immanent within, culture itself is, for the poststructuralists, to perpetuate the same cycle of domination and subordination that has afflicted Western metaphysics from the beginning. To Derrida and the others, all perspectives are equally illusory and thus equally meaningless, and any assertions to the contrary, either about perspectives within texts or about perspectives outside them, are "fictions" that ought to be deconstructed. Yet this only demonstrates that deconstructionism, both as a critical method and as an artistic mode, does possess a moral dimension in spite of itself. We must deconstruct all our little fictions, so the argument goes, because they belong to a metaphysical tradition of bigger fictions whose purpose is always to gain power over others through spurious claims to ethical or spiritual preeminence.

3

The difficulty with this observation, as critics like Gerald Graff and Hayden White have noted, is that deconstructionists lack the intellectual terms to recognize its validity. Even more serious, they have no way of satisfactorily explaining how deconstructionism itself can operate as an intellectual procedure without falling victim to the same processes of false consciousness it purportedly criticizes in others. If all epistemic standpoints, as deconstructionists argue, are equally privileged and biased, if there is no secure epistemological or ontological ground anywhere, then on what, it must be asked, can the deconstructionist stand as he or she mounts an assault on our specious habits of fabrication?

It is to Derrida's credit that he has acknowledged this problem even though, as we will see momentarily, he can propose no adequate solution to it. If the metaphysics of substance or presence has been undermined by the critical philosophy of the last three hundred years, the fact remains that these newest critics of culture can no more do without its assumption of an ontological center somewhere, of what Thoreau once called "a hard bottom and rocks in place," than can the most intransigent Platonist or neo-Aristotelian. The bottom may be false, as Walter Benn Michaels has pointed out,[2] but their own critique of Western cultural forms positively depends upon its postulation, and their own view of language as unable to "include within itself its own origin or its own end," as Derrida says, clearly presupposes it.[3]

Derrida concedes, in other words, that the Saussurean distinction between signifier and signified, which he and others use to such telling effect in dismantling the legacy of logocentricity, carries with it various metaphysical and theological sediments. As Derrida puts it,

> semiological or, more specifically, linguistic "science" cannot . . . hold on to the difference between signifier and signified—the very idea of the sign—without the difference between sensible and intelligible, certainly, but also not without retaining, more profoundly and more implicitly, and by the same token the reference to a signified able to "take place" in its intelligibility, before its "fall," before any expulsion into the exteriority of the sensible here below. As the face of pure intelligibility, it refers to an absolute logos to which it is immediately united.[4]

For Derrida there is no question of rejecting "these notions; they are necessary and, at least at present, nothing is conceivable for us without them."[5] Hence the project of deconstructionism is not to abandon such notions but merely—though it is a very large "merely"—to define their limitations and to outline their historical closure.

> Since these concepts are indispensable for unsettling the heritage to which they belong, we should be even less prone to renounce them. Within the closure, by an oblique and always perilous movement, constantly risking falling back within what is being deconstructed, it is necessary to surround the critical concepts with a careful and thorough dis-

course—to mark the conditions, the medium, and the limits of their effectiveness and to designate rigorously their intimate relationship to the machine whose deconstruction they permit; and, in the same process, designate the crevice through which the yet unnameable glimmer beyond the closure can be glimpsed.[6]

There now remains little secret about where the crevice lies or what can be glimpsed beyond it. The crevice is to be found in language, and more particularly in all that language masks, hides, or disavows, especially in the act of avowing it. Through this crevice one can obtain a glimpse of a light shed by what Derrida has named, in his essay on Levinas, the "unforeseeably-" or "infinitely-" or "absolutely-other," which Levinas locates at the very center of all religion and which Derrida aptly defines as "the religiosity of the religious."[7] Comprising that dimension of our experience which is "resistant to all categories," the "absolutely-other" discloses itself in what our concepts fail to encompass. This alterity is therefore nothing we can think, or even conceive by thinking in opposition to it, since "thinking the opposite . . . is still in complicity with the classical alternatives."[8] Yet thought and its language can be liberated "for the encounter beyond these alternatives" because the possibility of it is carried within the logic of our concepts, of our discursive practices, themselves.[9] Derrida is careful to state that this encounter with "transcendence beyond negativity"[10] cannot be experienced through direct contact but only through separation, rupture, differentiation, puzzlement. Yet the encounter is available, accessible, indeed unavoidable, at the heart of experience, and it takes the form of a radical question that experience puts to language, " 'at the point where neither no nor yes is the first word' but an interrogation."[11]

To suggest the totality of this interrogation, Derrida falls back, somewhat surprisingly, on religious language, and a religious language that however clearly it intends to echo Levinas, takes on a special urgency and power in Derrida's usage—"a distress and denuding, a supplication, a demanding prayer addressed to a freedom, that is, to a commandment: the only possible ethical imperative, the only incarnated nonviolence in that it is respect for the other."[12] At this point Derrida seems, but only seems, to save himself from self-contradiction by insisting that this total question posed by the failure of our concepts, our language, to encompass and include the "transcendence beyond negativity" is experienced "not as a total presence but as a trace."[13] However, he immediately goes on to claim that nonetheless this trace, or, rather, our encounter with it, constitutes "the only possible opening of time, the only pure future, the only pure expenditure *beyond* history as economy."[14] Moreover, he concludes that the trace of transcendence present in experience in what might be thought of as the sign of its absence proves that "experience itself is eschatological at its origin and in each of its aspects."[15]

To a more "traditional" critic like Gerald Graff, this argument only demonstrates that the "radical" structuralists are caught in a hopeless web of self-contradiction that effectively undermines their claim that reality is merely a construct of consciousness and art its willing or unwilling victim. Though the deconstructionists are correct in rejecting the view that reality exists wholly independent of mind, with literature serving to mediate between reality and mind by mirroring the truth about the one to the consciousness of the other, Graff still wants to hold out for the notion that the moral function of art consists wholly of its ability to express the truth about reality, the point being that now we need to change our conception of the way this occurs. Graff proposes that we join E. H. Gombrich's model of the artwork as a combination of "making" and "matching" with Karl Popper's contention that we obtain knowledge of the real only by disconfirming the hypotheses and conjectures we constantly construct about it. As works of art attempt, through their formal structures of plausibility, to "match" with reality those hypotheses or conjectures we continuously "make" about it, they disclose a range of facts that these hypotheses and conjectures fail to keep in view. In this manner they not only attest to a realm of being that exists outside of consciousness but presumably convey what can only be called "truth" about the nature of that realm, along with some hints about how to accommodate ourselves to it. Graff here wants to hold on to the Kantian notion that our minds constitute the world we perceive, or at least that they provide the frames through which we perceive it, without accepting the corollary notion, which the "radical" structuralists push to such an extreme, that the world we inhabit or interact with is thereby solely imprisoned within the constructions of consciousness. As Graff puts it, the world we inhabit is considerably more and other than the world we construct out of consciousness; in fact, we construct that world because our perceptual experience continuously reveals the failure of our attempts to impose our conscious constructions upon it. What exists outside of or beyond consciousness, then, are precisely those dimensions or facts of experience, those elements of the real world, that resist its impositions.[16]

There can be no question that Graff's revision of the mimetic model of artistic meaning represents an important advance in conceptualizing the mediating function that art serves between consciousness on the one side and what is called the world or reality on the other. The issue is whether it ever quite confronts the questions that deconstructionists, indeed, poststructuralists in general, want to raise. The kind of question a Derrida or a Blanchot or, for that matter, Thomas Pynchon and the later Wallace Stevens might well want to ask is how we can be certain that the dimensions of experience Graff thinks of as resisting the impositions of consciousness aren't just other conscious constructions. Couldn't one argue, in fact, that Gombrich's scheme of "making" and "matching," just like Popper's theory of testing reality through the disconfirmation of our hypotheses, is itself just another "fiction," or culturally contrived way of making sense, that has endured through time, not because in any absolute sense it is true, but only because in some more utilitarian sense it works?

But this line of inquiry can be carried one step further. If the question of truth is what is ultimately at stake in Graff's attempt to defend the notion that reality has an existence independent of mind and that art can still be conceived as an effective moral instrument insofar as it mediates that existence to us, then one can argue that it finally doesn't matter whether the world so mediated to us is real or only imagined. In either case, as the philosopher of history Hayden White has pointed out, the mode of making sense of it is the same.[17] Language provides us with only a limited number of ways to make sense of experience, and these mental configurations, or "tropes," as White calls them—he invokes Kenneth Burke's famous four (metaphor, metonymy, synecdoche, and irony)—are clearly figurative. This means that we can only make sense of experience through the interposition of conscious constructions; it also means that these conscious constructions are inevitably "fictive," or imaginative.

To clarify the implications that this radical refiguration of thought possesses for the question of truth we need only compare the methods of the historian with those of the poet or novelist. In a traditional view it is usually maintained, for example, that the truth claims of the one must differ from those of the other, because the historian is dealing with events assumed to be actual, the poet or novelist with events that instead are held to be fictive. We therefore typically conclude that the historian gives us knowledge of the certifiable, or what is true, and the poet or novelist gives us knowledge of the conceivable, or only of what is possible. "In point of fact," White counters, "history—the real world as it evolves in time—is made sense of in the same way that the poet or novelist tries to make sense of it, i.e., by endowing what originally appears to be problematical and mysterious with the aspect of a recognizable, because a familiar, form."[18] Each employs figurative strategies to confer meaning on situations that initially appear to lack it. In addition, both use the same, or virtually the same, figurative strategies, even though these similar strategies encourage us to draw different conclusions because of the distinctive situations they are respectively meant to encompass.

Historian and poet alike, it must be admitted, are confronted with situations that are interpretively problematic, that raise a question about "what these facts mean," about "what these events signify," but they go about answering such questions in different ways. The historian organizes such "facts" or "events" into a series that seeks to determine their presumed consequences by ordering them in relation to their probable causes. The novelist or poet, on the other hand, organizes the same facts or events into a series that tries to project their plausible implications and ramifications for further experience from an intuitive inference about their essential nature. But the strategies of order are fictive in either case. That is, the historian can only lift his narrative above the level of mere chronicle by finding the "story" in it, by devising an order for his events that suggests in its extreme their most plausible sense. Yet to emplot his narrative the historian must do more than arrange the succession of happenings into a beginning, middle, and end; he must restructure it in conformity with one of the basic types of story that his culture accepts as a credible narrative form. Following Northrop Frye, White is not prepared to concede that there are any more than four basic types or forms of narrative emplotment in the West—tragedy, comedy, romance, and irony—but whether there are four or four hundred is beside the point. The point is that history makes sense in the same way that poems and novels do: not by reproducing the things to which it refers in experience, but by calling to mind recognizable images of those things. Therefore it is not accurate to say that history, any more than fiction, copies or imitates "real" events: "it tells us in what direction to think about . . . events and charges our thought about . . . events with different emotional valences."[19]

If we thus return to our original interest in the question of truth, whether in history, fiction, or any other medium, it should now be apparent that we never respond to the respective contents of these expressive structures, distinctive as those contents may be, but rather to the culturally derived forms by which they organize those contents into meaningful configurations. Our response, in other words, is to the forms "by which consciousness both constitutes and colonizes the world it seeks to inhabit."[20] From this perspective, a position like Gerald Graff's—that truth claims, whether in literature and art or any other medium of expression, depend upon, and must faithfully describe, a realm of being that we somehow know independent of consciousness—creates a false issue and is potentially misleading. Though we doubtless become conscious at all only because of vexations that originate from beyond consciousness, we become sensible of those vexations and proceed to determine what they mean only through the interventions of consciousness itself. What this should tell us is that, just as the more traditional critics like Graff confuse the real argument, so the more radical poststructuralists make too much of only one side of the coin. The crucial question is not whether the constructions of consciousness must be subordinated to the real, nor whether the conventions of language have attained complete sovereignty over the actual, but whether we can ever know the real or the actual except by means of the imaginative or the fictive? And this, in turn, suggests that the essential moral question posed by our experience of works of art is not how to get beyond consciousness, nor how to get rid of it, but rather how to expand its scope or reach.

4

One of the more famous answers to this last question was first outlined by Immanuel Kant in his third *Critique* but has received a fresh and quite un-Kantian restatement by the social thinker and philosopher Hannah Arendt. According to Arendt, Kant's great insight into the moral life derived from his decision to construe all acts of judgment or interpretation as expressions of taste and then to argue that the faculty of taste is less a personal possession than a social acquisition, since it depends so largely not on our ability to seek for our opinions only within ourselves but also on our ability to develop our perceptions in reference to the feelings of others. Arendt uses this insight to lay the basis for a moral conception of cultural discourse by maintaining that differences of taste, far from remaining, as conventional wisdom has it, beyond dispute, are nearly the only things really disputable.

John Dewey, it is worth remarking, said nearly the same thing. Indeed, Dewey's convictions about the centrality of taste in the formation of cultural discourse and, further, about its status as the guarantor of the moral nature of such discourse are especially apt at this point because they demonstrate how one could just as easily arrive at Arendt's position with regard to the social and ethical dimensions of taste by proceeding from a point of origin very nearly the opposite of any represented by Kant. The passage in question deserves to be quoted entire:

> The word "taste" has perhaps got too completely associated with arbitrary liking to express the nature of judgments of value. But if the word be used in the sense of an appreciation as once cultivated and active, one may say that the formation of taste is the chief matter wherever values enter in, whether intellectual, esthetic or moral. . . . Instead of there being no disputing about tastes, they are the one thing worth disputing about, if by "dispute" is signified discussion involving reflective inquiry. Taste, if we use the word in its best sense, is the outcome of experience brought cumulatively to bear on the intelligent appreciation of the real worth of likings and enjoyments. There is nothing in which a person so completely reveals himself as in the things which he judges enjoyable and desirable. Such judgments are the sole alternative to the domination of belief by impulse, chance, blind habit and self-interest. The formation of a cultivated and effectively operative good judgment or taste with respect to what is esthetically admirable, intellectually acceptable and morally approvable is the supreme task set to human beings by the incidents of experience.[21]

What Dewey does not say here but everywhere presupposed is that taste is formed in collaboration with other people and in its very processes of formation helps create a community of these others. Arendt explains how this occurs when she writes that the disputes generated by arguments about taste are valuable because they cannot be adjudicated, much less resolved, without appeal to sentiments and sensibilities other than one's own. Hence such disputes possess the effect, whatever their intentions, of drawing individuals out of themselves and into a wider world of meanings they share with their fellows, even as they simultaneously clarify individual preferences. But the wider world of meaning created by such discourse is none other than the world of culture whose moral purpose, it can now be seen, is simply the further refinement of taste.

It should be obvious that Arendt, like Kant and Dewey before her but unlike many Kantians, clearly dissociates taste from the merely subjective or narrowly impressionistic. Representing the fruition of judgment as much as its source, taste refers primarily to the public sphere, the world we share with others, rather than to the private sphere, the world we share only with ourselves. Within this public sphere, Kant maintained and Dewey echoes, taste is as much a moral category as an aesthetic one because it derives from our capacity not only to judge for ourselves and from within our own frame of reference but also from our capacity to judge from the perspective of others, or, as Kant put it, "to think in the place of everybody else."[22] As Arendt explains,

> the power of judgment [as of interpretation] rests on a potential agreement with others, and the thinking process which is active in judging [or interpreting] something is not, like the thought process of pure reasoning, a dialogue between me and myself, but finds itself always and primarily, even if I am quite alone in making up my mind, in an anticipated communication [or conversation] with others with whom I know I must finally come to some agreement.[23]

Arendt does not mean that we can never judge as others judge or see what others see; she only means that we cannot judge at all unless we can put ourselves at least partially in their place and thus begin to comprehend what things look like, if not to them, at least to us if we occupied their point of observation. To do this is, quite obviously, not to see with their eyes but only to see what their eyes look at, which is a very different matter. To see through their eyes, to judge as they judge, would be tantamount to becoming them, which is clearly impossible. To perceive what is revealed from where they stand, to comprehend what is discernible from their perspective, is simply—though this is a great deal—to enlarge our own horizon of understanding. It may not change how we see or what we feel about it, but it does alter what we must now take into our purview and presumably respond to.

But this only underscores how aesthetic judgments expressive of even the simplest kinds of preference or dislike inevitably take on for Arendt the character of moral judgments—not because they involve approbation or reprobation but because they eventuate in what Kant so movingly called "enlarged mentality." "Enlarged mentality," as Arendt interprets it, represents the ability to think in the place of other people without thinking as other people think. A result of our capacity to imagine our way into frames of thought and forms of sentiment other than our own, "enlarged mentality" is not only what taste aims at but also its chief moral instrument.

For Arendt, then, the faculty of taste is to be located at the opposite end of the affective spectrum from personal prejudice or a sense of cultural privilege. Its basis lies in common and not uncommon sense, the sense we share with others of the meanings we can acknowledge together even when we interpret them according to our personal lights. The purpose of cultivating our sense of taste is to extend the public world of meaning, of interpretation, of significant experience we share with others by joining with them in the debate about what things shall be represented in that world and what attitudes shall be taken with respect to them. Without the constant and relatively free exercise of taste, this world of publicly acknowledged meanings would eventually disappear. With its active cultivation, however, this world, like those who create it out of their conversation, can be expanded and enriched, but only because questions of taste, like all matters of individual judgment, can never be resolved through coercion or the appeal to authority but only through moral suasion, only, as Arendt was fond of quoting Kant to say, "by wooing the consent of everyone else."[24]

5

This recommendation would only strike the poststructuralist as paradoxical and self-contradictory. How can consciousness be expanded, it would be asked, when the logocentricity of our theory of language has already guaranteed it complete sovereignty? And how can consciousness be made morally responsible when its expansion would only strengthen the proclivities to imperialism already latent within it? Indeed, doesn't Arendt's rhetorically suasive way of stating it undermine in advance the credibility of her case? She is determined to manipulate language for the sake of putting a more genial face on a tactic whose only purpose, after all, is domination and control?

Such questions as these serve, or should serve, as a sharp reminder of what in America we have too quickly forgotten, if we ever learned it at all: namely, that poststructuralism developed in Europe out of a political and not just an epistemological or metaphysical critique of Western culture, and that its natural evolutionary bent, as can be seen in the work of thinkers like Foucault and Said, has always been toward a more broadly social as opposed to more restricted literary theory. In America intellectuals have apparently been misled by the fact that this critique seems to center less on the self-aggrandizing tendencies of social collectivities than on those of linguistic and semiotic structures, but the central political insight of poststructuralism, following Nietzsche as much as Marx, is that these structures are essentially hegemonic. The poststructuralist assault on signification has thus amounted to a wholesale attack on the imperialism of consciousness. The "political" task is critically to subvert—the favored word is, of course, *decon-*

struct—all "traces" of such imperialism in whatever structures they have secreted themselves.

Nevertheless, there is something deeply troubling about the way that the discourse of poststructuralism survives the demolition of its own critique. It might be more accurate to say that its own discourse proves most troubling when the strategies of deconstruction it inaugurates— and so often carries to such extraordinary analytical lengths—leaves the authority of its own rhetorical performance somehow untouched. Even when the verbal play of the performance, instead of being "serious," is most whimsical and promiscuous, where it turns against itself and contemplates the absurdity of its own predicament, something about the exercise, if not disturbingly logocentric, is disconcertingly egocentric. If only because of the radical energy of mind and imagination required by its intellectual procedures, one is compelled to say that the discourse tends to focus an inordinate amount of attention directly upon itself. Thus while the language of the discourse is successfully subverting everything within it, the voice of the discourse is effectively subordinating everything outside it. In short, the discourse is always tending to become a monologue.

The problem this creates for poststructuralism in general is very serious indeed. Its enormity can be suggested, however, only if one remembers that poststructuralist philosophy and criticism are based on the premise that all discourse is inevitably composed of oppositional terms that are arranged hierarchically. Thus to deconstruct any discourse involves considerably more than simply reversing its hierarchy of oppositions, or even showing that such a reversal is already potentially immanent within the discourse itself. To deconstruct the discourse completely requires a displacement of the system on which the hierarchy is based. But such systems, which Foucault calls "regimes of power," can only be displaced if they are comprehended from a perspective completely external to them.[25] This, however, is impossible, as Derrida has pointed out, because the old hierarchical system will be partially maintained, even in the act of subverting it, so long as its oppositional repressions remain, as they must, the subject of one's argument. Hence the most one can hope for in deconstruction is to challenge the hierarchical opposition and the system on which it relies by showing how one's own discourse, even as it attempts to reverse the opposition and give it a different meaning and significance, constitutes but a further chapter in the history of repressions it has tacitly or explicitly authorized. To put this differently, since poststructuralist deconstruction is always dependent, as Jonathan Culler has recently remarked, on the system it would "breach," its success as a mode of critical inquiry can only be measured by the degree to which it places its own procedures and perspectives, its own epistemic authority, at risk. The question is whether this can be accomplished at all in a discourse as monologic as deconstructionism.

The Russian critic M. M. Bakhtin would say that it cannot. Bakhtin maintains that monologue is always associated with the voice of "authority," or, rather, represents the form that speech seeking "authority" is most naturally disposed to select for its own utterance. Monologue is a mode of discourse that, no matter how it is used, no matter what is "said" within it, tends to focus attention upon itself and to submit what Bakhtin calls the "heteroglossic," or multivoiced, character of language to the artificial and self-authenticating constraints of some system of understanding. As a mode of discourse, Bakhtin argues, monologue is brought to most complete expression in the genre of lyric poetry, which he sharply contrasts with the more dialectical and "polylogical" mode of discourse typical of the novel and prose in general. The rhetoric of fiction, Bakhtin contends, as indeed of all prose, is oriented not toward the speaker at all but rather toward his or her auditors. Because such rhetoric acknowledges both the plurisignificative character of language and the "polyglossic" character of speech,[26] Bakhtin can assert that the dialogism of prose is politically and intellectually disruptive and even subversive, in a way that the monologism of poetry is not, because the latter, unlike the former, depends upon recognition of, and interaction with, what is different and other and potentially oppositional.

There can be no doubt that Bakhtin's preference for the novel over poetry and the epic—like his interpretation of the novel as an essentially ludic literary mode that through parody, ridicule, laughter, and self-criticism exposes the lie behind every formal, systematic attempt to absolutize any discourse or to idealize any genre, including its own—will challenge longstanding literary and philosophical prejudices, but his grounds for repudiating monologism and embracing dialogism are germane to the present discussion. Essentially moral, they amount to asserting, to put them in the idiom of poststructuralism, that a mode of discourse in which there are no "others" (that is, no significant implied others whose very *différance*, in the full Derridean meaning—different, differing, defering—constitutes a challenge to the authority of certitude assumed by a critical mode that, in its tendencies to infinite regression, is inevitably so self-reflexive) belies what Derrida suggests elsewhere about the anxiety of authority that should attend every assumption of epistemic, moral, or ontological privilege—"of being implicated in the game being caught by the game, of being, as it were, from the very beginning at stake in the game."

This is clearly not the same thing as charging poststructuralism with a self-serving circularity of argument. Even if it remains true that deconstructionism, for example, is so closely bound to its own "governing theoretical premises," as Suresh Raval has claimed, that it "rather ceaselessly seeks to confirm those premises," the crucial problem is not, as she avers, "that the limits of what they say are defined by the concepts they hold . . . [that] the concepts determine the limits of their experience." The problem is rather that "the concepts they hold" are betrayed by "the limits of what they say," or, more accurately, by the limits of what they think their concepts, their premises, give them license to say.[27] In a world defined by a metaphysics of absence rather than of presence, there are few if any prohibitions or constraints interpretive or otherwise, as Nietzsche stated and Dostoevsky confirmed, and this confers upon even the most arbitrary or tentative actions, when they are undertaken deliberately, an enormous presumption of authority. Thus the real difficulty with deconstructionism, as with poststructuralism in general, arises precisely at those points where, as a critical mode, it is, in the words of Gayatri Spivak, most attractive:

> the recognition, within deconstructive practice, of provisional and intractable starting points in any investigative effort; its disclosure of complicities where a will to knowledge would create oppositions; its insistence that in disclosing complicities the critic-as-subject is herself complicit with the object of her critique; its emphasis upon "history" and upon the ethico-political as the "trace" of that complicity—the proof that we do not inhabit a clearly defined critical space free of such traces; and, finally, the acknowledgment that its own discourse can never be adequate to its example.[28]

Recognition of this paradox, that poststructuralist thinking is most assertive and manipulative where it seems most deferential and tentative, has not been entirely lost on some of its ablest representatives, but it is a paradox that can never be overcome or resolved. All one can do, they seem to say, is learn how to enjoy its effects through the play of associations and the startling connections they afford, hoping, perhaps, if that play is carried far enough and executed with enough ingenuity and wariness, to reach that "uncanny moment" of almost kinesthetic as well as cognitive release from the tyranny of signification that some people claim to experience in reading an essay by the later Barthes, or listening to a composition by John Cage, or following a story by Robbe-Grillet.

6

Randall Jarrell complained as long ago as the 1950s about the tendency of criticism to become a new religion, but he was only reacting to the way middle-class couples with a taste for the literary had permitted the critic to displace the poet as the arbiter of aesthetic taste. In our newest age of criticism, this shift of opinion has not been restricted to our conception of the locus of literary authority; it also reflects a change in our view of the source of creative energy. This newest displacement of literature by criticism is expressive of a belief—vigorously held by some, such as Harold Bloom and Geoffrey Hartman, more tentatively entertained by others, such as Frank Lentricchia or Jonathan Culler—that the artist *as artist* is no longer centrally in touch with the most representative or seminal experience of our time and that this experience is no longer necessarily susceptible to being rendered in the more traditional fictive forms. In fact, there seems to be at work in literary culture an active belief to the contrary: that the only forms capable of fully and accurately rendering the ironic, disjunctive, self-contradictory character of contemporary experience are critical, recursive, ratiocinative, and highly self-reflexive, just because the characteristic experience of our time centers on the human mind itself as it moves in brilliant but sometimes fitful and ever more disbelieving steps toward the end of its own tether.

Of fictive forms capable of rendering this experience, only the anatomy will do, that most untraditional of fictive forms deriving from Mennippean satire and organized around the exhaustive play of the mind as it exploits particular ideas or sets of ideas for the purpose of submitting an entire social world to critical scrutiny. More to the point, criticism itself is resorting to the anatomy, is in fact becoming the anatomy, in this excruciatingly intellectualistic age that is so obsessed with thought but so suspicious of ideas. In what might be called positive anatomies, we get historical and generic taxonomies like Northrop Frye's great study of classical and Christian myth, or Angus Fletcher's treatment of allegory, which produce the ironic effect of casting doubt upon the ontological status of the very intellectual systems they are designed to sort out and explain because of the sheer volume of material they amass in support of them. In what could be described as negative anatomies, we get Midrashic interpretations like Derrida's dissections of the classics of Western metaphysics and epistemology, in which the meticulousness of the analysis is carried to the point where the deontologization of the text under discussion leads paradoxically to something like a reontologization of the mode of discussing it.

We are thus left in the uncomfortable position of witnessing the displacement first of literature by criticism and now of criticism by itself in the direction of some newer hierophantic mode as yet unnameable. Still, there is no way out of this spiral, I am convinced, except by going through it. But the way through it does not lie in the direction of some deinterpreted or uninterpretable surd of signs, as the deconstructionists sometimes suggest, nor in the direction of some reinterpreted or overinterpretable system or signifiers, as the semioticians seem to argue, but rather in the direction of a fresh look at experience itself. The question that forces itself upon us is whether or not experience, in all its ragged impurity, vagueness, and improbability, cannot still serve, even in an age without absolutes, as a source not only for critical reflection but also for moral understanding.

their many cultural supporters who refused to limit the reality of experience to the experience of what particular individuals defined as reality. Convinced that reality encompasses at least all that we can know in experience, if not a good deal else besides, they quickly concluded that thought had traditionally attempted to establish the legitimacy of its own operations on the wrong basis and had proposed for itself the wrong objects. In response to the futility, as they perceived it, of isolating some absolute starting point for thought from which one could then proceed in systematic intellectual fashion toward conclusions that bore some correspondent, verifiable relation with the reality they signified, the pragmatists proposed that we change our model of intellectual inquiry. Develop a model, they suggested, that accepts the structural prejudices inherent in thinking but accordingly reconceives the purpose of thought. Instead of conceiving this purpose in essentially substantive or essentialist terms, as the confirmation of what is postulated as true or not true about experience, the pragmatists urged a more empirical, actually experiential conception, as a determination of the implications of specific conceptions of truth. According to the pragmatists, the question posed by experience is not "What is real as opposed to mere appearance?" but "What difference does it make, whether mentally, emotionally, or volitionally, to think so?"

Recourse to the philosophical method and theory of truth known as pragmatism may appear to some as too mild a remedy for the epistemological and ontological cancer diagnosed by poststructuralism, but only if we discount the metaphysical radicalism of the critique on which pragmatism was based. The American pragmatists were just as skeptical as any contemporary poststructuralist about all privileged— they called them "idealist"—claims to truth or meaning, and they were just as convinced that all such claims are based on a false metaphysics of substance or presence—they generally called it a metaphysics of "absolutes"—that had been critically dismantled by the end of the nineteenth century. This left them convinced that the only way to inquire into the truth or meaning of anything is to determine what difference its claim to being true makes to experience, or conversely, to determine, as William James put it, "what experiences will be different from those which would obtain if the belief were false." James went on to say that "Ideas (which themselves are but parts of experience) become true just insofar as they help us get into satisfactory relations with other parts of our experience."[2]

James called this procedure, somewhat unfortunately, the pragmatic method, intending to follow Charles Sanders Peirce, who proposed, in

"How to Make Our Ideas Clear," that the meaning of any idea can only be settled by determining "what conduct it is designed to produce," that conduct constituting, for Peirce, "its sole significance."[3] But when James revised Peirce's formulation by concluding that the pragmatic method was therefore designed to determine the meaning of ideas in light of their conceivable practical effects—"what sensations we are to expect from it, and what reactions we must prepare [for]"[4]— he moved away from Peirce's more behaviorist, or at least empirical, orientation toward one that was more explicitly interpretive and speculative. James assumed that he was remaining faithful to the spirit of Peirce's formulation, even if he changed its letter ever so slightly, but in reality he recast Peirce's definition of the pragmatic method in a somewhat different light, or, rather, invoked the necessity of an additional light, which, in turn, gave the method a noticeably different cast. Though James insisted that his definition of pragmatism accentuated the concreteness of its orientation and brought out the method's strong attachment to facts, actions, and results, the facts, actions, and results with which James believed pragmatism was concerned were more conjectural than confirmed, more constructed than established. That is to say, the pragmatic method, as James defined it, proposed to define the meaning of ideas not in relation to consequences already verified experimentally but only in relation to outcomes anticipated intellectually. Thus while James's pragmatism turned toward ends and conceived of ideas as means or tools, its methods for deciding the meaning and truth of ideas relied far less on empirical instruments of measurement than on conceptual and interpretive and, even more important, imaginative ones.

For this reason it might have been more suitable if James had renamed his version of pragmatism the experiential method or, still more precisely, the hermeneutic method. Had he done so he might then have perceived more readily the need for the kind of methodological shift in critical inquiry that Richard Rorty has recently called for in *Philosophy and the Mirror of Nature* and his newer study *Consequences of Pragmatism*. Rorty argues that in a world deprived of secure metaphysical standpoints, we must radically revise our conception of thought. To carry out the pragmatic program, he asserts, we must replace the old epistemological quest for universals, for foundations, for unchanging essences of which we can be certain and which our discourse is supposed to reflect or mirror, with a more hermeneutic model of critical inquiry as a form of conversation or dialogue, which our discourse is intended to extend and enrich.

Rorty's image of culture as a kind of conversation is heavily indebted to Michael Oakeshott's *The Voice of Poetry in the Conversation of Mankind*. The chief distinction on which this supposition depends is that a conversation is neither an inquiry that holds out the promise of being satisfied nor an argument that holds out the promise of being resolved. The key passage is as follows:

> In a conversation the participants are not engaged in an inquiry or a debate; there is no "truth" to be discovered, no proposition to be proved, no conclusion sought. They are not concerned to inform, to persuade, or to refute one another, and therefore the cogency of their utterances does not depend upon their all speaking the same idiom; they may differ without disagreeing. Of course, a conversation may have passages of argument and a speaker is not forbidden to be demonstrative; but reasoning is neither sovereign nor alone, and the conversation itself does not compose an argument. . . . In conversation, "facts" appear only to be resolved once more into the possibilities from which they were made; "certainties" are shown to be combustible, not by being brought into contact with other "certainties" or with doubts, but by being kindled by the presence of ideas of another order; approximations are revealed between notions normally remote from one another. Thoughts of different species take wing and play round one another, responding to each other's movements and provoking one another to fresh exertions. Nobody asks where they have come from or on what authority they are present; nobody cares what will become of them when they have played their part. There is no symposiarch or arbiter; not even a doorkeeper to examine credentials. Every entrant is taken at its face-value and everything is permitted which can get itself accepted into the flow of speculation. And voices which speak in conversation do not compose a hierarchy. Conversation is not an enterprise designed to yield an extrinsic profit, a contest where a winner gets a prize, nor is it an activity of exegesis; it is an unrehearsed intellectual adventure. It is with conversation as with gambling, its significance lies neither in winning nor in losing, but in wagering. Properly speaking, it is impossible in the absence of a diversity of voices: in it different universes of discourse meet, acknowledge each other and enjoy an oblique relationship which neither requires nor forecasts their being assimilated to one another.[5]

In this rather benign view of conversation, every voice is distinctive as well as equal, or at least no voice should be given priority over any other and each presumably has its part to play. The ability to participate effectively in conversation depends neither on the amount of one's information nor on one's skill in bringing other people over to one's own side; rather, it is a matter of learning how to recognize the different voices at work in any given exchange and the proper occasions and forms of utterance. No one, apparently, is ever at any loss for words, and everyone finds, or should be able to find, a way to have his or her say.

Oakeshott concedes that conversation, in this conception of it, can be subverted in one of two ways: first, whenever any of its participants, forgetting that every voice must remain wholly conversable, separate, or try to separate, what is said from its mode of utterance and thus reduce what is supposed to be a form of speech to a body of conclusions; second, if any voice contributing to it becomes overly obsessed with its own mode of utterance and therefore identifies the conversation with itself. Oakeshott associates the first problem with reductionism, where voice threatens to become eristic; the problem in the second instance is bad manners, where voice gives way to what he calls *superbia*.

Oakeshott is not unmindful of the liabilities of this way of conceiving culture. To some it is likely to appear frivolous, to others deeply skeptical, even cynical.

> This understanding of activity as composed, in the last resort, of inconsequent adventures, often put by for another day but never concluded, and of the participants as play fellows moved, not by a belief in the evanescence of imperfection but only by their loyalty and affection for one another, may seem to neglect the passion and the seriousness with which, for example, both scientific and practical enterprises are often pursued and the memorable achievements they have yielded. And the denial of a hierarchical order among the voices is not only a departure from one of the most notable traditions of European thought (in which all activity was judged in relation to the *vita contemplativa*), but will seem also to reinforce the scepticism.[6]

Oakeshott is clearly troubled by the moral relativism inherent in this view of cultural conversation, but he has no problem with the element of frivolity it implies because of his belief that playfulness is, or should be, ingredient even in the most serious of conversations. For Rorty it is just the opposite. The seriousness with which he takes the relativization of all hierarchies of value that give priority to one voice over another in cultural experience seems to exclude, or at least to limit severely, the ludic element in his conversational model of culture. His chief concern is whether we can carry the skepticism far enough, whether we can take the hermeneutic cynicism, if cynicism it is, seriously enough.

In any case, although Rorty himself doesn't quite say so, this conver-

sational relativization of axiological hierarchies amounts, epistemologically and politically, to a suspension of the search for the limits of the
knowable and for an unprivileged ordering of the known in favor of an
examination of the heuristic potential of the knowing process itself and
an exploitation of those social arrangements that encourage the widest
possible participation in it. Metaphysically and morally, this involves a
replacement of a world of total possibility, where, at least within hermeneutics, virtually anything goes, with a pluralistic world of limited
but necessary options, where the cost of everything is measured in
relation to the alterations of experience that must, as it were, be exchanged for it. From the pragmatic perspective, life is a series of
tradeoffs, almost as though it were a zero-sum game, where the value
lies in weighing every alternative by the shrewdest of calculations.
From the poststructuralist perspective, life is more nearly like a fixed
or predetermined set of choices that wait to entrap the unwary and
that require all the subtle dexterity and mental agility of the escape
artist to elude.

To reconceive critical inquiry along such lines as these is to realize
that the ethical issue in criticism cannot be confined to the question of
what to make of texts in the light of what they presumably say—
whatever else they may say—about us. It must be widened to encompass the question of what to make of ourselves in the light of what
texts say—no matter how indirectly they say it—about others. But this
puts the issue too obliquely. The central issue in a hermeneutic—or, if
you will, a pragmatic—theory of criticism is neither what texts say
about us nor what we say about them but what we can learn from the
forms of otherness they mediate to us. Hence the moral question for
criticism, the question implied by a pragmatic model, is not, to use the
fashionable locution, how to fix the "said" of the text in conceptually
stable or ethically absolute terms, but how to define the differences it
can, or should, make when the world of experience is constructed and
construed from perspectives, or, as we now say, privileged epistemic
standpoints, other than our own. The object, at least according to
Rorty, is "edification"—"to take us out of our old selves by the power
of strangeness, to aid us in becoming new beings."[7]

Edification is Rorty's word for the German concept of *Bildung,* or
self-formation. He extracts this concept from the philosophy of Hans-
Georg Gadamer where edification, which for Rorty and for Gadamer
is simply a better word for "education," displaces, without quite
wholly replacing, the acquisition of knowledge or truth as the actual
goal of thinking itself. What seems to be at issue in this substitution is

the question of what results from taking thought, even when the act of thinking is directed at something as specific as a determination of the real. Rorty's point, following Gadamer, is that the actual operations of thinking produce an alteration in the mind, indeed, in the very being of the thinker, and that this alteration is more consequential than any other more specific accomplishments that thought may want to claim for itself. For what is necessarily, if ever so slightly, changed by virtue of such activity is not merely the perspective of the thinker but his or her whole disposition. This addition, or enhancement, is normally produced, according to Rorty, in one of two ways: either through an interpretation of the connections between our own cultural mindset or discipline and another that is unfamiliar to us, or through the more imaginative invention of new terms or new disciplines to defamiliarize situations to which we have become overly habituated. In either case, an introduction of novelty or otherness in this process elicits change, and not only change, to recall Rorty's incipiently religious language, but renewal, rejuvenation, even rebirth.

1

As it happens, the strikingly antinomian, almost salvific, tone of Rorty's description of the aim of critical inquiry is echoed in other works of contemporary criticism that draw on the pragmatic tradition. In fact, this strangely Adamic, even religiously nostalgic intonation can be found in a book as shrewdly knowing as Geoffrey Hartman's aptly titled *Criticism in the Wilderness,* which calls for a new emigration of philosophical ideas from within America to balance the much heralded immigration from without. Hartman hopes that such a "swerve" away from Continental traditions and back toward American thinkers like Peirce, James, Royce, and Randolph Bourne will produce a new "transnational" base for American criticism. Hartman remains unclear about just what such a critical perspective will look like, but he is quite specific about what it will entail. Like Rorty before him, Hartman believes that we can only move beyond criticism in the direction of some new recovery of interpretive immediacy and encounter—toward what he terms "the presence of the fictive, and . . . the fiction of presence"[8]—by means of criticism, but a criticism that reverses the genteel fastidiousness of the New Criticism by moving in a revisionist direction back toward impurity, *bricolage,* and outrageousness. This criticism will attempt to reconnect modernism philosophically with its Romantic origins and thus to revise modernism in the direction of its religious foundations while at the same time renouncing the ambition either "to master or demystify its subject by technocratic, predictive or authoritarian formulas."[9]

In the light of his subsequent reflections in *Consequences of Pragmatism,* I believe, Rorty would respond by noting that you can't have it both ways. If one wants to opt for interpretive immediacy and encounter, as Hartman does—that is, to restore to criticism its own voice without permitting this voice to possess more normative authority than any of the other voices that potentially constitute the cultural conversation—then one must abandon Hartman's project of regrafting modernism to its Romantic roots, on the assumption that even if this were to retrieve for criticism the "right" to its "own tongue," that tongue could not be permitted, in a pragmatic culture at least, to accord criticism any priority of speech.[10]

To put this differently, Rorty would be likely to argue that Hartman has misconstrued the relation between Romanticism and pragmatism and is therefore attempting to push Romanticism in the wrong direction. As Rorty sees it, the point is not to reunite Romanticism with its spiritual roots but to appreciate the way that Romanticism has relativized our various discourses so that pragmatism could then place their appeals on a different footing. Romanticism therefore inaugurated the revolution that pragmatism, according to Rorty, has now completed. Where Romanticism demonstrated that no single discourse possesses privileged access to ultimate reality, that different discourses can get at the same essential truth, pragmatism, on Rorty's account, then suspended the quest for reality or truth as such and proposed instead that we differentiate between different discourses simply by determining what they can respectively do for us. Philosophical pragmatism, then, which is the same thing for Rorty as critical pragmatism, falls into place as the beginning of the last stage in the devolution, really the disintegration, of the Western tradition of metaphysical idealism.

Rorty's account of this collapse, a process that led to the creation of what he calls "post-philosophical culture," is sufficiently interesting and germane to warrant further comment. By Rorty's reckoning there were three stages involved. The first occurred at the end of the Enlightenment, when metaphysical idealism differentiated itself from all the more traditional forms of dogmatic or deistic supernaturalism by insisting, to paraphrase Maurice Mandelbaum's definition, that the clue to an understanding of ultimate reality lay within human experience and not outside it, and specifically in those traits that define human beings as spiritual.[11] The second stage occurred when Romanticism gave up the idealist assumption that reality possesses an ultimate nature whose essence is encompassable within a single vocabulary and proposed instead that different vocabularies furnish us with different routes of access to the real and different images of what constitutes its ultimacy. The third stage occurred when the Romantic notion that there are different modes of access to what is conceived as ultimately real was displaced by the arguments of naturalists like Nietzsche, on the one hand, and pragmatists like James, on the other, that different vocabularies are simply different ways of stating and sometimes getting what we want. At this point philosophy could no longer be viewed as the source of some Archimedean point from which to survey the whole of cultural experience, because all Archimedean points were now construed as parts of cultural experience and the philosophical search for them simply understood as one among a variety of ways of satisfying particular spiritual needs.

According to Rorty's calculus, this threefold development now places all philosophical criticism on the same level with all cultural criticism, and places all cultural criticism, at least when it is sufficiently pragmatic, on the same level with what he calls contemporary "textualism." Rorty then unites modern pragmatism with contemporary textualism because both repudiate the correspondence theory of truth, the picture theory of language, and the mimetic theory of art in favor of a view that all cultural forms can be construed as texts that exist not for what can be found within them but rather for what can be got out of them. Their meaning, in other words, is identical with their possibilities for use, and these uses are determined solely by the economics of the linguistic marketplace where, as Barbara Herrnstein Smith says, we transact our symbolic business.[12] Weak textualists—what most people would call structuralists—are those who think there is some deep structure encoded within the text that can be deciphered with the assistance of the proper methodological tools. Strong textualists—most people call them poststructuralists—are those who find the deep structure of their own vocabulary more interesting than any deep structure within the texts they examine and thus use texts to stimulate their own interpretations. Instead of attempting to decipher texts, strong textualists prefer to misread them, the object being not to do them "justice" but to make them more interesting.

Rorty's brief summary of the evolution of cultural criticism has much to recommend it. For one thing, his description of cultural criticism as a kind of displaced philosophy or metaphysics and philosophy as a kind of displaced theology or religious mythography clarifies the historical relation between traditional religious thinking, if there is such a thing, and this kind of critical discourse. If the one works out of a normative center and attempts to widen the authority of that center, the other develops in response to the collapse of such centers and constitutes itself as a discipline engaged in assessing the comparative merits of their various legacies. For another, Rorty's account sharpens our sense of the ethos of much contemporary cultural criticism by describing it as a discourse whose essential purpose is neither to confirm nor to console but rather, essentially, to sustain. The intent is to substitute for a science of criticism a hermeneutics of discourse and to argue, as Rorty does so effectively, that the main business of culture is, pure and simple, to keep the conversation going.

Nevertheless, it appears to me that there are serious problems with Rorty's view of postphilosophical culture and the kind of critical conversation that it comprises. On the one side, Rorty's definition of the current cultural situation and the place of critical inquiry within it fails to deal with the interpretive malady most simply diagnosed in the title of one of William James's most famous essays, "On a Certain Blindness in Human Beings." James was referring to the myopia we experience with respect to the perspectives of others because of the fetish we make of our own. And even when we manage to resist the temptation to fetishize our own perceptions, James realized, there remain so many other constraints besides conversational ones—linguistic, economic, social, and political—that seem to control the discourse that constitutes culture. On the other side, Rorty fails, so far as I can tell, to comprehend the contradiction within poststructuralism or textualism itself, a contradiction that prevents it from being either continuous with or parallel to his own version of pragmatism. He never acknowledges that Derrida and many who follow him, in contradistinction with the more radical pragmatists, continue to think metaphysically even when they repudiate metaphysics. John Searle is only the latest critic to have pointed this out, but his argument possesses the added interest of being defended exclusively on pragmatic grounds. Searle contends that Derridean textualists remain hostage to the very logocentric system they would dismantle because of their insistence that the collapse of metaphyics has changed everything. In point of fact, Searle maintains, for all the talk about an "ontology of presence" being displaced by an "ontology of absence," it has changed nothing at all; "as Wittgenstein says, it leaves everything exactly as it is."[13] Rorty, of course, would have no difficulty in accepting Wittgenstein's conclusion; he simply fails to see that it renders the whole textualist or poststructuralist critique of logocentricity deeply problematic and therefore obliges us to consider pragmatism not only as discontinuous with poststructuralism but, as I have already suggested, essentially an alternative to it.

Rorty is on more certain ground, and incidentally comes closer to providing a satisfactory explanation of the meaning of edification as the aim of critical inquiry, when he falls back on John Dewey's view of the destiny of philosophy in a postreligious, if not postphilosophical, world. Dewey argued that when philosophy relinquishes the attempt to transcend experience, it becomes instead a form of criticism whose purpose is to clarify the nature and implications of our attachment to the cultural constituents of our experience. Dewey realized that this could only be accomplished by what he called "the discipline of severe thought."[14] To understand such attachments critically—that is, in relation to the conditions from which they emerge and the consequences, whether actual or merely potential, to which they may give rise— Dewey perceived that it was necessary to examine our typical or habitual ways of viewing them.

> We cannot permanently divest ourselves of the intellectual habits we take on and wear when we assimilate the culture of our own time and place. But intelligent furthering of culture demands that we take some of them off, that we inspect them critically to see what they are made of and what wearing them does to us.[15]

But the aim of this strategy was not the recovery of some "primitive naiveté" of experience, which Dewey held to be impossible anyway, but rather the creation of what he described as a kind of "cultivated naiveté," and this required a rigorous act of what he called "intellectual disrobing."[16]

Dewey was here outlining in brief what we might now call his cultural hermeneutics, a hermeneutics not of suspicion, as in so much contemporary critical theory, but of replenishment. Dewey was fully prepared to view philosophy as but another theory of interpretation, but the goal of this interpretive theory was neither diagnostic nor, in the narrow sense of the word, remedial. Dewey did not believe that philosophy constituted either a better pathology than other disciplinary sciences or a more adequate surgical procedure. Its real momentum was all in another direction. As a restorative discipline, philosophy had the chief aim of recovering and critically renewing our relation to the constituents of our experience, not in the primitive immediacy of our first encounter with them but only in the "artful innocence" of our second. This was Dewey's way of affirming the now widely accepted dictum that we can only overcome the consequences of criticism by means of the correctives of criticism. It was at the same time to underscore what has since become recognized as one of the major insights of interpretation theory in general: that culture is not to be transcended from without but only from within, and transcended only by those possibilities for self-overcoming that are implicit in the very act of understanding, or, as Dewey preferred to call it, communication itself.

To argue that understanding entails self-effacement and precipitates self-transcendence is not only to acknowledge, at least implicitly, that conversation, dialogue, even dialectic, is integral to the processes of culture, but also to assume that the aim of culture is finally heuristic or, as Dewey preferred to say, educational. The question posed by every cultural conversation or transaction for Dewey is what can be learned from it, how it can teach us; this concern sprang from the heart of his belief that in a democracy the highest ambition that culture, and the conversations of which it is comprised, can set for itself is to bring every individual "into the full stature of his possibility." Dewey thus concluded his path-breaking book of 1920, *Reconstruction in Philosophy,* by noting that "Democracy has many meanings, but if it has a moral meaning, it is found in resolving that the supreme test of all political institutions and industrial arrangements should be the contribution they make to the all-around growth of every member of society."[17]

In saying this, Dewey was prepared to concede that, as he put it elsewhere, "A Democracy is more than a form of government; it is primarily a mode of associated living, of conjoint communicated experience."[18] But unlike Richard Rorty, who otherwise shares his sentiments about the moral value of democracy, Dewey was perfectly aware that the associated forms of communicated experience that democracies attempt to cultivate are not always accessible to everyone, that not all people, or even most people in a democracy, actually enjoy the opportunity to realize the full measure of their possibility. Thus for Dewey the most serious difficulties posed by a pragmatic view of culture as a particular kind of conversation were not ontological or epistemological, as they are for Rorty, but political and ethical. Rorty seems to forget, or at any rate refuses to consider with sufficient seriousness, what Dewey never failed to remember: that discourse is rhetorical, that rhetoric is a form of persuasion, and that persuasion is a form of power, an instrument of social manipulation and control. Thus Rorty is unable to discern, as Frank Lentricchia has recently pointed out so vividly in *Criticism and Social Change,* that by concentrating almost exclusively on the aesthetics of the conversation that constitutes culture—that is, on the way individuals can be revivified by it, rejuvenated, almost reborn—he has not only ducked the political question about who gets to participate in the conversation but also the moral question about whether these suasive processes serve the social and other interests of some groups at the expense of others. In other words, while conceding the danger in every cultural conversation to hypostatize "some privileged set of descriptions,"[19] Rorty never quite manages to ask if one of the motives generating such conversations in the first place might be the opportunity they provide certain classes to essentialize their own interests through the privileging of particular ideas and idioms.

Lentricchia proposes that the only thinker within the pragmatic tradition in American thought who has fully confronted these issues is Kenneth Burke. In Lentricchia's reading, therefore, Burke provides the perfect radical corrective to Rorty's overly sanguine and admittedly bourgeois meliorism because his theory of critical inquiry simultaneously acknowledges the political nature of all cultural forms, including critical and artistic ones, and yet resists the essentializing tendencies in every theoretical attempt to make thinking more systematic, including his own.

2

The politics of Burke's critical program is suggested by the title of his first book, *Counter-Statement,* where he takes up a position from within modernism to launch a criticism of modernism itself. In doing so Burke produces what Geoffrey Hartman would rightly call a "revisionist reversal" of modernist aesthetics.[20] Burke's strategy is to counter the modernist claim that art is opposed to science, or that art constitutes a world unto itself, or that art is self-referential and autotelic, with the statement that art is rather "a type of oppositional activity" whose "discordant and disruptive voice [is] out to 'undermine any one rigid scheme of living' "[21] To fulfill his own oppositional and disruptive function as a critic, and further to display the political coloration of his own pragmatism, Burke then proceeds by raising the pragmatic question about the kind of social structure that is implied in, or could be produced by, the aesthetics of modernism.

Lentricchia throws Burke's radicalism into even greater prominence by contrasting it with the deconstruction of Paul de Man, which Lentricchia characterizes as "conservatism by default."[22] What becomes clear to Lentricchia as a result is the way Burke anticipated structuralists and poststructuralists alike by conceiving of art, and all other expressive objects, as but another form of interpretation, of reading, while still holding firmly to the basic Marxist axiom that all expression is equally a form of praxis. This perception of the correlation between discourse and action, between hermeneutics and power, constitutes the heart of Burke's pragmatism, so far as Lentricchia is concerned, and provides the chief source of Burke's crucial insight into the social ends culture serves if Burke, and with him Lentricchia, is correct in believing, contrary to Rorty, that the conversation that constitutes culture is always historically freighted with social privilege and inevitably directed toward constituting and maintaining social elites that seek to essentialize themselves. Lentricchia's own argument with Rorty is that the latter's view of culture as discourse altogether overlooks these concrete historical and empirical constraints on the conversation that constitutes culture and instead concentrates only on those that define the structure and ethos of the conversation itself. From Lentricchia's perspective, Rorty's understanding of culture and its conversation is therefore too free, detached, and personal. Rorty's view suggests that we are essentially at liberty to say what we want in the conversation and to want what we say, when, on Lentricchia's reading, it seems manifestly obvious from an inspection of history that the nature of human desire is largely delimited not only by the available forms of human expression but also by the exigencies of our social situation.[23]

But Lentricchia is also of the opinion that Burke's position possesses its own Achilles heel. In fact, Burke's Achilles heel can be defined in either of two ways, depending on Lentricchia's argument. When Lentricchia is absorbed with the metaphysics of his argument, then he perceives Burke's weakness as a residual essentialism that threatens to undermine the otherwise antiessentialist thrust of his whole system of Dramatism. "Dramatism" is Burke's name for a theory of motives that attempts to interpret all human actions in relation to a fundamental grammar. Burke has been very careful, however, to make certain that this grammar is not reductionist, by organizing it around terms that seek to exploit ambiguities rather than avoid them, by locating the particular places in any theory of action where they naturally arise. Nor is this grammar intended to be essentialist, because Burke has restricted his interest to the terms alone (Act, Scene, Agent, Agency, and Purpose) and not to the utilization of their potential for formulating actual statements about motives themselves. Still, Lentricchia believes that he can discern a trace of essentialist thinking in Burke's assumption that there are universal patterns of human subjectivity from which all behavior springs.

Lentricchia views this trace as evidence that Burke has never successfully managed to overcome his own modernist humanism; Burke still seems to think, as Lentricchia reads him, that there is an essence to our humanity that enables us to develop adequate explanations of our action. But Lentricchia then turns around and embraces something very much like the latent essentialism he attributes to Burke when, in response to Paul de Man's claim that the death of humanism means that we can no longer be held responsible for our actions, Lentricchia eloquently protests: "We may never wholly know what we are doing, as de Man argues, but in some part we do, and to that part at least we must hold ourselves to political account."[24] But isn't Lentricchia's assertion itself humanistic? In fact, couldn't someone like Saul Bellow say very nearly the same thing—as, indeed, in *Mr. Sammler's Planet,* he actually does?

Despite the rigor of his analysis, Lentricchia's case against the metaphysics of Burke's argument never manages to answer such questions; but when Lentricchia turns instead to the social and political dimensions of his argument, then Burke's weakness, and thus the vulnerability of his pragmatism as an adequate model of critical inquiry, appears in a very different light. The problem with Burke's position then turns for Lentricchia on the character of Burke's radicalism. Like any committed Marxist thinker, Lentricchia naturally believes that the central political task is not merely to interpret the world differently but also to change it, and from this perspective Burke's pragmatism has much to recommend it. Not only does Burke explain the social and political implications of all expressive actions and forms; his pragmatism assumes from the start that ideas have social consequences, that interpretations produce material effects. But the question that lingers with Lentriccia is whether Burke's pragmatism also does justice to the fact that interpretations *reflect* material circumstances, that ideas *represent* empirical conditions. Does Burke's critical pragmatism fully comprehend, Lentricchia wants to know, the role that material forces play not only as a source of cultural discourse but also as one of its principal determinants?

In a sense, this question is more problematic than the ambiguity of any answer Lentricchia can provide for it. The question reveals a residual essentialism on Lentricchia's part, as in the thought of many Marxists, that is far more troublesome than any residual essentialism we can detect in Burke. The chief difficulty with Lentricchia's question has to do with the model of culture on which it depends. Culture, it seems to assume, is in considerable part the product or expression of material conditions, which are imagined to stand over against it. But if Lentricchia is to avoid the trap of essentialism himself, he must be prepared to question the entire base-superstructure conception of the relation between cultural formations and empirical realities. For as Marshall Sahlins has demonstrated, in *Culture and Practical Reason,* there are no "material conditions" that in the classic Marxist sense stand over against "culture"; the concept of "material," like the notion of "conditions," is merely a symbolic construct that may, it is true, prove determinative of social structure, but not because it is other than cultural.[25] Sahlin's point, one that much Marxist thinking has yet to absorb, is that it is simply incorrect to assert that material conditions have priority over cultural constructs in the formation of society; rather, as Sahlins points out, in our society at least—the same would not necessarily remain true in relation to various others—the symbolism of material conditions, particularly in their economic form, has proved "structurally determining." Thus it would be more accurate to say that social structures are not determined by what exerts authority over cultural constructs from outside them, or rather, as in the Marxist image, from what lies "beneath" them, but instead by how the various elements of experience that such constructs designate are hierarchically arranged and institutionally integrated within them.[26]

This is precisely where Burke's pragmatism is most pertinent to a criticism committed, as Lentricchia rightly is, to social change. Burke's critical method is designed explicitly to take account of those conditions that are material to, in the sense of being constitutive of, whatever is constructed or produced culturally. Burke's pragmatic criticism, or critical pragmatics, is accountable to such factors because it proceeds from the assumption that all symbolic actions and forms can be viewed as responses to situations that are at once concrete and empirical in the full Jamesian sense. But these responses are not automatic or instinctive; they are calculated, stylized, and strategic. Their purpose, in a word, is to seek some control or power over the situation that prompts them by projecting some strategy for encompassing or transcending it. As strategic responses to situations, symbolic actions and forms typically proceed, first, by sizing up the situations they confront; next, by defining their structure and essential ingredients; and, finally, by defining or naming them in a way that conveys an implicit attitude toward them.

One of the most important points about this conception of symbolic or cultural forms, including critical ones, is that it is as far from personal subjectivism as it is from historical relativism, and it outlines a critical method that is both empirical and, within certain limits, fully generalizable. As Burke stated in one of his earliest formulations of his theory: "The situations are real; the strategies for handling them have public content; and in so far as the situations overlap from individual to individual, or from one historical period to another, the strategies possess universal relevance."[27]

From this Burke deduced at one point in his career that it might be possible "to provide a reintegrative point of view, a broader empire of investigation encompassing the lot."[28] But this metacritical impulse, which might have entailed essentializing risks of its own, has always been frustrated by Burke's steadfast repudiation of categories that attempt to "place things" in favor of categories that emphasize their active nature. Hence his search for categories, as in his theory of Dramatism, that are precise without being reductionistic, that, so to speak, "lie on the bias," that cut across all the disciplines and concepts of modern specialization without blurring the kinds of differentiations they sometimes respectively enable.[29]

A second point worth making about Burke's theory of cultural and critical forms, and one that further protects it from essentialism even while confirming its political thrust, is that the strategic encompassment or transcendence afforded by symbolic actions and constructs is designed not to propel us "beyond culture" in any sense, no matter how metaphorically qualified, but rather to take place wholly within it. The transcendence made possible by Burke's critical theory is a transcendence of culture by means of culture itself, that is, a transcendence of terms alone, or of what Burke now prefers to call "terministic screens."[30] Implied in this possibility of intra- as opposed to supracultural transcendence is the political possibility that if we can never wholly master our destiny, we can become, once we learn how to think "grammatologically" rather than metaphysically, arbiters of the destiny of some of our masters.[31] Which is simply to say that if we can't ever manage to escape material conditions, we can at least alter some of their social and cultural uses.

Burke's method for turning cultural criticism into an instrument of social change is fundamentally, and often maddeningly, comic. But the underlying purpose of his resort to a method of comic inversions and juxtapositions is neither to disarm his enemies nor to gull his friends. It is rather to create an intellectual idiom supple and quixotic enough to resist the seductions even of its own performance. Thus if Lentricchia, like the poststructuralists, is correct in thinking that one of our chief problems as human beings is the temptation to reify or essentialize our own insights, then Burke has discovered that the best strategy for resisting and thus surmounting this temptation is to learn how to laugh at our own foibles. Whether the ability to laugh at ourselves involves a "transcendence upward," as Burke might call it, or a "transcendence downward," Lentricchia is undoubtedly sensitive to Burke's mastery of this mode but nonetheless rather curiously leaves all the humor out of the Burke he presents to us. The result of such an omission in a book otherwise so probing and forceful—Wayne Booth's treatment of Burke as a theoretical pluralist in *Critical Understanding* suffers from the same lapse—is clearly disappointing. Burke's comedy is no mere stylistic embellishment of his thought but part of its very substance, and contributes in crucial ways to its credibility in a time so disingenuous as our own. Thus to deprive Burke of his jokes, his puns, and his sly winks, to say nothing of his burlesques of the serious and his parodies of the banal, is to rob him of much of the machinery that makes his thinking radically critical and his criticism radically social and political.

3

Burke's criticism is founded on the belief that insight or perspective is most often afforded by improbable juxtapositions and unlikely, often outrageous, comparisons. The basis of this belief lies ultimately in the tropological nature of language itself, where metaphor and its variants, metonymy and synecdoche, attest to the necessity of naming things in terms of what they are not. But this deeply ingrained tendency in our speech to call things, as it were, by their "wrong" name is even more dramatically revealed in what Burke calls "exorcism by misnomer," the verbal tactic by which we cast out "devils by misnaming them." The example that comes to mind is the way we comfort the frightened child who cannot fall asleep in the darkened room because of a vague shape in the corner by showing the child that the forbidding object is merely an old coat hanging on a hook. "One has not thereby named the object which struck the terror but misnamed it. Thus one casts out demons by a vocabulary of conversion, . . . by calling them the very thing in all the world that they are not."[32]

Burke's belief in the utility of startling terminological inversions and combinations is most effectively expressed in the lucid improvisations that he performs both on and with his own critical language. Burke has developed an entire lexicon, or menagerie, of critical terms to furnish him with what he calls "perspective by incongruity"—*naming, counterweighting, corrective discounting, maneuvering, charting, investment, mergers, frames of acceptance, coordinates of thought, secular conversions, demoralizing, remoralizing, exorcism by misnomer, bureaucratizing the imaginative, stylistic infections, ritual reidentification, scapegoating, critical debunking,* and a whole zoo of other marvelous creatures that help characterize what Burke elsewhere calls "the human barnyard." The purpose of this lexicon is to give critics what Burke says art gives to the rest of us, namely "a greater complexity of coordinates," so that we can "see around the corner," "figure out what's coming next."[33]

These tactical terms are necessary because Burke assumes that culture constitutes a conspiracy against the self, even though we all play our part in it. The conspiracy that culture foments and supports is a conspiracy of piety, according to Burke, a conspiracy about "what properly goes with what." But the word *piety* in Burke's critical lexicon represents more than a sense of propriety, of fittingness, of taste in the narrow sense; it also constitutes the source of essentialism itself because it "contributes to the desire to round things out, to fit experiences into a unified whole."[34] Burke therefore calls piety our chief "system-builder" and explains its mode of construction as follows:

> If there is an altar, it is pious of man to perform some ritual act whereby he may approach this altar with clean hands. A kind of symbolic cleanliness goes with altars, a technique of symbolic cleansing goes with cleanliness, a preparation or initiation goes with the technique of cleansing, the need of cleansing was based upon some feeling of taboo—and so on, until pious linkages may have brought all the significant details of the day into coordination, relating them integrally with one another by a complex interpretive network.[35]

Piety, of course, need not be associated only with solemnities, according to Burke, even if Santayana provided the best definition of it as "loyalty to the sources of our being." This would help explain the connection Burke discerns between the range of piety and childhood experiences, "since in childhood we develop our first patterns of judgment, while the experiences of maturity are revisions and amplifications of these childhood patterns."[36] It may also suggest why the maintenance of piety can be so painful, "requiring a set of symbolic expiations to counteract the symbolic offenses involved in purely utilitarian actions."[37]

But Burke strongly resists identifying piety exclusively with religion. In fact, his most effective demonstration of its operations is to be found in his witty speculation about what Matthew Arnold would have done if he had suddenly found himself standing on a corner in the company of the gashouse gang watching the parade of local pulchritude pass by. Everything about him, Burke notes, would have been wrong: he would have misunderstood the conventions about swearing, he would have given offense by his reactions to the commentary on feminine comeliness, and he would have wholly failed to appreciate the etiquette of spitting.

The moral question thus raised by the ubiquity and sovereignty of piety, Burke might say in echo of the poststructuralists, is how to keep from being wholly seduced. But where poststructuralists have sought to resist seduction by attempting, futilely as I see it, to disavow and dismantle the system as a whole, Burke settles for the more prosaic task of presenting as many counterinfluences as possible. Here Burke's terminological operations come into play: they help us resist the enticements of cultural piety through intellectual manipulations that challenge the connections it would enforce. If the essentializing and privileging tendencies of cultural behavior always encourage what Burke elsewhere calls an attitude of "Holier than Thou," Burke's critical tactics—some would call them critical antics or hijinks—are designed to promote an attitude of cultural irreverence.[38]

But if Burke's criticism, or any other for that matter, is to escape the hypostatization of its own attitudes and biases, it is not enough for its language to be iconoclastic and culturally blasphemous; in fact, such language is far too easily produced. To be fully effective in resisting the pull of its own pieties, criticism must reflect what Burke calls "our fundamental kinship with the enemy."[39] But this recognition requires the development of a critical language that not only challenges the privileging of its own terms but also seeks to undermine such symbolic activity everywhere by revealing the strategies in which we are all implicated. For this purpose only a comic language will do, one that thrives on the possibility of comic reversals and absurd, or at least unexpected and unlikely, linkings and comparisons. Thus all of Burke's critical terms—*socialization of losses, condensation and displacement, transubstantiation, counter-morality, transcendence downward*—operate as modes of convertibility that simultaneously permit him to bring strikingly different things into unanticipated relations and to keep his readers off balance.

This principle of comic convertibility, of terminological metamorphosis, is not only the essence of Burke's critical method but also the basis of his social and political hope. Burke is convinced that if we cannot wrench things loose enough from their conventional linguistic and axiological moorings to imagine them in new valuational configurations, then we are indeed captives of a closed system and there is, as it were, nothing to be done. But Burke believes we can do this; he believes, both literally and figuratively, in transformation, in the possibility of symbolic rebirth. Indeed, he is continually converting himself into a kind of quick-change artist, masquer, magician, trickster, whose disguises, far from intending to hide his sleight of hand, are all designed as provocations and come-ons to bring his readers into the game and to show them how to play.

These ludic improvisations and performances give to much of Burke's writing an almost liminal quality. One is always in the process not only of transgressing against cultural shibboleths but also of transversing the boundaries of propriety between them. The moment of illumination for Burke—he might almost call it the moment of "epiphany" or "revelation"—comes in those passages of transition where one set of critical coordinates is discarded for another. Burke speaks of such coordinates as a kind of "calculus" for mapping or charting events and for clarifying their implications and effects. And if such coordinates could ever be gathered into a larger system, that system would ideally take on the form of a metacritical glossary or dictionary of terms. But Burke's metacritical dictionary would be self-consciously conceived and constructed as a devil's dictionary, not only because its categories would violate so many protocols of traditional classifications but also because its overall intention would be to refute the privileging and essentializing assumptions on which all other taxonomic and classificatory schemes are based. Thus even in its lexicographical aspects, Burke's criticism takes on the stylistic character of a lawyer's brief and, like any legal argument, depends for its proof on its suasive capacities to appeal to common, and not uncommon, sense, or, as Burke might describe it, on its possibilities for "gainful employment." The commercial imagery is no accident. Though Burke relies less upon the language of finance and the marketplace than he once did, his recourse to a heavily economic vocabulary not only follows the verbal tactics adopted by earlier pragmatists, such as William James, but also represents a strategic attempt to write in the idiom of his contemporaries while at the same time parodying it. In justification of such a strategy, one can almost hear Burke quoting a line Melville gives to Ishmael early on in *Moby-Dick:* "Not ignoring what is good, I am quick to perceive a horror, and could still be social with it . . . since it is but well to be on friendly terms with all the inmates of the place one lodges in."

4

If Burke has spent the whole of his life attempting to formulate such a metacritical system, it is hardly surprising that he has never been satisfied with the formulations he has achieved. Instead, the attentive reader of Burke has had to make his or her way through a bewildering variety of successive nominees for the office of definitive system— symbolic action theory, sociological criticism, Dramatism, grammatology, logology—without ever feeling that Burke has finally come to rest. The truth, of course, is that he cannot, and the reason for it has everything to do with Burke's comic realism, which has taught him that every perspective is limited, every position vulnerable to attack and revision; his favorite example is "the trout who becomes a critic when his jaw is ripped, learning then a nicer discrimination between food and bait."[40] Thus at every point where Burke might have terminated his quest for an adequate conception of his "criticism of criticism," for a theory of critical inquiry that would reintegrate the lot, he has been compelled to abandon it in favor of a conception presumably more inclusive in the reach of its categories but—because these categories focus actively on precisely those aspects of experience where ambiguity, indeterminacy, instability, even otherness (all that poststructuralists mean by "undecidability") are more in evidence—less susceptible to essentialization or reification. Developing more comprehensive kinds of critical calculus has always been Burke's object, and this has entailed an effort to move continuously toward those areas of experience where the edges are most blurred, the meanings least transparent.

What is astonishing is that Burke has accepted without serious complaint the necessity of abandoning former theoretical positions once carefully defined and defended for still higher, or at least more strategically encompassing, ground. This might well be explained by his long-held opinion that in criticism it is the thinking and not the thought that counts. Yet Burke, never one to leave a proverbial expression alone, would be quick to add that "perhaps no man can, by taking thought, add a cubit to his stature, but he clearly can, by revision, remove much that lowers the general average."[41]

In this, as in all of Burke's writing, there is a picaresque sense of being embattled, of fighting against the odds. For Burke, life is clearly an affair of coping, of major gaffes and minor adjustments. As he suggests at one point, recalling Oakeshott's and Rorty's image of culture as conversation but giving that image an entirely different interpretation, the conversation is already under way when we enter the room, and it will continue long after we have left. All we can hope for, during the time we are present, is to catch the gist of the argument and then try to put in our own "oar" before we are compelled to depart:

> Someone answers; you answer him; another comes to your defense; another aligns himself against you, to either the embarassment or gratification of your opponent, depending upon the quality of your ally's assistance. However, the discussion is interminable. The hour grows late, you must depart. And you do depart, with the discussion still vigorously in progress.[42]

To view life in this way is to see all action as reaction and all reactions as either temporary holding actions or as limited sorties into potentially hostile territory. Yet Burke's vision of this guerilla warfare, it seems to me, is Cervantean. It is Cervantean precisely because Burke would have us do battle with words against forces that seem so much more powerful than words, yet he goes on to argue that the things that constitute our enemies are so often created out of, or at least represented by, words, and very often consist of nothing but words. The explicit challenge for Burke, one that requires all his resources as a verbal artist, is to outmaneuver language, or something language does, so that language, words, terministic screens, do not become the prisonhouse of thought. Burke therefore risks the essentialization of his own ideas, one might say, only at the level of the proverbial, because the proverbial is the one consistently cautionary mode of discourse.

If Burke's critical theory is vulnerable, then the problem arises not from the way he secures his categories vertically but from the way he stretches them horizontally. As R. P. Blackmur once noted, Burke's categories seem to provide no way of differentiating between William Shakespeare, Dashiell Hammett, and Marie Corelli. Burke was quick to concede the point, once he had finished wincing, but was equally quick to offer a counterargument:

> You can't properly set Marie Corelli and Shakespeare apart until you have first put them together. First genus, then differentia. The strategy in common is the genus. The *range* or *scale* or *spectrum* of particularizations is the differentia.[43]

On one level, then, Burke would argue that there is really no difference at all between those symbolic forms and actions that we regard as monumental, that are accepted as decisive shapings or representations of human experience, and those images and events we come into daily contact with on television programs, in the newspaper, through the anecdotes of our children, or from the gossip of our neighbors. All such forms and actions belong to what Burke calls the genus of strategies, "strategies for selecting enemies and allies, for socializing losses, for warding off evil eye, for purification, propitiation, and desanctification, consolation and vengeance, admonition and exhortation. . . ."[44] Yet Burke maintains that we not only can, but also must and do, differentiate between and among them, in terms of the seriousness and complexity of the situations they respectively confront, the practicality and efficacy of the strategies they recommend for encompassing those situations, and the aptness and humaneness of the attitudes they urge us to take towards them.

If this method of critical discrimination has yielded in Burke only the wariest of pragmatisms, that critical pragmatism is nonetheless capable of measuring real compensatory losses and gains. The key to this pragmatic wariness is a kind of critical humility—and this is no coincidence—wholly absent from postmodern textualism because it teaches one how, as radical textualism or poststructuralism cannot do without self-contradiction, "to get off before the end of the line."[45] Burke wants to claim that this kind of humility serves as a corrective for the effects of pride, but its emphasis is not, as in tragedy, on the criminality of pride but rather on its stupidity. Comedy depicts people not as vicious, according to Burke, but only as mistaken. Nevertheless, he continues, "When you add that people are *necessarily* mistaken, that *all* people are exposed to situations in which they must act as fools, that *every* insight contains its own special kind of blindness, you complete the comic circle, returning again to the lesson of humility that underlies great tragedy."[46]

Burke contrasts the critical wisdom associated with comedy, a wisdom bred of fear, resignation, and a realization of limits, with "the modern tendency," which Richard Rorty seems prepared to embrace: the disposition "to look upon intelligence as merely a *coefficient of power* for heightening our ability to get things, be they good or bad."[47] Needless to say, Burke finds this modern disposition seriously deficient when compared to traditional comic wisdom; he regards the comic perspective, as opposed to the modern, the most humane and enlightened outlook yet attained by human beings. But Burke would be the first to admit that without corrective discounting, the comic perspective can also become a fetish, indeed, can become essentialized. Comedy only remains a cure-all because it does not rest in its own realizations but rather contains the seeds of its own counterstatements within itself.

But if comedy is curative, the critic's medicine, Burke maintains, is somewhat different from the artist's. While the artist's method, as Burke notes in one of his more famous analogies, is homeopathic, since he or she tries to immunize us "by stylistically infecting us with the disease," the critic's method is allopathic, since he or she tries to combat the disease by providing us with remedies that counter its effects.[48] Where the artist tries to cure us by giving us an attenuated case of his or her own piety, the critic tries to cure us by supplying us with an antidote of irreverence or at least of skepticism. Yet the two strategies eventually come to roughly the same thing: both are ways of protecting us, even of arming us, against the privileging, the hypostatizing, ultimately the essentializing, of our own limited senses of what goes with what.

"One must watch the mind," Burke writes in *Towards a Better Life,* "as you would eye a mean dog."[49] Yet it is still possible, he might add, to keep from being bitten. To change the figure of speech, it all comes down to whether we are occasionally willing, and even more than occasionally, as Burke says, "to look a gift horse in the mouth."[50] Burke's advice seems to boil down to the admonition to "keep your weather eye open."[51]

5

If the foregoing could be described as Burke's minimalist position, his maximal position is indicated by one of his mottoes for Dramatism: "By and through language, beyond language." Call this, if you will, Burke's vision of transcendence; it comprises the basis of his radicalism and also of his humanism. As what William James called a "live" or "vital option," it concedes, among other things, that human beings are enmeshed in language, that they live in a reality of words, that they view everything through a "fog of symbols."[52] Burke developed Dramatism and his other "techniques of trouble," as R. P. Blackmur once called modern literary and cultural criticism, as methods for penetrating this fog by examining the uses to which human beings put language and thus by extension for exploring the nature of human beings themselves by analyzing the drama of their relations with words. Dramatism, like Burke's other critical methods, helps us see that while the fog is ubiquitous, it is not wholly blinding; the treachery of the fog is due not to its own opacity but to our all-too-willing disposition to make ourselves and our world over in the image of its distortions. Burke's critical theories and methods are essentially techniques for getting us to see the fog as what it is and for helping us adopt a more constructive attitude toward it, so that we may better contemplate the irony of our situation as symbol-using animals without, as so many contemporary intellectuals have, being driven to complete distraction by this discovery.

We move by language and through language "beyond language" when Burke's critical theories, each in their turn and each in their own way, "make methodologic the attitude of patience."[53] But beyond the "beyond" of patience as a constructive attitude we get, says Burke, "glimpses into the ultimate reality that stretches somehow beyond the fogs of language and its sloganizing."[54] The phrase "ultimate reality" is in many ways regrettable and in any case misleading. Burke is not thinking in spatial or essentialist terms here, however inevitable the associations are with some Great Good Place or some primordial bedrock. Burke seems to fall back on such language only as a way of suggesting that the dramatistic study of the principles of discourse, the functions of language, the relations of terms, all seem to yield timeless —or, if not timeless, at least perennial—secrets about man as a symbol-using animal, and these secrets revolve endlessly for Burke about the notion of a total or encompassing idea of Order. Order may simply be the last in the progressive series of terms from which Burke started and beyond which it is impossible for him to think. In any case, Order is the term that naturally suggests itself to a mind such as Burke's, which has always been so fascinated with categorization, and not just with categorization as such, but with the infinite rearrangement and reconstruction of categories, terminologies, conceptualizations.

But Burke's idea of Order, like the quest for it, is anything but static. In fact, one of his most arresting images of both the idea and the quest appears in his amplification of what he elsewhere treats as a synonym for them, "comprehensive, summarizing truth"; the progress toward this truth, "like a spring under the skyscrapers of Manhattan, must somehow still go on—truth, still welling forth, down there in the dark, the brooks still wholesomely flowing, unstoppable, in the dark, down there, somehow."[55] As Burke's metaphor suggests, this notion of Order, or summarizing truth, can only be intuited, and intuited in the teeth of the reality we see with our symbols—indeed, the reality we actually see *as* our symbols—as something that must be imagined, assumed, even against all evidence, as source and fulfillment of those reifications of desire, those hypostatizations of spirit, represented by the Manhattan skyscrapers.

Still, it would be entirely out of character for Burke to rest content with such an abstraction, even one so fluid and dynamic. Besides, he has always said that "this is a time (because it is always such a time) for us to remind ourselves that All the Returns Aren't in Yet. . . . To doubt this is to doubt the very essence of culture, as a mutual search for truth." Thus Burke urges upon his readers, who are always addressed implicitly as fellow citizens, the creation of a cultural dialogue in quest for truth that would include "more voices than just two flatly pitted against each other."[56] And the chief rhetorical instrument in such a dialogue should be dialectics, which Burke defines as a verbal method for transforming any "troublesome *either-or* . . . into a *both-and*."[57] The object of this dialectic, to say it one more time, is discussion, not debate. What it seeks to achieve is a more complete realization of the voices that contribute to it, not the silencing of some to secure the supremacy of others.

These observations about the conversation that constitutes culture are perfectly consistent with Burke's view that truth—especially in its summary or comprehensive form, if such a form exists in any other modality than a motivational one, to inspire the quest for it—is constantly changing and becoming more inclusive and encompassing, like Burke's increasingly generalized terms for it. They also follow, however, from the fact that, like Dewey, Burke pays allegiance not to a hierarchy of values but to a hierarchy of problems. And if the only constants in this hierarchy of problems derive from man's use and misuse of symbols, the only constant in Burke's preoccupation with them is his resistance to the inevitable drift toward Armageddon, which is induced by our capitulation to symbol systems that deprive us of both the freedom to create, or at least to improvise, and our responsibility to choose, or at least to act in behalf of "a better life." The poet is Burke's image of the first of these values, the critic or intellectual his symbol for the second. Both exist to show us that if we cannot change all of our circumstances, we can change the way we think of them and the power we symbolically grant to them; in short, if we cannot emancipate "truth from every system of power," we can liberate "the power of truth," as Foucault said, "from the forms of hegemony, social, economic, and cultural, within which it operates at the present time."[58]

From this it should be obvious that Burke's entire critical corpus constitutes a response to a specific social and political situation, that it is comprised of "verbal acts upon a historical scene." But this response is not merely intellectual but also strategic, since it is designed, as a "humanist's counter-statement," in William H. Rueckert's fine phrase,[59] to encompass the crisis caused by a world lurching toward the lunacy of self-destruction out of a sense of what might be called misplaced piety, which is another name for symbolic solipsism. Burke's writing is predicated on the hope that, whether or not this malady can ever be cured, it can at least be arrested, possibly indefinitely, if we humanists attend to our proper business. With the wit born of wisdom that constitutes his full comic measure, Burke has perhaps most succinctly defined that business, and expressed the hope that underlies it, in a passage from his unfinished *Symbolic of Motives:*

> Whatever may be the ultimate ground of all possibility, the proper study of mankind is man's tendency to misjudge reality as inspirited by the troublous genius of symbolism. But if we were trained, for generation after generation, from our first emergence out of infancy, and in ways ranging from the simplest to the most complex, depending upon our stage of development, to collaborate in spying upon ourselves with pious yet sportive fearfulness, and thus helping to free one another of the false ambitions that symbolism so readily encourages, we might yet contrive to keep from wholly ruining this handsome planet and its plentitude.[60]

II

The Culture of Criticism

and

the Moral Imagination

5

The Semiotics of Culture and the Diagnostics of Criticism: Clifford Geertz and the Moral Imagination

In an essay in progress at the time of his death, Lionel Trilling initiated an unusually fruitful dialogue with the social and cultural anthropologist Clifford Geertz.[1] The ostensible reason for Trilling's interest in Geertz's work was the way it confirmed certain suspicions Trilling had come to entertain, as a result of a course he had recently taught on Jane Austen, about the traditional assumptions of humanistic scholarship. However, his unfinished meditation and Geertz's subsequent response[2] possess a critical importance that far transcends the particular circumstances of their origin. By setting the discussion of literary as well as anthropological interpretation in the wider context of intra- and cross-cultural understanding, their dialogue sheds significant light on what a semiotic theory of culture like Geertz's has to do with a moral theory of criticism like Trilling's, and also suggests along the way what cultural semiotics, if I may use so modern a term to describe Geertz's method, has to learn from literary hermeneutics, to employ a description awkwardly récherché for Trilling's. More than this, their dialogue provides a welcome relief from the mystifications of much recent criti-

cal theory, mystifications that have almost succeeded in removing critical discussion from the plane of public discourse altogether.

1

In his typically canny way, Trilling had been both disturbed and challenged by the experience of teaching Austen's major novels to an
audience so culturally distant from her own because it raised certain
troubling questions about the conventional assumptions of humanistic
pedagogy and research. Central among those assumptions, as Trilling
pointed out, is the notion that the products of other minds, the expressions of other selves, possess a crucial relevance to our own moral
existence and that they can be placed in the service of our moral lives
precisely because, no matter how distant in time or how different in
temperament, they are more or less fully accessible to us. This purported accessibility is possible, so the conventional argument goes,
because the humanist has traditionally been convinced that beneath all
the surface differences and apparent variations between one mind and
another, one mode of being and its neighbor, there exists both within
cultures and across them an unbroken continuity. And from this derives the humanist's whole theory of the past "as a source of remedial
wisdom, a prosthetic corrective for a damaged spiritual life."[3] As
Trilling put it,

> Humanism does not in the least question the good effect of reading
> about the conduct of other people of one's own time, but it does put a
> special value upon ranging backward in time to find in a past culture the
> paradigms by which our own moral lives are put to the test. In its
> predilection for the moral instructiveness of past cultures, humanism is
> resolute in the belief that there is very little in this transaction that is
> problematic; it is confident that the paradigms will be properly derived
> and that the judgments made on the basis they offer will be valid. Hu-
> manism takes for granted that any culture of the past out of which has
> come a work of art that commands our interest must be the product, and
> also, of course, the shaping condition, of minds which are essentially the
> same as our own.[4]

Yet is was just this comforting reassurance about the essential continuities between minds other than our own that had been put in question by Trilling's recent experiences in the classroom. If any such continuities exist—and no study of other selves, much less other cultures,
could proceed without assuming that they do—Trilling's problems in
placing Jane Austen's world before a group of students so culturally

ill-equipped to grasp its general outlines, much less its deeper nuances, still convinced him that there are real discontinuities as well. And it was in the interest of understanding the nature of, and the reason for, these discontinuities and disjunctions that he was initially drawn to the work of Clifford Geertz.

He focused on an essay in which Geertz disputes the view widely shared by humanists and social scientists alike that our knowledge of other peoples depends in large part on our capacity to empathize, to imagine our way into the subjective life of someone else. On the contrary, Geertz argues, our ability to empathize has very little to do with it; the anthropologist is not engaged in learning how to think and feel as others do but how to define and assess what, so to speak, they are up to. The task is not to put oneself in their place but to learn how to comprehend the symbolic forms in which they represent themselves to each other. And this is accomplished, Geertz goes on, in the same way one undertakes any other act of understanding: by submitting oneself to what has been acknowledged since the time of St. Augustine and referred to since the time of Wilhelm Dilthey as "the hermeneutic circle."

The "hermeneutic circle" is but a complicated way of referring to a comparatively simple process. We cannot understand the parts of anything without some sense of the whole to which they belong, just as we cannot comprehend the whole to which they belong until we have grasped the parts that make it up. Thus we are constantly obliged to move back and forth in our effort to understand something "between the whole conceived through the parts which actualize it and the parts conceived through the whole which motivates them" in an effort "to turn them, by a sort of intellectual perpetual motion, into explication of one another."[5] Hence the understanding of other peoples, as of other minds, normally proceeds by way of a dialectic in which knowledge increases as we alternately press two kinds of questions, the first having to do with the general form of their life, the second having to do with the specific vehicles in which that form is embodied. From this perspective, the goal of the anthropologist, Geertz reasons, cannot be to achieve communion or identity with those lives but only to enter into a kind of conversation with them. While we cannot assume their mode of being or take on their form of existence, we can at least establish a relationship with them by attempting, from our own vantage point, to comprehend what they are about.

It was just here, however, that Trilling began to express reservations concerning Geertz's formulations. While he could respect Geertz's real-

ism about the staggering problems involved in any act of cultural interpretation and found this realism a salutary antidote to humanism's customarily facile indifference to such problems, he was stlll perplexed and
alarmed by Geertz's apparent refusal to concede that the imagination
plays any determinative role in this hermeneutical transaction. Since
Trilling's reflections break off when he became too ill to proceed, it is
difficult to be certain of all Trilling intended to say in response to
Geertz's view of the way we gain knowledge of other minds, of different
sensibilities, but the gist of his argument seems to be as follows: Even if
we can never succeed in imagining ourselves so completely into the
innerness of lives other than our own so that we can take on their modes
of thought and feeling, put ourselves in their place, nevertheless we can
learn how to think more and more like them, to think more intelligently
and concretely and sympathetically about them, as we learn, to borrow
an expression from Archibald MacLeish, how to put our thought in the
place where our imagination goes. And the proof that we can do this is
provided by our own experience of being able to think against ourselves,
of being able to overcome, or at least to resist, the movement of our
own sensibilities by responding imaginatively to alternative modes of
being that threaten to disrupt or destroy them.

The example that offered itself to Trilling was the one Geertz himself had employed in his essay on "From the Native's Point of View,"
namely, Keats's "Ode on a Grecian Urn." But where Geertz reads
the poem as constituting an assertion of the priority of the aesthetic
over the historical, Trilling read it instead as an effort to assimilate,
without subordinating, the historical to the aesthetic, and to do so by
seeing pastness as an essential attribute of beauty. In such terms as
these, Trilling in fact believed that Keats's poem spoke directly to the
question currently in dispute between Geertz and himself. For if the
aesthetic incorporates the historical within itself and thus refers to
something finished, completed, and, to that degree, static and even
deathlike, then by effecting a transmutation of what is living and
changing into a state of fixity and inertness, the poem actually invites
us to repudiate the essence of the Western ideal of personality, of
self-realization, by conceiving the goal of life as something dependent
not on the exercise of the will but on the negation of it. Such a
reading did not mean to Trilling that Keats had succeeded in undermining certain of the most cherished spiritual aspirations of Western
culture; it only signaled that he had been responsive to, and in turn
been able to make his readers aware of, the paradoxical character of
that ideal itself. And by the use of this example, Trilling therefore

seemed to be winding his way back to his initial reservations about Geertz's skepticism concerning the role of the imagination and to be preparing to ask whether the very dialectic of our own imaginative life in culture isn't itself the surest, if not the only, guarantee that we can obtain a knowledge of what we are not—namely, of other minds, even of alien cultures.

2

In his otherwise sensitive and probing response to Trilling's essay, Geertz never quite succeeds in facing the issue Trilling raised. Yet he does manage, and that very effectively, to clarify the nature of their common enterprise. Referring to that enterprise in his subtitle as "the social history of the moral imagination," Geertz defines it most succinctly as the question of how other peoples' imaginations enter into and color our own. Like Trilling before him, Geertz finds this an immensely difficult question to answer for at least two reasons: first, because of the suspicions aroused by historical relativists that there may be no connections at all between the lives of others and the way we live now; second, because of the awareness urged upon us by cultural historicists of the interfering glosses between. But if Geertz rejects the relativist argument on the grounds that we can certainly know as much about the minds of others as we can know about anything else not our own, he finds equally reasonable grounds for dismissing the historicist argument on the assumption that, if we can never go around those glosses or see behind them, we can still look through them.

For Geertz this means that there is a deep and undeniable "equivocality" about the things studied by the literary critic and the anthropologist. Each is continually confronted with objects that "speak with equal power to the consoling piety that we are all like one another and to the worrying suspicion that we are not."[6] This paradox cannot be evaded or dismissed but only confronted and accepted. To confront it, however, is to realize that everything that comes to us from the past, everything that crosses to us from other minds, reaches us in the form of a translation, as something that has been filtered through, perhaps, countless intervening readings. And to accept this paradox is to resist the temptation to remove these filters and instead try to learn how to see by them, to discover what modes of insight they afford as well as deny, enhance as well as obscure. If we are all "lost in translation," as James Merrill suggests in the poem that Geertz takes as the point of departure for his remarks, then the way out is not through some form of intellectual escapism where (as for the deconstructionists, for example) all translations are deprived of any validity but that which attests to their own willful subjectivism, but through submission to what Conrad's Stein would have called "the destructive element," that hermeneutical tangle of interpretations that constitutes the filtered character of virtually everything we encounter in culture. To continue the Conradian analogy, in culture you learn how to "make the deep, deep sea keep you up" by "getting straight," as Geertz puts it, "how the massive fact of cultural historical particularity comports with the equally massive fact of cross-cultural and cross-historical accessibility— how the deeply different can be deeply known without becoming any less different; the enormously distant enormously close without becoming any less far away."[7]

Without blinking the extent of the problem, Geertz holds that the only possibility of coming to grips with it, much less of resolving it in individual instances, lies in the exercise of what he refers to as "the moral imagination," and in the broadest sense his whole theory of culture is an attempt to define the scope of this imagination and explain its task. Geertz's theory of the symbolic forms that constitute culture is in effect an attempt to lay the basis for a moral analysis of culture itself, and what unites the cultural analysis of symbolic forms— in our case predominantly aesthetic forms—with the moral analysis of culture is the interpretive character of both. But to understand how interpretation operates culturally, it is necessary to see how culture for Geertz is an interpretive system, or a series of such systems; this leads one back from the question of what other peoples' imaginations have to do with our own to the question of what characteristic forms the imagination uses to express itself, and of how those forms relate to the others that comprise culture and to the particular function all cultural forms serve in human experience.

3

As Geertz would be the first to concede, neither his ideas about art and its relation to culture nor his views of the semiotic nature of culture are in any way novel. Their theoretical importance lies elsewhere: in the way he has combined them into a coherent system that attempts to "cross the border" and "close the gap," as Leslie Fiedler once put it, not only between high culture and low but also between individual expressions of mind, collective forms of experience, and the immense thicket of social and historical fact that surrounds them. By doing so, Geertz has mounted what may well become a significant modern alternative to all theories of art and culture that attempt to isolate them from the practical contexts that give them life—either as the old New Critics did, through their definition of the self-interpreting text, or, to employ Geoffrey Hartmann's phrase, as the "new New Critics" do, through their notion of the self-deconstructing text. On Geertz's reading, such "pure" theories are almost inevitably misleading because they typically obscure the very problem they were designed to overcome—for the old New Critics, the problem of how the totally distinctive can be known at all if it is so unique; for the new New Critics, the problem of how the essentially indeterminate can be deconstructed when it is unstable and self-canceling to begin with.

Geertz's theory of culture, and of the imaginative forms in which it has its being, so to speak, is therefore partially conceived as a response to certain widespread misconceptions. For example, against those who, like many modern formalists, tend to view culture as a more or less self-contained and historically transcendent reality with purposes and procedures intrinsic to itself; or, again, in reaction to those who, like certain historical positivists as well as behavioral psychologists, typically associate culture only with those most explicit patterns of behavior that are observable in any identifiable community; or, yet again, in response to those who, like many contemporary Marxists as well as ethnoscientists, come close to reducing the notion of culture to the ideas and assumptions one must share in order to operate in a manner deemed acceptable by the dominant social group or class—over against all these various misconceptions, Geertz conceives of culture as an imaginative world (or worlds) in which acts are constantly being translated into signs so that human beings can attach a meaning to things that the things themselves do not intrinsically possess. The purpose of such translation, especially as individual signs become absorbed into the interrelated system of significant signs or symbols we call culture, is to provide a context in which the raw materials of experience—events, objects, acts, persons, other signs—can be interpreted. Thus the concept of culture Geertz wishes to advance is a semiotic one. "Believing, with Max Weber, that man is an animal suspended in webs of significance he himself has spun, I take culture to be those webs, and the analysis of it to be therefore not an experimental science in search of law but an interpretive one in search of meaning."[8]

But the interlinked system of significant signs and symbols Geertz calls culture—*sign* and *symbol* being roughly interchangeable words to refer to "any object, act, event, quality, or relation which serves as a vehicle for a conception"[9]—does more than help make sense out of what would otherwise remain opaque and threatening. Taken as a whole, it also furnishes a set of patterns, blueprints, programs (Geertz also calls them "templates") by which many social and psychological processes can be organized in advance. Thus cultural symbol systems do a kind of double duty both to interpret the "already" and to antici- pate the "not yet."

The necessity for such strange behavior, Geertz maintains, derives from the fact that human beings are unequipped genetically to deal with the environment in any other fashion. Other animals possess suffi- cient internal sources of information to make their actions and reac- tions effective in response to the outer world; our internal sources of information, our genetic endowment, is in some ways deficient and must therefore be supplemented by what we can receive or acquire externally. And this is precisely what cultural symbol systems provide us, in the form of models or templates that help familiarize the strange and regulate behavior in relation to it. Often overlooked, however, is the fact that the information these templates provide is not only mental or conceptual but also affective and emotional. As human beings, we need not only to acquire various kinds of information but also need to determine how the information feels to us and how we feel about it before we can successfully negotiate our relations with the environ- ment. And this is the service rendered by those particular cultural symbol systems we typically think of as aesthetic—myth, ritual, art. By providing us with public images of sentiment and sensibility, they help us to know what we feel and to feel what we know.

Geertz is here drawing upon what he terms the "control mechanism view of culture," which associates culture with the set of mechanisms that govern behavior rather than with the concrete patterns of behav- ior that result from such governance. And there are several important corollaries to this. The first is that thinking is essentially a public rather than a private affair and therefore one that has less to do with events that occur outside the head than with events that result from man's interaction with what George Herbert Mead once called "sig- nificant symbols," referring to "anything, in fact, that is disengaged from its mere actuality and used to impose meaning upon experi- ence."[10] Such symbols are for the most part inherited rather than created and thus constitute the commercial tender by which individu- als as well as groups transact their business with the world. The second corollary is that, without the intervention of such symbols and symbol systems, human beings would be completely at the mercy of events and their behavior therefore utterly chaotic. Cultural symbol systems give their actions specificity and purposefulness and thus are essential components of human existence rather than mere adornments. The third is that, according to this view, man is to be defined neither in terms of his capacities alone, nor in terms of his actions, "but by the link between them, by the way the first is transformed into the second, his generic potentialities focused into his specific performances."[11] As Geertz puts it elsewhere, in addition to being "the tool-making, laughing, or lying animal, man is also the incomplete— or, more accurately, self-completing animal" who must create "out of his general capacity for the construction of symbolic models the specific capabilities that define him."[12] Hence the clue to man's nature is not to be found in the commonalities of human behavior as they are exhibited throughout history and across cultures but in the processes and procedures whereby his inherent capacities are transformed into the concrete form of his actual accomplishments. Man's nature is to be inferred from his career "in its characteristic course" and not vice versa, Geertz likes to assert, "and though culture is but one element in determining that course, it is hardly the least important."[13]

The most dramatic support for this control mechanism view of culture comes from recent advances in the field of physical anthropology, and particularly from new discoveries about the nature of human origins. Three of the most significant advances have to do, first, with the abandonment of a sequential view of relations between physical evolution and the emergence of culture in favor of an interactive or overlap view; second, with the discovery that the most important biological changes associated with man's evolution from his immediate progenitors seem to have occurred in the central nervous system, particularly in the brain; and, third, with the growing realization that what differentiates man from the other animals is not so much the scope of his capacity to learn as the scope and character of what he must learn in order to get on in life at all.

What all these advances suggest is the close correlation between the evolution of man and the emergence of culture, on the one hand, and between the emergence of culture and the development of the human mind, on the other. Indeed, Geertz sees the growth of human mentality as not only instrumental to the creation of human culture but in significant part the result of it. The relationship between culture and mind is therefore more than complementary; it is integral. Thinking is but the ability to translate experiences into symbols in order to make sense of them. Culture is but the accumulated system of significant symbols by which this process of making sense is accomplished and furthered.

This distinctively functional but antibehaviorist view of mind and culture can be traced back through Talcott Parsons and Max Weber all the way to Giambattista Vico, but it is also compatible with the phenomenological perspective of such thinkers as Maurice Merleau-Ponty and Michael Polanyi and owes an even larger debt to the later philosophy of John Dewey. Geertz is drawn particularly to Dewey's redefinition of mind as neither an object nor a thing but an organized set of dispositions, capacities, propensities, abilities. But Geertz is equally attracted to Dewey's emphasis upon the essentially directed or pragmatic character of thinking. Mental activity begins in puzzlement and terminates in its resolution. Thought results from what sociologists sometimes refer to as an information deficit; it ceases when the deficit is, so to speak, overcome. Or, to use another paradigm, which Geertz borrows from Galanter and Gerstenhaber and which converges more directly with a theory of culture that places so much emphasis upon images and symbols, thinking can be conceived as "neither more nor less than constructing an image of the environment, running the model faster than the environment, and then predicting that the environment will behave as the model does. . . ."[14] In both cases, thought is related to the solution of a problem, and the discovery of the solution depends upon the mind's ability to exploit certain resources with which it is not genetically endowed to provide the information that is lacking.

For this reason Geertz is inclined to define all the forms of mental activity that can be differentiated culturally, from the scientific to the ideological and from the commonsensical to the religious, as "symbolic strategies for encompassing situations." This phrase is, of course, from Kenneth Burke, who uses it in his dramatistic theory of art and criticism to describe all forms of symbolic expressive activity, discursive as well as imaginative, physical as well as mental. What differentiates the various kinds of symbolic expression from one another is, according to Burke, the distinctive way they "size up" the specific situations they are designed to encompass: by naming their structure and essential components, and by naming them so as to convey a particular attitude toward them. The advantage of this definition of symbolic expression is that, in addition to stressing the purposeful intentions and implications of such actions, it leads away from personal and historical subjectivism toward what might be considered a kind of cultural empiricism. And it does so, Burke insists, because "the situations are real; the strategies for handling them have public content; and in so far as situations overlap from one individual to another, or from one historical period to another, the strategies possess universal significance."[15]

Thus Geertz can define ideology, for example, as a response to the loss of social and political orientation. The resultant confusion about what to make of the civic world of rights and responsibilities in the absence of suitable models for comprehending it sets off the frantic search for alternative models that will provide fresh images through which the opportunities and conditions of the civic realm can be sensibly grasped. As cultural systems designed to provide new maps to a world become strange and new sets of directions by which to find one's way, ideologies should be thought of as highly figurative solutions to very concrete problems. But in this they are no different from other cultural symbol systems like science or religion. What separates these systems is the particular procedure each employs to define the structure of situations, and the specific manner in which this process of defining, or "naming," as Burke calls it, determines the range of attitudes that can be taken in response to those situations. Thus science defines the structure of situations in such a way as to promote an attitude of disinterestedness toward them, whereas ideology defines them in a manner that elicits an attitude of commitment.

By virtue of the oft-repeated claims made in behalf of their cultural uniqueness, aesthetic forms might seem to represent the one exception to this rule. Ever since the appearance of texts like I. A. Richards's *Practical Criticism* and T. S. Eliot's *The Sacred Wood,* it has been modish to suppose that if aesthetic forms are not uniformly self-referential and, as Paul Valéry believed, autotelic, they are in any case far more responsive to the complications of their own nature than they are to forces associated with the social and historical world surrounding them. As we shall see, however, Geertz is prepared to dispute this; indeed, it is aesthetic forms in general, and art forms in particular, that represent for him the essential paradigms of a theory that conceives of culture as an interwoven system of functional, which is to say meaningful, symbolic forms.

4

Geertz's aesthetics rests on the premise that art forms typically deal with dimensions of experience that are normally well hidden from view. These forms organize those dimensions into an encompassing structure that throws into relief some specific understanding of their essential nature. The purpose, or at least the effect, of such strategies of representation is not so much to depict the way things literally are in experience as to portray how, from certain perspective, they might be. Thus the range of attitudes that can be indicated or provoked through such procedures is delimited by the nature of the imaginative situations they define. Dealing with what could be or, under certain circumstances, just may be the case, rather than with what necessarily and, under all circumstances, almost certainly is the case, they are intended to give expression to certain suppressed, or at least partially obscured, facets of human subjectivity and not to provide evidence for a specific argument or to validate a general view of life. As Northrop Frye suggests, we go to *Macbeth* not "to learn about the history of Scotland" but "to learn what a man feels like after he's gained a kingdom and lost his soul."[16] By bringing selected experiences or dimensions of experience to a focus, art forms give us what Aristotle designated as the typical or recurrent or universal human event, or what Geertz prefers to describe as the "paradigmatic human event—that is, one that tells us less what happens than the kind of thing that would happen if, as is not the case, life were art and could be as freely shaped by styles of feeling and states of mind as *Macbeth* and *David Copperfield* are."[17]

It is no coincidence that these comments about art are to be found in Geertz's widely quoted essay on the Balinese cockfight, an essay that, until the publication of "Art as Cultural System," was his most sustained discussion of aesthetics. Geertz's notion of art in fact extends to cultural forms built out of any materials, including social ones. The key to their peculiar nature lies in the effects of the imagination that produces them, for it is the imagination, Geertz believes, that permits artists to render the ordinary experiences of everyday life in terms of acts and objects dissociated from their practical consequences so that we can perceive their potential as opposed to their actual meaning. As Geertz puts it elsewhere,

> if there is any commonality among the arts in all the places one finds them. . . . that justifies including them under a single, Western-made rubric, it is not that they appeal to some universal sense of beauty [but that] certain activities everywhere seem specifically designed to demonstrate that ideas are visible, audible, and—one needs to make up a word here—tactible, that they can be cast in forms where the senses, and through the senses the emotions, can reflectively address them.[18]

Thus Geertz views the Balinese cockfight as he would any other aesthetic form: as an effort to place a construction on certain themes drawn from everyday life, to "make them, to those historically positioned to appreciate the construction, meaningful—visible, tangible, graspable—'real,' in an ideational sense."[19] What thereby sets the cockfight apart from any other events with which it might be compared is not that it performs certain social functions, such as the reinforcement of status discriminations, but that it serves a hermeneutic function, by disclosing certain partially concealed dimensions of Balinese experience. "An image, fiction, model, metaphor, the cockfight is a means of expression; its function is neither to assuage social passions nor to heighten them . . . , but, in a medium of feathers, blood, crowds, and money, to display them."[20]

Inherent in this way of putting the relations of art to experience is the danger, as Geertz realizes, of placing too much emphasis on the mimetic and expressive character of art and too little on the generative and creative. For if art forms refract and express certain meanings, they also help shape and sustain them. Art not only imitates life but equally influences it, by providing, often for the first time, a significant form for those very aspects of subjective human experience it purports only to reflect.[21] Here one confronts what Geertz takes to be one of the great paradoxes of aesthetic theory, what Eliseo Vivas meant by the dialectic of "creation and discovery."[22] Art objects seem to do no more than reorganize aspects of experience in terms of styles of feeling and states of mind that were presumed to exist before. Yet the most highly valued among them, as one reason why they are so highly valued, succeed simultaneously in convincing us that those same styles of feeling and states of mind never fully or "truly" existed until they were cast in an aesthetic form that shed significant new light on their essential nature. Hence Geertz can conclude that "quartets, still lifes, and Balinese cockfights are not merely reflections of a pre-existing sensibility analogically represented; they are positive agents in the creation and maintenance of such a sensibility."[23]

This realization that art forms are generative as well as refractory, creative as well as mimetic, clearly leads away from the notion, popularized by the New Critics, that art objects cannot be talked about but only enjoyed, that their function is not to mean but simply to be. Even if most art forms leave us with the impression that they can say in their own behalf far more than we can say about them, no one—and least of all artists themselves—can resist the temptation to talk incessantly about them. Except when this talk is purely technical, its purpose is somehow to situate the discussion of works of art within those larger contexts of meaning that endow the rest of our experience with sense and significance. The corollary is that there is no such thing as a purely aesthetic definition of art. To the degree that all talk about art demands to be assimilated into the patterns of meaning by which we lend import to everything else we experience, any theory of art is implicitly a theory of culture as well.

But this broadly cultural view of art and of our talk about it is also to be contrasted with the notion most often opposed to "pure" theories of the sort espoused by the New Critics. I refer in this case to the more functionalist view, associated with many anthropologists and sociologists, that has now been taken up in a variety of refined but not always consistent forms by the literary structuralists—the view that works of art are highly complex verbal mechanisms that define semantic worlds, or sustain linguistic codes, or strengthen the grammar of values sedimented into the syntactical components of speech itself. In setting his own theory of art over against this functionalist-structuralist view, Geertz is not proposing that art lacks a social function but only redefining it. Where many structural anthropologists and their literary compatriots tactily assume that aesthetic forms help to support social systems that would begin to collapse without them, Geertz wants to argue that aesthetic forms simply permit certain things that are felt partially as a result of those systems to be said within their confines. And when those things can no longer be said, then they may in time no longer be felt, whereupon life suffers diminishment, impoverishment. Hence the office of aesthetic forms is not, at least primarily, to sustain social structures, much less to reify them, but to "materialize a way of experiencing" within them, to "bring a particular cast of mind out into the world of objects, where men can look at it."[24] Their relation to society is thus ideational rather than mechanical, semiotic rather than instrumental. They are what Geertz would call, borrowing a term from Robert Goldwater, "primary documents; not illustrations of conceptions already in force, but conceptions that themselves seek—or for which people seek—a meaningful place in a repertoire of other documents, equally primary."[25]

The typical objection to this line of argument is that it may very well apply to the art of so-called primitives, or people who are unreflective generally, but that it has little bearing upon most of the more complex forms of Western art, which are sufficiently sophisticated to operate according to laws internal to their own nature. Geertz finds this to be a wholly specious distinction and one that can be readily discredited by examining some of the more complex forms of Western art. Taking as his example quattrocento Italian painting, Geertz notes that such painting existed not only to depict spiritual concerns but also to deepen them. The artist was interested in doing more than presenting religious material on his canvas; he was also anxious to invite the beholder to reflect on it in a religious manner. The artist's aim, in other words, was not merely illustrative or even exegetical but evocative; his object extended beyond the transcription of certain concerns to include the creation of an artistic situation in which others would be obliged to respond to those concerns. What the painter was attempting to do, Geertz observes with the help of Michael Baxandall's *Painting and Experience in Fifteenth Century Italy,* "was to construct an image to which a distinctive spirituality could forcibly react." His public did not need what it already possessed; what it needed, Geertz continues, "was an object rich enough to see it in, rich enough, even, to, in seeing it, deepen it."[26]

In this most complex of art forms, then, the relation between the painter and his audience, and, more precisely, the relation between his painting and the wider culture to which it was addressed, was complementary rather than expository, interactive rather than merely expressive. The beholder was in effect to complete the image presented to him in the painting by reflecting on it in the light of his religious experience and then by adjusting that experience accordingly. " 'For it is one thing to adore a painting,' as a Dominican preacher defending the virtuousness of art put it, 'but it is quite another to learn from a painted narrative what to adore.' "[27] Yet this capacity "to learn from a painted narrative what to adore" was not in the fifteenth century, and is not in the twentieth, the result of individual gifts of subjective intuitions only, but a wider collective form of experience of which this capacity is one component. Put another way, the distinctive sensibility to which the quattrocento painter addressed his art was not the creature of his own invention but one that the whole of the life of his time had participated in forming.

Such observations lead inescapably to a conclusion as germane to secular art as to religious, to what we like to think of as wholly imaginative forms as well as to didactic: the artist does not so much produce a reflection or imitation of the thing he would have his audience know and feel, and know through feeling, as create an object capable of eliciting in response those feelings that will enable his audience to learn what he wants them to know. In this sense, then, the meanings of his art might fairly be described as being determined by that art without, as many structuralists contend, being imprisoned within it. These meanings, which his art as fully draws out of his audience as renders for them, clearly belong to a larger field of experience than any that either the art form itself or its audience may be said to define, refract, or epitomize. And this wider realm of meaning that supervenes our experience of art is every bit as real a datum of consciousness as our sense of the poverty of mind that compels us to intervene by interpreting it. But this is only a roundabout way of asserting that artist, audience, and aesthetic form alike are part of a collective experience that considerably transcends them and that it is out of their mutual participation in this larger collective experience of meaning we call culture that, as Geertz says, their participation in the particular form of it we call art, "which is in fact but a sector of it, is possible."[28]

5

With this background, Geertz's critical theory, or theory of criticism, makes a good deal more sense. What we require, Geertz believes, is a semiotics of art, a science of aesthetics, concerned with how signs signify. What differentiates his own semiotics from almost all contemporary variants is that it would not be a formal science, like mathematics and logic (the models for structuralism), but a social science, like history and anthropology (the models for hermeneutics). This distinction is crucial to Geertz, for he believes that it is one thing to describe the structure of a work of art but quite another to account for the sources of its spell. The former activity can content itself with the definition of relationships; the latter must undertake the investigation of meanings and the assessment of their significance. In pressing this distinction, Geertz has no intention of discounting the importance of the formal analysis of works of art; he only wishes, like Trilling before him, to delimit the scope of that analysis on the grounds that "one can no more understand aesthetic objects as concatenations of pure form than one can understand speech as a parade of syntactic variations, or myth as a set of structural transformations."[29]

By a semiotics of art Geertz therefore refers to "a kind of natural history of signs and symbols, an ethnography of the vehicles of meaning."[30] Such a semiotics or ethnography must move beyond the study of signs dissociated from the uses to which they have been put in society and toward a study of signs defined in relation to those uses. Instead of regarding signs as assertions to be deconstructed, codes to be deciphered, or messages to be demystified, Geertz wants to conceive of them as idioms to be interpreted, texts to be read. The first approach leads only to "a new cryptography" in which one kind of sign is replaced by another more opaque. The second issues in what Geertz wants to call "a new diagnostics" where signs are investigated in terms of the circumstances of their significance."[31] The clinical overtones of this last phrase should not be allowed to discredit its utility. In calling for "a new diagnostics," Geertz intends to point to a procedure concerned with heuristics, not pathology, with signification, not symptoms. Insofar as it can be called a science, this "new diagnostics" will be concerned not with determining the nature and causes of disease but with determining "the meaning of things for the life that surrounds them."[32]

Geertz's proposal for "a new diagnostics" provides the link between the cultural analysis of artistic forms and the moral analysis of culture. By shifting the analysis of cultural forms from the analogy of dissecting an organism, decoding a message, or dismantling a system to that of interpreting a text, and by viewing all cultural texts, whether they be constructed of social materials or imaginative, as symbolic strategies for encompassing situations, Geertz intends to argue that such strategies can never be adequately understood without sufficient comprehension of the situations they were designed to encompass. The moral analysis of culture is therefore ingredient within the cultural analysis of art because the study of culture in all its forms involves a study of the social uses these symbolic strategies serve, or the social uses to which they can be put, in man's continuous effort to make sense of, and find significance in, the great variety of things that happen to him. The study of such uses is what Geertz means by "the social history of the moral imagination" and what, like Trilling before him, he assumes to be the one subject common to all students of culture.

As I observed earlier, Geertz has a highly sophisticated sense of the complexity of that history and thus of the devious ways our imaginations are influenced by those of others. The process by which the imaginations of others insinuate themselves into our own involves a subtle but continuous series of interpretive translations that we can never comprehend by reversing, in the hopes of reaching some ultimate goal of deinterpreted immediacies, but only by penetrating, in an effort to discover how the immediacies of one form of experience are translated into the metaphors of another. For Geertz, the key to rendering this metamorphic process intelligible is to set its successive phases in their social frames, to place its stages of evolution in the practical contexts in which they occur and from which they derive their meaning.

Yet it is just here that Geertz's semiotics becomes vulnerable to criticism. Those social frames in which he urges us to set the translated object in the various phases of its existence so as to make it intelligible—what are they but another translation of our own, and one that is just as susceptible to manipulation and distortion as any other? Fredric R. Jameson has recently argued that if the Burkean model of the text is to be applied with critical consistency, then it must be realized that the attempt to establish social frames within which to place the existential phases of the interpreted object represents in its turn a strategy of our own for encompassing situations—the situation in this case being the necessity of making sense out of the text before us.[33] We do so, it would seem, only by supplying a secondary text to interpret the primary one, the secondary text being a fabrication constructed out of that collective fund of wisdom which happens, for whatever reason, to serve us best in making sense out of the past.

To assume, then, that we can always successfully differentiate between the interpreted transformations of the translated object and the social contexts of its various forms of existence is as treacherous as supposing that we can work our way back through the phases of translation and recover the immediacy of experience from which it springs. The meaning of the object, at least for us, is the meaning it possesses as a result of, and not in spite of, its particular career of translation; the social contexts we supply to make comprehensible to ourselves the several successive episodes of that career are but an additional chapter in the history of its translation, a chapter colored by our own needs and biases as translators. Thus Geertz is surely correct when he argues that "the application of critical categories to social events and sociological categories to symbolic structures is not some primitive form of philosophic mistake, nor is it another mere confusion of art with life."[34] But he can go on to argue that "it is a way into the thing itself" only if he is willing to concede that the act of social framing, of "bordering" the phases of that career "with the tenor of the life around them," constitutes a translation of our own, and that, like the others, ours is conditioned by a hermeneutical setting in whose tenor one presumably finds much of its meaning.

Even more serious, perhaps, is the ambiguity latent in Geertz's use of those slippery words *moral* and *imagination*. When Trilling challenged the axiom so dear to humanistic scholarship by raising questions about "the moral instructiveness of past cultures," and of other cultures generally, the real issue for him was ethical and not epistemological. He was nowhere near as anxious about the possibility of obtaining knowledge of other minds, of other sensibilities, as he was about the problem of deciding what such knowledge is good for. And what simultaneously interested and worried him was not the kind of recognition such knowledge affords but the kind of changes such knowledge does or, more alarmingly, doesn't effect. Geertz, on the other hand, seems to have reversed the order of importance of these issues. He does not lack interest in the effects of such knowledge, but his interest is more severely circumscribed than Trilling's. While Geertz is willing to admit that exposure to other minds, as to other cultures, can (or at least should) considerably expand the range of our own, and often "at the expense of its inward ease,"[35] he is less interested in the consequences of such expansion than in the mystery on which it is based. What evokes his greatest curiosity is not the difference other peoples' imaginations make to the moral constitution of our own, but "how it is that other peoples' creations can be so utterly their own and so deeply part of us."[36]

If Geertz is here inclined to subsume moral considerations under aesthetic ones, it could be justifiably argued that this is merely of a piece with a semiotics that conceives of "the interpretation of cultures," as Geertz suggests in his essay on anthropological understanding, on the model of reading a poem. But this analogy presents a problem that derives from Geertz's rather restricted notion of poetic interpretation in the same article. Interpreting a poem, he argues, is of the same order of activity as grasping a pun, solving a riddle, appreciating a proverb, or getting a joke. Or, as he says in explaining his rather narrow conception of the hermeneutic circle as a dialectical process of reading parts in relation to wholes and wholes in relation to parts, interpretation is like understanding baseball: "In order to follow a baseball game one must understand what a bat, a hit, an inning, a left fielder, a squeeze play, a hanging curve, or a tightened infield are, and what the game in which these 'things' are elements is all about."[37] Up to a point this is true. It becomes false precisely where the quotient of knowability and the character of the knowable change in works of art.

In verbal games no less than physical ones, complete knowability is at least hypothetically possible and depends upon understanding the "principle" at stake in the play when that play is conducted in conformity with an acknowledged structure of "rules." The principle and the structure go together, the principle demonstrating one version of the "wisdom" embodied in the structure, the structure serving, if you will, as the ontological ground of the "insight" or meaning epitomized by the principle. In works of art, by contrast, complete knowability is never possible since part of the point of the interpretive "play" is to use the structure to explore meanings that are in no sense contained by it or mirrors of it but only potential to it. Reading a poem or interpreting any other aesthetic object, except in those exegetical exercises that typically try to account for their power by formally explaining it away, has little do with "finding a solution," as in puzzles and riddles, or "getting the point," as in puns, jokes, and proverbs. It has far more to do with what Paul Ricoeur describes as "the direction of thought opened up by the text," which discloses "a possible way of looking at things" suggested by the text but in no sense restricted to or represented by the text.[38]

Thus, as Trilling hinted in his nuanced reply, Geertz's attempt to discount the importance of empathetic understanding in literary and cultural interpretation alike, whatever its merits on anthropological grounds, is questionable on literary grounds. If as readers we cannot put ourselves completely in the place of others, we can, as a result of our exposure to some of their representative forms of life, their characteristic modes of being, at least become engaged with them in ways that were never before possible for us; if we cannot fully absorb forms of humanity alien to our own, we can at least tolerate the intrusion into our own of forms of humanity that are by no means identical with it, and we can creatively respond to them. And we can do this, as Trilling might have added if he had been familiar with more of Geertz's other work, on the testimony of Geertz's own aesthetic theory. For according to Geertz's aesthetics, what makes communication between poem and reader possible to begin with is their mutual participation in a field of symbolic experience wider than any that either comprises alone. Yet what do the variations in that wider field of experience suggest if not that the relations between poem and reader, as between poet and the broader historical audience to which his poem is addressed, need to be reconceived as reciprocal rather than merely representational, as interactive rather than simply expressive?

If cultural interpretation can be conceived on the analogy of literary interpretation, then it would be fair to say that elsewhere Geertz quite properly construes artistic interpretation generally in terms of the rhetorical model of utterance and response, of argument and reply, or, more specifically, in terms of the dramatistic model of a reaction to a situation. In either case, the interpreter is confronted with a symbolic form that purports not simply to convey something but to stimulate and challenge something, that seeks not just to inform but also to influence and incite, in short, to move. And it does so, in the example of quattrocento painting no less than that of the Balinese cockfight, by casting ideas, conceptions, notions in forms where the feelings are not only attached to them but can, as Geertz says, "reflectively address them."[39] Art not only *is* something for Geertz but also, as for Trilling as well, *does* something. And what it does is to furnish us with forms that, far from merely reflecting a consciousness already created and complete, enable us to enter into a relationship with that consciousness and, through our dialogic effort to answer the utterance we think it makes, to keep alive that portion of it which is still meaningful to us.

This aesthetic position is a far cry from the narrowly textual theory of poetic interpretation that Geertz advances in the essays on anthropological understanding to which Trilling responded; in that essay, reading a poem amounts to no more than determining what it is about, to no more than understanding the relation between its generalized view of life and the specific vehicles in which that view is embodied and communicated. If Geertz is to be consistent with the larger implications of his own theory of culture, then reading a poem, figuring out what the poem "is up to," entails at the very least a comprehension of the sorts of claims it makes on us as readers and an assessment of how, accordingly, we should respond. More typically, it involves a confrontation with modes of being, with forms of life, other than our own and an attempt to make the necessary adjustments.

Reading a poem, like interpreting another culture, thus depends upon a fundamental, if also fundamentally unstable, distinction between all that we think we are at any given moment and all that we know we are not, or, better, between all that at any given moment we think we could be and all that we are certain we cannot be or should not be. It is this "dialectic," to use one of Trilling's favorite words, that occasions those interpretive workings and reworkings that Geertz rightly perceives as the essence of cultural life and the central subject of cultural study. Yet the impact such interpretive reworkings have upon the moral lives of those who undertake them and those who respond to them tends to remain an unresolved issue for Geertz. Not that he doubts that they have an impact or make a difference; only that he has been reluctant, in every instance but that of the Balinese city-state, which is the subject of his book *Negira,* to say whether that impact, that difference, is for good or ill. And while Geertz's restraint on this point may well be an indication of his own moral integrity, it remains, as I think Trilling sensed, the most troubling feature of his whole theory of culture and continues to constitute the chief threat to its moral basis.

Geertz would respond that the usual humanistic way of resolving this issue, perhaps even Trilling's way of resolving it, is bought at too dear a price, one that attempts to purchase the reunification of our fragmented cultural, and perhaps political, life in the twentieth century at the expense of the very humanity it seeks to protect. For however one might judge, in any given instance, the value of the translation of the idioms of one people into the images of another, such assessments are for the humanist premised on the notion that underneath all the superficial differences between human selves and societies there is a fundamental oneness that all interpretive or hermeneutic activity ultimately helps to display. For Geertz, this is putting things the wrong way around. If humanistic understanding has advanced at all over the centuries, that advance has surely been toward an enlarged appreciation of the greater diversity and variety of life forms that can now be comprehended and accepted as definably human. But this only makes clearer than before what many humanists have disregarded or dismissed for too long: that the only basis for humanistic understanding lies not in reducing human experience to its lowest (or highest) common denominator but in discovering how it is possible for human beings inhabiting inevitably different and often conflicting, even contradictory, worlds to still have "a genuine, and reciprocal, impact on one another." Even if it were true, as Geertz has recently mused (though I, for one, remain dubious), that "there is a general human consciousness," it could only consist "of the interplay of a disorderly crowd of not wholly commensurable visions. . . ."[40] And this consciousness will grow stronger not by attempting, however delicately and subtly, to merge the perspectives that make it up but only by creating conditions under which the interplay among them can more constructively occur. What currently stands in the way are the enormous pressures now being generated in many humanistic (and even some social scientific) circles to ground recent discoveries of human variousness in a new and more capacious but still unitary humanism. To resist these pressures, Geertz recommends a kind of moral counterstrategy: "the first step is surely to accept the depth of the differences underlying often superficial similarities that characterize the ways human beings have chosen to express their nature; the second is to understand what these differences consist of and amount to; and the third is to construct some sort of vocabulary in which they can be publically formulated"—one in which all parties to the discussion are permitted to "give a credible account of themselves to one another."[41]

Thus the goal of humanistic understanding is not to bring about a reunification of humankind in allegiance to a wider humanism but to enable its members to converse with one another even across the divide of historical time and cultural space. Such conversation is salutary, even crucial, not because human beings need to exchange identities with someone else, much less because they need to assume an identity in common with everyone else, but because, as Erich Heller has pointed out, "one of the things that sets man apart from all other beings is that the sum of his potentialities by far exceeds the measure of their realizability in one human life or even one historical epoch."[42] In addition to being that creature who to cope with the environment must translate its contacts with that environment into symbols, the human animal seems to be the one creature in the animal kingdom that cannot reach its full potential without interacting with the inevitably different and sometimes conflicting symbolic constructions that other individuals put on those same contacts. In part, this is simply to say that human beings cannot realize themselves except socially; in part, it is to suggest that human beings always experience such realizations in terms that run the risk of solipsism. Either way, the key to the realization of their potentialities lies in the process by which they not only interpret those contacts for themselves but also relate the interpretations of others to their own.

This, in sum, is what the moral imagination does—in fact, defines what the moral imagination is. And while the knowledge it affords can never provide us with a wholly adequate understanding of any people or their traditions, much less put us in the same position occupied by those people and represented by their traditions, the moral imagination can provide us with something no less essential to our sense of solidarity as human beings: not only can it help us comprehend what creates any particular people out of a group of different and distinct individuals and allows them to share on the plane of experience what they have never necessarily undergone together in the realm of action or perceived together in the realm of ideas; it can also help us determine what they gain thereby and lose, or, at least from our own perspective, what as a result they acquire and what they give up, and, again from our perspective if not theirs, why such things matter in the first place. This kind of knowledge is extremely hard to come by in an age so heavily ideological, logocentric, and monologistic as our own, but it may well prove indispensable not only to the study of human culture but also to the survival of the human species.

6

The Humanities and
Their Discontents: Mikhail Bakhtin
and the Recovery of Alterity

The humanities in our time are in considerable trouble. Almost every-where one looks in American institutions of higher education, one finds them in a state of enforced retreat to the far edges of the academic curriculum, and they are marginalized in the wider society. This retreat within the academy and growing obsolescence outside it are the more notable for two reasons: first, because they are continuing in the midst of a much publicized "return to basics" that is supposedly reviving general education requirements in undergraduate programs and restoring an ideal of "civility" to the theory of education in general; second, because they are occurring despite a host of what were once regarded as promising developments for the humanities, such as the creation, during the administration of Lyndon B. Johnson, of National Endowments both for the Arts and the Humanities; the subsequent establishment of various institutes for advanced study in the humanities all the way from the Carolinas to California; the development in Washington, D.C., of a professional organization committed to lobbying solely for programs and funding for the humanities; and, finally, the appearance of a variety of new interdisciplinary journals, from the *Raritan Review* to *Representations,* concerned with humanistic issues. The reasons for this state of affairs are numerous. The pressures of the economic marketplace are one factor; the careerism of a new generation of students is often cited as another; national priorities that obviously favor science, technology, and social engineering are a third; and the pervasive materialism, as Tocqueville called it, of the American people, which makes them so indifferent to, if not hostile toward, pleasures whose gratifications are not immediate as well as direct, no doubt constitutes a fourth. But an additional factor primarily located within the gates of the humanities rather than outside them is currently exerting a more corrosive effect on their present conception and actual application than any of the factors just mentioned. I refer to the pervasive sense of suspicion with which they are now regarded within academic life itself, and not only by such traditional intellectual detractors as behaviorists, positivists, and quantifiers, but also by many of their most able and eloquent exemplars. And the suspicion is blanket: it is not simply the utility of the humanities that is being questioned, their intellectual or practical bearing, but their very legitimacy as a mode of intellectual inquiry.

Edward Said has indicated something of the basis of this suspicion by pointing out that humanistic study, especially within the university, has become an "experience more or less officially consecrating the pact between a canon of works, a band of initiate instructors, and a group of younger affiliates," all reproducing "in a socially validated manner . . . the filiative discipline supposedly transcended by the educational process."[1] In certain respects, Said is not an accurate barometer of this suspicion since he has no quarrel with many of the traditional methods and aims of humanistic scholarship. His own quarrel is with the almost exclusively Eurocentric bias of humanistic learning in the West, which now "represents," as Said rightly observes, "only a fraction of the real human relationships and interactions taking place in the world," and, further, with the way this bias dissociates the objects of its inquiry from the social circumstances of their creation and influence.[2] But a far from inconsiderable number of other skeptics and critics are notably less circumspect or judicious. Their objections are raised directly against the kinds of privileges claimed or assumed by the humanities as presently conceived, and strike at the heart of the procedures and protocols represented by the humanities as presently practiced. These objections stem from two different evaluations of our current cultural crisis, but they eventuate in a common assessment of the complicity of the humanities in that crisis.

The humanities have come under attack, on the one side, from those radical hermeneutical skeptics who believe that human beings are hopelessly entangled within webs of cultural meaning and practice that are simultaneously ubiquitous, unstable, and solipsistic; all they can ever presume to do, so the argument goes, is to discover the self-serving and ultimately self-canceling character of such webs of meaning, which are so often masked by fogs of humanistic piety, and set about trying to demystify and deconstruct them. The humanities have come under attack from the other side by those radical historical pessimists who believe that such modern phenomena as the rise of totalitarianism, the growth of terrorism as a social and political policy, the perpetration of (or, in certain other "official circles," tacit acceptance of) the Holocaust, and now the threat of thermonuclear war have destroyed the credibility of all our previous categories of thought and standards of judgment. Caught in the gap between a past we are compelled to spurn and a future we dare not imagine, all of our familiar moral and ontological guideposts have rotted from within.

Central to both groups is the assumption that we now live in an unprecedented historical situation. Ours is a world bereft of transcendent meaning or purpose and from which we are totally alienated, either imprisoned within grammars of discourse whose warrants and usages afford us no contact with anything outside and independent of them, or held captive by an escalating politics of violence whose foreseeable conclusion is the annihilation of human life as we know it. Either way, the current historicocultural situation has disclosed the bankruptcy of our intellectual and linguistic inheritance, and the humanities as currently established in the academy only deepen our arrears by preserving and protecting a legacy of ideas and values that, as a matter of historical record, has often been employed, if not to precipitate these delusions, at least to rationalize them.

1

This indictment is not easily dismissed. Whatever the lines between contemporary history and the development, evolution, and refinement of humanistic study—and the examination of those lines has only just begun—there is no doubt that the humanities represent a set of ideas, and a way of regarding them, and even a cast of mind formed by them, that have deep historical implications precisely because they have been assumed to exist above history, to survive the successive changes of time in, as with T. S. Eliot's concept of tradition, a timeless present of perennial significance and value. Even a humanist as sensitive to the remorseless alterations of time as the author of *The Sense of an Ending* is driven in his latest book, *Forms of Attention,* to fall back on the notion that there is a classic body of texts whose meaning and pertinence escape the demolitions—or, as these most severe critics of the humanities might put it, the deceptions—of historical existence.

But Frank Kermode is not alone. The assumption that the humanities represent a body of timeless truths dies a very slow death because it was present at their conception. First defined as a kind of learning distinct from divinity, and then as well from natural science, when Bacon, in the *Advancement of Learning,* differentiated the "three knowledges, Divine Philosophy, Natural Philosophy and Humane Philosophy, or Humanitie," the humanities have always been associated with the notion of the classics; only at the beginning of the eighteenth century in France did they acquire their further traditional associations with modern literature and philosophy. But the concept of the humanities acquired additional complications when it subsequently became affiliated with the term *humanist.* A significant Renaissance word from the early sixteenth century, by the end of that century *humanist* had established a connection between the notion of the classicist and that of a person who studies human as opposed to divine matters. And latent in the notion of the human in its relation to classicism was a disctinction between pagan and Christian learning as well as a difference between those who are learned in the classical languages and those who are not. In any case, by the middle of the seventeenth century these ambiguities were resolved when the term *humanist* came to refer at once to the revival of classical learning and to the new interest in man in his ideal form.

However, the notion of the humanities did not acquire its modern complexity until it was linked not only to the idea of the "humanist" but also to the idea of "humanism." This latter notion developed independently of the other two terms from the German word *humanismus,* a general concept that appeared in the late eighteenth century to represent a spiritual alternative to orthodox Christianity. But the broader sense of the term derived from post-Enlightenment notions of history as the realm of human self-development and self-perfection, which, when combined in the nineteenth century with the older notions of "humanist" and "the humanities," yielded our modern conception of humanism as a particular kind of perspective dependent upon a special kind of learning, a perspective or way of seeing that, if not embodied within the humanities, is at any rate produced by them and is in the custody of the humanist. And what characterizes this perspective, and distinguishes it as a mode of learning from all others, is its peculiar tendency to valorize culture by associating it with the realization, and often the consummation, of human perfection.[3]

This historical privileging of the concept of the humanities has inevitably permitted all manner of social, political, and moral outrage to be committed in its name, or at least condoned, and is obviously one reason—perhaps the most important—why the humanities are now viewed with such marked suspicion, and often more than occasional hostility, even among humanist scholars themselves. There are other reasons, however, no doubt colored by this privileging, that have more to do with the way the humanities have been conceived within and beyond the academic establishment not only by some of their most severe critics but by their most vocal defenders. What one sees in this instance, time and again, is massive evidence of what can only be called intellectual as well as moral failure. Failure of mind is evidenced in the way those who profess the humanities have consistently evaded so many hard disciplinary questions about the relations between the humanities and the other branches of learning, even about the relations among the various components of the humanities themselves. Not only have they failed to spell out the relations between the humanities and the sciences, natural, social, and physical; they have generally made a practice, almost an art, of evading questions about what literature has to do with philosophy, or what language study has to do with historical understanding, or what understanding in the visual arts can teach about the arts of composition. Failure of moral responsibility—it would be more accurate to call it failure of moral imagination—is displayed in the fact that proponents of the humanities have rarely been able, despite their facility for explaining everything else, to develop cogent and publicly compelling explanations of what the humanities are ultimately good for, of how they constitute, in Kenneth Burke's phrase, a kind of "equipment for living." Instead of constructing arguments for their general relevance, humanists have mounted arguments for their special uniqueness. Instead of developing methods for their practical application, humanists have refined techniques that restrict their broader accessibility.

The cumulative effect of these failures has been to encourage the tendency, already under way for other reasons, to idealize the humanities as special enclaves of intellectual privilege, and at the same time to sever various specialized expressions of humanism from their roots in the common soil of ordinary experience. Imaginative literature, it has been insisted, is not to be confused with the life around it and should be studied solely in relation to the terms of its own origination and expression. History, it is often maintained, must be restricted to a study of events in relation to their antecedent causes and subsequent consequences and should never be extended to an examination of its possible uses and potential dangers. Philosophy, it has customarily been asserted, is not about the meaning of existence or the nature of wisdom, but about the study of language and what can be asserted, or not asserted, with its assistance. The performing arts, it has been assumed, exist somewhere outside the humanities altogether, since the disciplines they require and the forms they serve have nothing whatsoever to do with general ideas. And so it has gone, with a good many subjects and modes of critical inquiry simply left out of account. Folklore is overlooked because it is neither history nor literature. The crafts are discounted because they are not art. Ethics and theology are omitted because they are not disinterested. The theoretical sciences are dismissed because they have led to practical discoveries.

The wonder in all this is how reasonably intelligent human beings can tolerate, much less commit, such lapses. Surely Gregor Mendel's early experiments with genetics are just as extraordinary a human achievement, just as profound a contribution to the relief of man's estate, as William Shakespeare's experiments with tragic form. Surely the New England shipwright's design for the American clipper ship, or the Yankee wheelwright's design for the New England trotting wagon, are, on their own scale, just as astonishing a marriage of aesthetic form and human function as Bernini's *David* or the Library of San Marco in Florence. But the primary issue isn't one of intelligence or technique alone. If it is far from being conceded or even understood by the general public at large, there is still a large measure of consensus among professional humanists that what Charles Darwin, say, undertook aboard H.M.S. *Beagle* is no less a part of the humanities than what Marcel Proust undertook in his cork-lined room. Yet one will rarely find the *Origin of Species* or *Descent of Man* on the same syllabus with any volumes from *Remembrance of Things Past,* and the reason is at least twofold. Darwin and Proust, representing different and somewhat opposed conceptions of what the humanities are, serve the interests of different guilds, different "regimes of power," as Foucault calls them, in the profession, however informal and heavily masked their rule may be. Moreover, humanists no longer possess, if they ever had it, a language capable of bridging the gap between the two, much less of simultaneously encompassing all that both together still leave out of account.

The current inability to perceive such connections, much less to incorporate them structurally within the educational curriculum, testifies to just how timorous and purblind humanistic study remains in America. It is not simply a matter of reluctance to remove the humanities from the closet of cultural elitism and resituate them in something approximating the workaday, or at least the empirical, world. Nor is it a question of breaking down the Eurocentric biases of humanistic scholarship in the West through concentrated exposure to non-Western cultures and methods of analysis. The problem is, rather, to overcome the kind of heuristic skepticism that the privileging of the humanities both protects and nourishes, a dubiety not only about those disciplinary matrixes that structure such prejudice but about the kinds of knowledge and the sorts of ability they furnish or make possible— whether those kinds of knowledge be Occidental or Oriental, whether those abilities be "civilized" or "primitive." And having lost faith in the kinds of learning and the sorts of competencies that the humanities should, or could, represent and enable—programming a computer does not involve the same sort of challenge, challenging though it may be, as mastering the subtlety of a Bach cantata or the Japanese art of puppetry known as Banraku; acquiring the ability to read a corporate financial statement does not raise questions of the same order of magnitude or personal menace as do *Moby-Dick* or Aztec rituals of human sacrifice—humanists simply no longer possess a conceptual language, or at least a conceptual language free of clichés, to discuss such things. And without an adequate language of concepts to discuss and debate them, humanists no longer know how to think about them intelligently, much less how to pose their challenge adequately to students.

2

Sometimes we talk as though the humanities referred to a kind of subject matter like the "great books" or the "great ideas," sometimes as though they suggest a particular set of procedures or methods by which to study such things. At other times we seem to refer by the word *humanities* to the effect that a particular kind of study of certain sorts of subjects can have on human beings themselves, such as making them more civilized, more humane, more intelligent, or better balanced. At still others we seem to mean by the humanities those specific qualities that are the civilizing agents themselves and that are sometimes produced by a particular kind of study of selected sorts of material.

Each of these senses of the word *humanities* has its integrity and its uses, but each also has a way of encroaching upon its neighbors. The problem arises when in our discussion of the humanities one of these senses is established as arbiter of the place and meaning of the other three. Take, for example, the tendency to define the humanities in terms of a particular subject matter, and let us suppose that we try to erect a fairly generous definition of what that subject matter includes. Even if we could agree on a definition as broad, say, as those arts of thought and feeling, those traditions of reflection and expression, in which the meaning of being human is somehow centrally at issue, then what are we to make of Goethe's work on colors or Lamennais's treatise on scientific classifications? Are such texts as these, which did so much to facilitate thinking and discovery in all areas of intellectual life in their time—are such texts as these to be excluded from the canon of the humanistic tradition simply because one of them is ostensibly concerned with optics and the other with insects?

The same quandary arises if we identify the humanities too closely with any particular method of analysis or mode of critical approach. Even if by method we mean nothing more precise than a demonstrable concern with qualities as well as measurable quantities and a refusal to rest content in an attitude of neutral detachment with regard to questions of value, then what are we to make of a work like Sigmund Freud's "Fragment of an Analysis of a Case of Hysteria," otherwise known as his study of "Dora," which was based so largely on empirical observation and scrupulously attempts to maintain an attitude of scientific disinterestedness in relation to the implications of its findings? Surely Freud and Lamennais and Goethe were doing something that falls within the sphere of the humanities inasmuch as they managed, through these works, to change conventional understandings of the human world and our relation to it. Yet most definitions of the humanities, which associate them with interpretive disciplines that are principally sensible of subjective factors, as opposed to objective ones, would rule such works out of account.

3

For many people in the humanities, the Victorian writer and critic Matthew Arnold seemed to have provided a way out of this dilemma by inviting us to associate the humanities, not only as a subject matter and a method but also as a set of qualities, with what he called forthrightly "the best which has been thought and said in the world."[4] Yet Arnold's way of putting this, for all its pertinence at the time, had its difficulties. Arnold was of course referring by his magniloquent phrase to culture rather than to the humanities, which he recommended "as the great help out of our present difficulties."[5] The new middle classes had recently come to economic and political ascendancy in England without experiencing a commensurate spiritual development, and Arnold hoped to "Hellenize" the "Philistines" by exposing them to the cultural monuments and style traditionally associated with the aristocracy. Through association with what Arnold described in another context as "the best culture of this nation," the middle classes, to whose fortunes he was so devoted, might acquire "a greatness and a noble sprit, which the tone of these classes is not of itself at present adequate to impart."[6] Trusting too blindly in externals and mechanically relying upon habit, routine, and precedent, Arnold hoped that knowledge of "the best" might turn "a stream of fresh and free thought upon . . . stock notions and habits, which we now follow staunchly but mechanically, vainly imagining that there is a virtue in following them staunchly which makes up for the mischief of following them mechanically."[7]

Among the various difficulties with Arnold's way of formulating his conception of culture, at least three are pertinent to this discussion. For one thing, it seemed to accentuate the importance of things thought and written at the expense of things made or done. The great deed and the material construction were obliged to accept a very secondary position in relation to the literary masterpiece or the philosophical masterwork. For another, it treated the products of humanistic achievement as monuments to be appreciated rather than as models to be emulated, as performances to inspire practices.[8] Arnold's rhetoric favored a view of the humanities as a repository of texts that comprise some of "the jewels in life's crown," to borrow a distinction from Edmund Wilson, but are not conceived as among "the great springs of life." Third and finally, there was, and is, something at once distastefully high-toned and self-consciously obscure about Arnold's formulation. What precisely was meant by "the best," and who made such determinations anyway? Needless to say, Arnold's memorable formulation encouraged the temptation, now almost epidemic in many American quarters, to think of the humanities as something produced solely, to turn Thorstein Veblen on his head, "for the leisure of the theoried classes," and then to foster a definition of those "classes" primarily related their tendency to convert the humanities into a theory of their own entitlement.

On this reading, Arnold might have been better advised to replace the word *best* in his definition of culture with another of his favorite words, *critical*, but he would have to had to dissociate *critical* from all those relations it possesses in his own writing and elsewhere with notions of "taste" and "cultivation," relations that achieve objective expression in the need to develop durable and lasting standards of "judgment" and that achieve subjective expressions in the interest to which this leads in the formation of something called "sensibility." Criticism in this sense expresses the prejudices of a particular class and eventually a profession. As Raymond Williams has pointed out, it is ideological not only in the sense that it places the critic in the position of a consumer but also because it masks this metamorphosis "by a succession of abstractions of its real terms of response."[9] Williams correctly objects to this view of criticism because it circumscribes the kind of response criticism entails and misleadingly distorts it. The purpose of such an observation, however, is not, as Williams remarks,

> to find some other term to replace it, while continuing the same kind of activity, but to get rid of the habit, which depends, fundamentally, on the abstraction of response from its real situation and circumstances: the elevation to judgment, and to an apparently general process, when what always needs to be understood is the specificity of the response, which is not a judgment but a practice, in active and complex relations with the situation and conditions of the practice, and, necessarily, with all other practices.[10]

On this view, criticism is not without prejudice and cannot be understood apart from the social and political circumstances of its significance. But when it is placed in relation to other social practices, we can see its prejudice for what it is: a prejudice that exists not for the sake of promoting better and more informed judgment, more discriminating taste, or more cultivated sensibility, as in the Arnoldian model, but for the sake, as John Dewey stated, of "instituting and perpetuating more enduring and extensive values."[11] In short, the practice of criticism, to use another of Dewey's phrases, is the "critique of prejudices," but the "critique of prejudices" does not involve the supercession of privilege so much as its self-criticism.

4

If this view of criticism is applied to the theory of the humanities, then it becomes apparent that the humanities are critical in a double and not in single sense. The humanities refer, on the one hand, to those traditions of inquiry and expression where our civilization, indeed any civilization, places its own presiding assumptions, rituals, and sentiments under the most searching intellectual scrutiny in the act of giving them formal realization; they refer, on the other, to those critical methods in which civilizations attempt to repossess those traditions of understanding inherited from the past and readapt them to the changing needs of the present and the future by developing the arts and sciences of appropriate response to them. From this perspective, the humanities should not be restricted as to content and cannot be reduced to a single method. While they refer to something objective enough to study, their value lies equally in the kinds of responses they evoke in those who study them, in the sorts of practical activities and consequences to which their study leads.

So saying, I mean to resist the temptation to limit the humanities to some holy trinity like art, history, and philosophy, or even to some looser triumvirate like the verbal arts, the fine arts, and the critical arts. In addition, I mean to challenge the view that the humanities are material for reflection only and not for performative replication. Finally, I intend to contradict the notion that the humanities are reserved exclusively for the intellectually elect and are thus inaccessible to what Whitman called "the democratic en-masse." If some of their formal expressions seem to exist on a plane somewhat removed from that of our everyday experience, this is only because they seek to challenge the reach of our more customary interpretations of everyday experience and can only mount this challenge by developing forms that carry us beyond its ken.

By the humanities, then, I refer to one of two indissolubly connected things. If we are considering the humanities as a kind of subject matter or body of material, I refer to all those traditions of investigation and reflection—scientific as well as philosophic, social as well as artistic, anthropological as well as religious—in which any given civilization has conducted its own self-scrutiny and, where necessary, has attempted to revise itself in behalf of a more capacious present and future. As a "field of inquiry," then, humanistic studies involve considerably more than an analysis of all those exemplary forms in which this commentary has been conducted throughout history. They also involve an examination of the factors that have compelled the creation or modification of such forms at certain historical moments and encouraged the neglect or hastened the repudiation and suppression of such forms at other moments. But this is not all. Humanistic studies would be seriously incomplete if they did not simultaneously entail an exploration of the differences such forms have made to the societies, and the people living within them, whose imaginations they have helped shape and whose lives they have helped control.

If, on the other hand, I mean by the humanities a specific set of intellectual procedures or a discriminable method of approach, they then encompass all those disciplines where, or any disciplines when, questions of value are simultaneously ingredient in, and determinative of, the form of the investigation. By values, however, I do not mean anything as restrictive as ideals or norms, conscious or otherwise. Rather, I refer to the categories of significance, of assessed meaning, by which we arrange experience—any experience, all experience—hierarchically. We do so, apparently, because we have to. Life continually confronts us with choices, options between which we must decide. We decide only on the basis of preference, which requires valuation and produces rankings. Thus wherever experience is ranked, wherever it is assigned a place in some vertical ordering, we are in the presence of valuations and can presumably examine values. But the mere raising of questions of value does not mark a discipline as humanistic. Disciplines are organized in relation to values, and thus become humanistic, only when valuing, or valuation, is central to what is being questioned. Hence insofar as the term *humanities* designates a mode of inquiry rather than a subject of study, it points not to disciplines that are concerned with values as such—as though, say, art history was humanistic but marine biology was not—but to disciplines that, whatever their stipulated subject matter, make processes of valuation constitutive of the kind of inquiry that defines them.

To make this more concrete, does this argument mean that there is a canonical list of "greats" for the humanist, whether texts, individuals, ideas, or actions? The answer is both Yes and No. Yes, texts like the *Iliad,* the *Odyssey,* or the *Aeneid* have a kind of indispensability because for hundreds of years they have embodied, in our civilization at any rate, much of what it means for human beings to be mighty in force and rage, to be resourceful in survival, or subordinate themselves to the interests of the state or empire. Yet to study these texts humanistically is not to accept their normative status uncritically but to reassess that status continuously, both by critically comparing them with all the other paradigms that have defined our view of the human or affected our attitudes toward experience and by seeing them as themselves the outcome, the result, of a similar process of paradigm criticism and revision in which options were weighed, choices made, preferences expressed. To examine these texts with an eye to their humanistic meaning and import is to see them as responses to situations, responses that seek to deal with those situations neither by seeking to replicate the circumstances of their occasion or to direct the course of their future development, as in science, nor by attempting to define their nature through a delineation and systematization of their component parts, as in philosophy, but by exploring symbolic strategies for encompassing them, strategies that simultaneously mute, or at least contain, their potential for personal disruption and explore their possibilities for understanding. But such strategies as these can never be less than tentative, provisional, even precarious, because they are devised as critical solutions to problems whose conceptualization is inextricably related to the prejudices of the mind that so construes them and the predispositions of the mind that interprets them.

This may be no more than belaboring the obvious: whether as a kind of study or as a source of things studied, the humanities are not about the worship of a single list of texts that are considered repositories of more or less absolute truths that admit of but one correct set of interpretations. As a discipline of inquiry, the humanities are equally concerned with the reasons why, and the ways in which, such texts as these have given a meaningful shape and coloring to the experience of particular peoples; with why these texts, and not others, have determined the hierarchies of significance by which these peoples organize so much of their experience; and with how these texts might be read differently if one were more attentive to the process of paradigm deconstruction and reconstruction that is going on within them. In other words, the debate about these texts, like the debate within them, is not incidental to their study but coterminous with it, part of the *res* and not merely about it.

The question that remains is whether these texts and the traditions of interpretation they embody and comprise, however susceptible to change those traditions inevitably prove to be, serve any other heuristic purpose? What bearing, what concrete relevance, it is fair to ask, do they possess beyond the provision of models for the relationship between consciousness and life that are at least partially imitable, or if not imitable, then instructive, provocative, disturbing? The answer is to be found in the particular responses they bring into play, the specific aptitudes and skills they activate in their comprehension and enjoyment. Their practical "cash value," as William James would have called it, is in no small measure a result of the cognitive and affective procedures they enable and the pleasures those procedures provide.

Barbara Herrnstein Smith has developed an analogy between the procedures of humanistic interpretation and the character of a game. This analogy is rooted in the fact that while some meanings of any humanistic text are interpretively indeterminate, all are potentially inferable. Thus part of the pleasure of "reading" such texts derives from the opportunity they provide us to hypothesize such meanings and then see if we can confirm them. Indeed, the more fictive, or imaginative, a text is, the more it will invite and even compel such speculative play, and the more this play will, in turn, determine and even constitute our interpretation of the text. Literary or artistic works, it might be said, simply afford the most extensive use of creative aptitudes and skills, but such aptitudes and skills are requisite in some measure to the interpretation of any partially indeterminate object and inevitably comprise a portion of its experience.

The importance of this creative element in interpretation, which is not simply subjective or solipsistic, may well be related to the fact that, as Smith goes on to say, we are constantly the subject, during every moment of our lives, of potential "experiences" that we never have the time or energy to take full cognizance of, unless some subsequent occasion provides us with an opportunity to recover what has been suppressed or to acknowledge "what we did not even know we knew: a perception never before quite articulated, an emotion we had sustained on the periphery of consciousness, a sense—barely grasped before—of the 'import' of some incident."[12] We bring such experiences "back to mind," and thus grasp more of what was always potentially knowable to us, only when we are furnished some reason for repossessing them. Humanistic texts might well be thought of as providing us with just such occasions, really inducements, because of their interpretive open-endedness. In compelling us to supply some of their meaning to make full sense of them, humanistic texts encourage us to draw upon our store of unexploited experiences and thus find a genuine use for it—and not simply a use but also a vehicle for experiencing what would otherwise have been permanently lost to us.

This process of collaboration with the text, whereby we often have to complete its sense with the help of meanings drawn from our own repository of unrealized experience, is of course anything but freeform. The text that evokes such activity also seeks to shape it and, indeed, as Smith remarks in the case of imaginative literature, "to resist it. Even as certain possibilities of interpretation are opened, they are also directed, lured, and redirected . . . through the verbal structure" of the work itself.[13]

But the analogy between interpretation and games can be extended

even further to suggest how the humanities resemble a kind of spectator sport in which all critical "readings" become rehearsals or reenact-
ments "of a game that has already been played":

> And since there can be masters on both sides of the board—great
> readers and great . . . [writers or thinkers or actors], matches for each
> other in the boldness or subtlety of their moves—there can also be
> master games, as engaging for the spectator as those he plays himself, or
> even more engaging. Thus . . . we have the achievements not of [say]
> literary historians or explicators as such but, precisely, of literary inter-
> preters, those who offer not to give us the [for example] the poem—
> which often means taking it away—but rather to take it on for us, as one
> plays a match with an opponent.[14]

To admit the place and play of such activities as these in their
conception of the humanities, humanists will have to break free of
the Arnoldian model. Having situated their materials at such a remove from the precincts of ordinary experience, and having placed
upon that material valuations that are often considered, as it were,
inviolate, many students of the humanities have forgotten that much
of this material came into existence only by violating the customary
canons of valuation and only in order to reassess the elements of the
ordinary. In other words, what lent such works their original power
of disturbance was their ability to challenge conventional understandings of experience in behalf of a new valuation of its constituent
elements. What they represented had practical bearing precisely because they disclosed new bearings of and within the practical. But
this, according to hermeneutic theory, is the way that advances occur
in almost any field of intellectual endeavor. It is not that we keep
experiencing things beyond the ken of our experience; it is only that
the ken of our experience keeps enlarging as we discover new ways to
construe its components.

5

Though *hermeneutics* is currently one of our most fashionable, or, if
you prefer, despised, critical buzzwords, interpretation theory possesses a noble lineage, going back at least as far as Aristotle's *On
Interpretation* and beginning to assume its modern form in the early
writings of Friedrich Schleiermacher at the end of the eighteenth century. It was then carried forward a century later in the work of Wilhelm Dilthey, from which it subsequently passed in our own century to
Martin Heidegger, Hans-Georg Gadamer, R. G. Collingwood, and

Paul Ricoeur. Originating in its early modern form as a discipline devoted to establishing the rules for understanding scripture, hermeneutics, or interpretation theory, now refers more generally to the set of assumptions that guide the interpretation of virtually anything that can be "read" as a "text," from single words or phrases to whole cultures.

But this way of putting it is misleading. Interpretation theory takes its rise in the modern period from the problem of understanding other minds, and more particularly from the difficulty of understanding minds, or the expressions of minds, separated from us historically and culturally. Where Schleiermacher's and even Dilthey's aim was to develop a set of procedures for overcoming such distance in order to effect an identification of the mind of the interpreter with the mind of the text, that is, the mind of the text's author, for modern theorists this distance itself is what must somehow be "understood." But in this case, understanding does not lead to a unity between the mind of the interpreter and what Ricoeur calls "the thing in question." He continues, "It is not kinship of one life with another that hermeneutics requires, but a kinship of thought with what the life aims at. . . ."[15]

Most modern theorists of interpretation assume that the establishment of this kinship follows a circular course exhibiting the dialectical structure of question and answer. Interpretation begins with the attempt to ferret out the question to which any given text is presumed to be an answer. This inquiry is complicated, however, by the fact that it has already been initiated by a question that the text was felt to have put to the interpreter, and the interpreter's response to this question inevitably colors his or her attempt to reconstruct the question the text is supposed to have originally put to itself.

This does not mean that understanding is futile, only that it represents a vastly more complex process than is commonly supposed. If every interpretive effort to understand the text in its contextual integrity is delimited by the very different context from which it is being interrogated, and if, indeed, the only way to overcome this difference, really this distance, is to exploit it by alternately using the question the text is assumed to put to the interpreter to try to unearth the question to which the text is itself a formulated answer, this circular process, involving, as it does, the preunderstanding of the reader to obtain what might be called a postunderstanding of the text, does lead somewhere. Though roundabout, the process of understanding is not closed. However different the horizon of assumptions possessed by the potential interpreter and the horizon of assumptions expressed by the text, and however necessary it is to use the first to disclose the second, understanding can, and does, occur if these two horizons of assumption or meaning can be made to converge, or at least to overlap; when this occurs, the result, the enacted interpretation, is usually assumed to be potentially disruptive. For what must eventually intersect and interact in the "event" of understanding, as it is sometimes called, are what the art historian E. H. Gombrich has described as two different and often disjunctive mindsets, and this intersection of mindsets produces a subtle but inevitable alteration in which the identity of each is supposedly expanded and revised through exposure to the other. How this occurs is never made entirely clear in most hermeneutic theory, but that it occurs is usually explained by reference to the incomplete and fragmentary character of the interpretive process itself. Since no two horizons of understanding ever perfectly converge, there is always some possibility for understanding left over, which serves as a lure, an incitement, for subsequent reciprocal contact and influence.

Hermeneutic theory traditionally acknowledges this surplus of the knowable that is attendant upon every act of understanding, and that forever exceeds our conscious grasp but still lies within the horizon of our conscious awareness, as that element or dimension in human experience that William James designated the "More."[16] But where James and much hermeneutic theory, particularly that associated with the work of Hans-Georg Gadamer, links this element of the "More" bordering every act of understanding with those higher transcendental or salvific powers operative in the universe outside us and of which we purportedly become aware in religious experience, I would give this element a wholly immanental and nonsupernatural reference, calling it that dimension of inexhaustibility, of excess, of remainder, that resists all our categorical attempts to integrate or incorporate it in understanding itself. Put more positively, this element of the "More," the inexhaustible, the elsewhere beyond language, reveals itself in the way we experience our interpretations when we become sensible that the realm in which we undertake and undergo them seems to thicken and deepen the more we become responsive to it.[17] In this manner, the "More" engenders the possibility of a transcendence *within experience* rather than a transcendence *beyond it* by so often encouraging us, almost compelling us, during the interpretive event itself, to think harder, to imagine further, to feel more intensely, just when such possibilities seem to have been played out. Instead of eventually being put off by obstacles to sense, by barriers to comprehension, the

"More" functions within experience as a lure, an inducement to begin thinking all over again.

But as for explaining how we are changed (if, in fact, we really *are* changed) when we take the trouble to extend our horizons of understanding in the direction of another, or why we take the trouble to submit to such extensions in the first place when our commerce with the "other," any "other," is so rarely achieved without considerable disorientation and discomfort—about this, hermeneutic theory has surprisingly little to say. Nor does it have much to say about why this process is so easily and so frequently diverted, corrupted, or aborted just when we try to bring it to some kind of intellectual closure by attempting to formulate, with all the intellectual resources at our command, exactly what it means and why it matters. These issues are crucial to the study and theory of the humanities, but to gain some assistance in addressing them we will have to see how the model of understanding inherited from hermeneutics has now been given a powerful new extension and complication in the writings of Mikhail Bakhtin.

6

Bakhtin's contribution to the theory of understanding derives finally from the way he challenged the whole notion of the circularity of hermeneutic reasoning and the possibility of overcoming the distinction between subjects and objects, self and other, with a new comprehension of the place of alterity in interpretive experience. Far from construing understanding as circular, Bakhtin maintains that understanding is dialogical and that the aim of the dialogue is not to merge, or at least to integrate, self and other, subject and object, but to differentiate and, in a particular way, to distantiate them. In sum, the key to Bakhtin's theory of understanding, and thus to his conception of those arts and sciences by means of which understanding is cultivated in behalf of a fuller humanity, is otherness.

Though Bakhtin gave thought to these matters at virtually every point of his career, his book on Dostoevsky probably affords the best introduction to his conception of the relation between hermeneutics and alterity. *Problems of Dostoevsky's Poetics* proceeds on the assumption that Dostoevsky precipitated a fundamental restructuring of artistic thinking in his creation of the "polyphonic novel." But this restructuring, Bakhtin contends, extends far beyond the parameters of art to encompass what amounts to a fundamentally new model of

experience and of the possibilities for understanding within it. Dostoevsky's revolutionary perspective derives from what Bakhtin defines as
"the chief characteristic of Dostoevsky's novels":

> a plurality of independent and unmerged voices and consciousness, a
> genuine polyphony of fully valid voices. . . . What unfolds in his works is
> not a multitude of characters and fates in a single objective world, illumi-
> nated by a single authorial consciousness; rather a plurality of conscious-
> nesses, with equal rights and each with its own world, combine but are
> not merged in the unity of the event. Dostoevsky's heroes are, by the
> very nature of his creative design, not only objects of authorial discourse
> but also subjects of their own directly signifying discourse.[18]

To say that characters have become the subjects of their own discourse
rather than remaining objects of the author's is to assert that their
voice has the same ontological weight as that of their creator's. Instead
of being subordinated to the author's voice, the character's voice
sounds alongside it, as it were, "and combines both with it and with
the full and equally valid voices of other characters."[19] What results is
a true plurality of voices, each with its own perspective on the world,
all with their own claims to integrity.

Bakhtin thought of this as in its way another Copernican revolution,
since it

> transferred the Gogolian author and narrator, with all their accumu-
> lated points of view and with the descriptions, characterizations, and
> definitions of the hero provided by them, into the field of view of the
> hero himself, thus transforming the finalized and integral reality of the
> hero into the material of the hero's own self-consciousness.[20]

But its deeper meaning produced consequences far beyond the world
of art that belonged to a different order than the aesthetic. Its deeper
meaning was essentially moral and reached directly into the worlds of
politics and social theory:

> a living human being cannot be turned into the voiceless object of some
> secondhand, finalizing cognitive process. In a human being there is al-
> ways something that only he himself can reveal, in a free act of self-con-
> sciousness and discourse, something that does not submit to an external-
> izing secondhand definition.[21]

Some might be tempted to think that Bakhtin is here merely defending the benighted ideal of bourgeois liberalism with its special emphasis on the uniqueness of the free and uncoerced self, but he is rather
defining a new "form of life," as Wittgenstein might have put it, in

which voice has become the instrumentality of consciousness, and consciousness, in its interior resistance to finalization, is viewed as the essence of the human. Furthermore, Bakhtin means consciousness not merely in its gravitations toward itself but also in its reciprocal interactions with other consciousnesses, all contributing together to "a genuine polyphony of fully valid voices." These voices are not only the true medium of the human but the appropriate form of the social, and their social and cultural instrumentality goes a long way toward explaining how we acquire experience of the world in the first place and then attempt to lay claim to our portion of it. For Bakhtin that process is vocal and aural long before it is verbal and textual, and its reality as speech, as Wayne Booth has put it, always retains priority over its reality as script:

> We come into consciousness speaking a language already permeated with many voices—a social, not a private language. From the beginning, we are "polyglot," already in process of mastering a variety of social dialects derived from parents, clan, class, religion, country. We grow in consciousness by taking in more voices as "authoritatively persuasive" and then by learning which to accept as "internally persuasive." Finally we achieve, if we are lucky, a kind of individuality, but it is never a private or autonomous individuality in the western sense; except when we maim ourselves arbitrarily to monologue, we always speak a chorus of languages. Anyone who has not been maimed by some imposed "ideology in the narrow sense," anyone who is not an "ideologue," respects the fact that each of us is a "we," not an "I." Polyphony, the miracle of our "dialogical" lives together, is thus both a fact of life and, in its higher reaches, a value to be pursued endlessly.[22]

But polyphony, Bakhtin is convinced, is always threatened by monologism, and monologism ultimately denies otherness. Monologism repudiates the possibility of any other consciousness outside itself capable of responding to it on equal terms. "For a monologic outlook," Bakhtin writes, "the other remains entirely and only an object of consciousness, and cannot constitute another consciousness."[23] This is not to say that monologue repudiates the existence of other selves, only that it fails to give any credence to their reality.

> No response capable of altering everything in the world of my consciousness, is expected of this other. The monologue is accomplished and deaf to the other's response; it does not await it and does not grant it any *decisive* force. Monologue makes do without the other; that is why to some extent it objectivizes all reality. Monologue pretends to be the *last word*.[24]

In this, however, monologism not only thwarts the possibilities of dialogue but also subverts its own pretensions. By refusing to concede
reality to any other consciousness but its own, it cuts itself off from any
possibility of understanding itself.

Here is where Bakhtin's ideas are most daring and most novel. Understanding, he insists, can never be undertaken from the point of view
of the self but only from that of the other. This is not the same thing as
saying that we can only understand ourselves by understanding what
we are not. It is instead a way of asserting that we cannot know
ourselves, or anything else, except from a perspective outside, independent. In truth, we do this all the time:

> we appraise ourselves from the point of view of others, we attempt to
> understand the transgredient moments of our very consciousness and to
> take them into account through the other . . . ; in a word, constantly
> and intensely, we oversee and apprehend the reflections of our life in the
> plane of consciousness of other men.[25]

But this exercise is not adventitious. Bakhtin's word *transgredient* is
intended to suggest that there are elements of consciousness external to
it that, as Tzvetan Todorov notes, "are absolutely necessary for its
completion, for its achievement of totalization."[26] Not only do we require someone else's gaze to give us the feeling that we form a totality;
our own sense of what constitutes a whole person can only come from
our perception of someone else and not from our conception of ourselves. Beyond this, as Bakhtin observed in connection with his Dostoevsky project, "I achieve self-consciousness, I become myself only by
revealing myself to another, through another and with another's help."[27]
In these respects, otherness no longer refers to something we see outside ourselves and either acknowledge or overlook at will, but something outside by which we will to see, among other things, ourselves.

Todorov coins the term *exotopy* to designate this sense one acquires
only through the consciousness of "finding oneself outside," and explains that it achieves its full meaning when Bakhtin employs it, in
relation to Dostoevsky, to refer not to "a transgredient exteriority"
that encompasses the other but to "an elsewhere beyond integration or
reduction. 'No fusion with the other but the preservation of his exotopic position and of his excess of vision and comprehension, that is its
correlative.' "[28] Understanding is here conceived neither as empathy
nor as sympathy but as the transformation of the other into a "self-
other" and of the self into an "other-self." The result of this exotopic

transformation is that each—both self and other—retains its sense of privilege:

> If there are two of us, what matters from the point of view of the actual productivity of the event is not that alongside of me there is *yet one more* man, essentially *similar* to me (*two men*) but that he is, for me, an *other* man. In this way, his simple sympathy for my life is not tantamount to our fusing into a single being and it does not constitute a numerical duplication of any life, but an essential enrichment of the event. Because the other co-experiences my life in a new form, as the life of an other man, perceived and valorized otherwise, and justified in a way other than this life. The productivity of the event does not lie in the fusion of all into one, but in the tension of my exotopy and my nonfusion, in the reliance upon the privilege afforded me by my unique position, outside other men.[29]

Yet Bakhtin could never be wholly satisfied with any model of understanding that was exclusively personal. Most understanding, he insisted, occurs, or is baffled, at the more general level of collective experience, where exotopic relations involve those larger ways of experiencing that we call cultures, and sympathy, or, as it is typically described in cultural anthropology, "seeing from the native's point of view," takes on an even more incidental role in understanding and alterity an even larger and more crucial one.

> There is an enduring image, that is partial, and therefore false, according to which to better understand a foreign culture one should live in it, and, forgetting one's own, look at the world through the eyes of this culture. As I have said, such an image is partial. To be sure, to enter in some measure into an alien culture and look at the world through its eyes, is a necessary moment in the process of its understanding; but if understanding were exhausted in this moment, it would have been no more than a single duplication, and would have brought nothing new or enriching. Creative understanding does not renounce its self, its place in time, its culture; it does not forget anything. The chief matter of understanding is the exotopy of the one who does the understanding—in time, space, and culture—in relation to that which he wants to understand creatively. Even his own external aspect is not really accessible to man, and he cannot interpret it as a whole; mirrors and photographs prove of no help; a man's real external aspect can be seen and understood only by other persons, thanks to their spatial exotopy, and thanks to the fact that they are other.
>
> In the realm of culture, exotopy is the most powerful lever of understanding. It is only to the eyes of an other culture that the alien culture

reveals itself more completely and more deeply (but never exhaustively, because there will come other cultures, that will see and understand even more).[30]

Todorov correctly notes that Bakhtin is here conceiving of interpretation as ethnology, but an ethnology that involves a good deal more than what is generally labeled "thick description." As Todorov points out, Bakhtin is calling for something more like a "dialogics of culture" that wholly abandons pretensions to neutrality or objectivity in favor of creatively attempting to exploit the irremediable facts of cultural privilege to comprehend cultural difference. Thus Bakhtin would seek to fulfill the hermeneutic ideal to establish a kinship not of "one life with another" but "of thought with what the life aims at" by exactly reversing the traditional hermeneutic maneuver: by showing us how to use our own historical and cultural exotopy to understand that of another. The hermeneutical ideal, however, can never be fulfilled; understanding always remains incomplete, partial, unstable:

> There is no first or last discourse, and dialogical context knows no limits (it disappears into an unlimited past and in our unlimited future). Even past meanings, that is those that have arisen in the dialogue of past centuries, can never be stable (completed once and for all, finished), they will always change (renewing themselves) in the course of the dialogue's subsequent development, and yet to come. At every moment of the dialogue, there are immense and unlimited masses of forgotten meanings, but, in some subsequent moments, as the dialogue moves forward, they will return to memory and live in renewed form (in a new context). Nothing is absolutely dead: every meaning will celebrate its rebirth.[31]

7

The critical, not to say cultural, implications of Bakhtin's work are extraordinarily far-reaching. In addition to challenging prevailing notions of everything from interpretation and intertextuality to epistemology and metaphysics, they suggest a distinctly different conception of the nature and purpose of all humanistic learning. This becomes abundantly clear when one brings Bakhtin's ideas into conversation with some of the other contemporary theoretical options for organizing the study of the humanities.

For example, Bakhtin shares with historical scholars otherwise as different as Erich Auerbach and M. H. Abrams a commitment to the study of literature as a form of the study of man in his historical changes and a belief that the study of man in his historicity is a study of his changing views of reality. But where Auerbach and Abrams assume that the particular office of literature and the other arts is formally to explore and render actual the experience of these changes in the constitution of reality, and to do so through aesthetic devices and stratagems that are essentially mimetic or representational, Bakthin insists that the fundamental humanistic issue in history is not the experience of reality in its changing forms but the formal changes in the reality of experience, changes that literature has been able to mediate only when it has broken free of mimetic or representational constraints. Though this means that all three take seriously the formal conventions through which art conveys its meanings, Auerbach and Abrams associate the conventional in art with stylistic techniques and narrative structures that render, or try to render, ways of conceptualizing something like a way of seeing or a frame of mind, while Bakhtin associates the conventional instead with generic forms that try to communicate something more nearly like a sense of life.

A still larger difference between them is revealed in the methods they employ as literary and cultural historians. Auerbach and Abrams seek to penetrate the felt world of their subjects and comprehend it, so to speak, from the inside, as that interior space is defined by the historicocritical perspective their subjects lack but they (Auerbach and Abrams) can furnish; Bakhtin, by contrast, wants to use his historical perspective to cultivate a peculiar kind of dialectical exteriority to his subjects so that, instead of entering into them, he can, as it were, hold a conversation with them, or at any rate overhear the conversation they carry on among themselves. In other words, Bakhtin wants to deprivilege his critical medium for the sake of reprivileging his subjects. Auerbach and Abrams risk depriviliging their subjects for the sake of almost overprivileging their critical perspective.

But what is merely a risk or a temptation in the work historical critics and scholars like Auerbach and Abrams becomes a general tenet in the writings of a myth and archtype critic like Northrop Frye. This is not, of course, to imply that Frye and other critics like him lack a historical sense or flout the importance of conventions. Indeed, one of the most obvious interests that Frye shares with Bakhtin and all other historically minded critics is a preoccupation with explaining how modern literary forms derive from ancient practices. But where Frye, for example, prefers forms like epic, tragedy, and the lyric, which possess a kind of theoretical or generic coherence, Bakhtin is drawn to forms like the fabliaux, farce, melodrama, satire, and dialogue, which are irregular, deviant, and conceptually untidy. So, too, with the contrast between Frye's preoccupation with legend and myth and Bakhtin's own preference for folktale, street song, anecdote, invective, and discursive prose generally. Bakhtin dismisses the former as solipsistic and prefers the latter because it is more responsive to the disorderly world outside and more readily disposed to treat language as a mask, a game, an illusion.

But this discrepancy is fully consistent with the way Frye and Bakhtin divide over the whole question of open and closed systems. Frye values literature precisely because he thinks it constitutes a formal system with a coherence and integrity all its own. Bakhtin values it precisely because he believes its forms open out onto the marvelously diverse and irreverent panorama of experience beyond. To Bakhtin, the whole of Frye's enterprise to organize the study of literature around categories supposedly intrinsic to the constitution of literature would seem not only self-defeating but monophonic. Indeed, from a Bakhtinian perspective, what Frye, or at least the scientistic side of Frye, seems to want is both to take over the languages of criticism by subsuming them in his own discourse and to keep the voice of texts, and their authors and characters, wholly out of it.

Many, but by no means all, of these same strictures would color Bakhtin's response to a thoroughgoing structuralism. Often classified as a structuralist of sorts himself—he is usually grouped with the Russian formalists—Bakhtin views structure very differently than its recent votaries do. Instead of dehistoricizing structure, Bakhtin rehistoricizes it and then proceeds to contextualize it socially and politically in a manner that pure structuralists never dream of doing. To borrow a formulation of Ralph Waldo Emerson's, Bakhtin wants to interpret the form or structure for the life within it and not the life for the form or structure of it. In this sense, Bakhtin would find much contemporary structuralism both reductionistic and reactionary. In fact, Bakhtin would look upon every attempt to organize and unify all verbal or semiotic experience in terms of some system of oppositions as not only futile, and, in that sense, self-deceived, but also as potentially destructive, even perverse. Thus Bakhtin repudiates the whole idea that, according to Robert Scholes, lies behind structuralism: that the fundamental problem of life is incoherence and that the fundamental solution to this problem is the metaphysical discovery of a true and absolute order.[32] Bakhtin would, I think, be disposed to reply with someone like Erich Heller that the only true order of life may be incoherence itself, or at least the realization that there is no such thing as true order to begin with; then he would go on to observe, again with Heller, that the hope of solving something called "the problem of life" is probably beside the point. If life, in fact, has any point at all, that point cannot be reduced to a "problem" awaiting "solution"; the point of it all lies in what Heller and Bakhtin would describe as another dimension.[33]

Among all the other theoretical candidates for organizing humanistic study, none has worked harder to determine precisely where that dimension lies and in what it consists than the method known as phenomenology. For the phenomenologist, the point of it all, or, rather, the point of experience, is inextricably related to the question of consciousness, and consciousness reaches its fullest expression in the works of poets and other imaginative artists. But for the later Heidegger, or even Poulet, consciousness is valuable not for what it represents in and of itself—the realization of a singular and valid, if still infinitely various, point of view—but for what it reveals beyond itself, for what it discloses of transcendence. Consciousness is the medium through which Being is revealed, and in the work of many phenomenologists, consciousness increases in value in direct proportion to the degree of its transparency to its own absolute ground.

Bakhtin would have problems with this way of construing consciousness because of his conviction that there is equal phenomenological evidence that consciousness may constitute its own ground. But this is not where Bakhtin would most likely take up his argument with the phenomenologists. The real phenomenological issue, he would maintain, is not where consciousness is grounded but how it is perceived or known in experience. Consciousness is known in experience, perceived experientially, only from outside itself, but only in the sense that there is within consciousness a capacity to be external to it. Thus while Bakhtin would agree that consciousness is a fundamental datum of literary experience and the crucial factor in artistic creation, he would dispute the way phenomenologists typically privilege, hypostatize, almost reify consciousness, arguing that the effect of this strategy is the very opposite of its intention: it merely succeeds in reducing consciousness to the status of an object by ideologically insisting that its status as subject depends upon its transparency to a mode of Being that is sovereign to it. Beyond this Bakhtin would, I think, be inclined to question any claims that consciousness represents either the aggregate of something or the essence of something. In its manifestations, he would be likely to point out, consciousness is perhaps best compared to something like a culture whose identity can be inferred neither from a single act, nor from an articulated pattern of actions, but only from an integrated way of living. And on this basis he would further question whether a writer's consciousness expresses itself with the kind of consistency we associate with the notion of a coherent personality, as is usually supposed in phenomenological criticism, or again whether, as in much phenomenological criticism, consciousness can be comprehended in isolation from the historicity of its particular realizations in society.

This is obviously not a problem for hermeneutic theory, which supposes with Bakhtin that cultural experience is analogous to the process of responding to a text and that this process entails not only an interaction between text and reader but also a transaction between this text and other texts, between this discourse and other discourses. Bakhtin also shares with hermeneutic theory in general the belief that this culturally mediated process of interaction and transaction between reader and text, and, through this text, between reader and other texts, requires for its completion a determination of how the reader has been changed in the interpretive process, of how he or she has been "read" by the text. Therefore "reading," interpretation, involves a dialectical process of distantiation and appropriation. But where someone like Ricoeur identifies this process with the semantic autonomy of the text itself, an autonomy that estranges the text from its author and can only be dialectically overcome when the reader makes this semantic otherness his own, Bakhtin maintains that the otherness of the text, semantic or otherwise, is not so much overcome in "reading" as made comprehensible by being made, as it were, conversable. Understanding can only occur, Bakhtin would say against Ricoeur and most other hermeneutic theorists, if the text remains in the most literal sense alien and other. Ricoeur and hermeneutic theory in general often sound as if they want to absorb alterity, to interiorize it; Bakhtin, on the other hand, is convinced that the aim of interpretation is to try to fathom it by extending and deepening the dialogue both about and with the distance, the unfamiliarity, the strangeness it implies.

Bakhtin and Ricoeur would thus agree that interpretation deals with matters that are at once ineffable and, at the same time, discussable; they differ over the terms in which that discussion can be conducted and the ends to which it ideally leads. For both Ricoeur and Bakhtin, texts are viewed ideally as devices that open up directions for thinking, possibilities for reflection, that transcend their own ostensive references. But Ricoeur typically describes this as the difference between what the text says and what it talks about, and he claims that the movement from one to the other is precisely the transition enabled by hermeneutics. This transition is accomplished for Ricoeur by means of what he calls an act of appropriation, whereby we demonstrate that we understand the author better than he understands himself because of our ability to "display the power of disclosure implied in his discourse beyond the limited horizon of his own existential situation."[34] Bakhtin would reply that the power to see beyond the author's limited existential horizon may well be available to us as readers, but only because it has already been projected by the author into characters or forms of consciousness that, in polyphonic art at least, are thus endowed with a humanly valid way of looking at things that is all their own. Bakhtin would add that the availability of this power is determined not, as it is for Ricoeur, by our ability to formulate in cognitive terms the extensions it gives to our previous understanding, but rather by our ability to enter into a relationship with it through the dialogic possibilities that all true pluralities of voice, whether within texts or outside them, hold out to us.

This is precisely the dimension of our textual experience that is viewed with greatest suspicion by the whole school of thinking associated with Jacques Derrida and deconstruction in general. The differences between deconstructionism and Bakhtinism are in many respects irreconcilable and proceed from what each takes to be primary. For Bakhtin what is primary is the living word, spoken and heard, and not the inscribed word to be deciphered or the abstract ciphers of which it is composed and the empty spaces between them. The word as uttered, as speech, has primacy over writing for Bakhtin, because discourse, voice, can often convey meanings, significances, senses of life, that are not, strictly speaking, dependent upon or restricted by the language in which they are expressed.

> Discourse lives, as it were, beyond itself, in a living impulse toward the object; if we detach ourselves completely from this impulse all we have left is the naked corpse of the word, from which we can learn nothing at all about the social situation or the fate of a given word in life. To study the word as such, ignoring the impulse that reaches out beyond it, is just as senseless as to study psychological experience outside the context of that real life toward which it was directed and by which it is determined.[35]

Thus to lay the problems with discourse at the door of language, or rather linguisticality, as Derrida does, rather than laying the problems of language at the door of discourse, is to commit what Alfred North Whitehead called "the fallacy of misplaced concreteness." Language becomes the prisonhouse of thought and the distorting mirror of experience only when it is employed in a discourse that is monologic, totalitarian, closed. But monologism is no more inevitable or irremediable than logocentricity is. Both deny the operative potential of that ontological surd which for Derrida grounds both discourse and script, namely, the concept of difference. But difference, or *differance,* and the otherness it implies and to which it leads, is not only the precipitant of alienation but also the prerequisite for understanding, and when polyphonically exploited, Bakhtin believes, it can just as easily become the basis of a new humanism as of a new nihilism.

Both convictions may be, and probably are, a form of prejudice, but Bakhtin was clear as to why he preferred his own to any other. His preference had everything to do with the kind of world he hoped it would produce, a world whose future would be determined by how completely our various cultural discourses are willing to put their own authority at risk for the sake of continuing the dialogue among them and enlarging its scope. Bakhtin possessed a further prejudice that this dialogue is often advanced by parodistic and comically subversive forms, but he differentiated sharply between those forms that deflate ideological pretensions by drawing upon the carnivalesque vulgate of experience and those that seek a similar end by moving in the direction of cynical self-cancelations. Where the first tries to burst the constraints of socially approved or politically sanctioned speech by letting in everything it customarily excludes—everything crude, gross, excessive, and irregular—the latter, he would have said, tends to collapse into solipsism by merging its subject with its object.

Discourse should be bounded, Bakhtin assumed, with a sense of the unexpressed, the unnameable, even the absent, because these constitute at least a portion of our experience of presence; the undecided, the unexpected, the unknown are all a part of our experience of voice, of polyglot discourse. And not only do they comprise a substantial measure of our experience when it is genuinely polyphonous, they can be known. But they are not known or knowable only at that point where all our verbal formulations break down and we peer over the edge of their failure into the abyss beneath; they are also capable of cognitive apprehension in the very processes by which we are taken hold of by language, voice, texts themselves, and enter into the unpredictable and indeterminate life they dialogically open up for us.

8

How, then, is one to construe Bakhtinism? Culturally, it means that the most appropriate model for human experience is discourse or conversation, but the aim of this conversation or discourse is anything but unanimity or truth; its aim is rather the enlargement of consciousness through dialogic engagement with alterity. To put this differently, because heteroglossia and not monoglossia is the normal condition of speech, text is always subordinate to context, and every meaning is related to a larger putative whole in which each has the potential of conditioning, as well as being conditioned by, others.

Socially, Bakhtinism amounts to something like a true democracy of individuals in which our shared life with others is the premise and possibility of our private lives with ourselves. And the quality of our private life with ourselves, like our shared life with others, depends at least in part on the range of otherness with which we are willing to interact. This is not primarily a question of developing greater tolerance and appreciation for whatever deviates from and violates the social or personal norm; it is rather a question of how much one is willing to take into one's purview as representative not only of the genuinely but also of the exigently human.

Politically, Bakhtinism asserts that any form of authority that frustrates dialogue within and among human communities must be resisted with all the cunning of what Santayana meant by "animal faith," and that the chief office of politics is to ensure that every party to all the conversations that constitute culture gets to contribute and to enjoy its fair share. The negative side of this is that ideology is monologic, and monologism, which represents the attempt to suppress discourse, and thus human interaction, is found wherever the natural plurality of utterance is compelled to efface itself in the interests of a unitary language.

Religiously and metaphysically, Bakhtinism assumes that the ideal goal of human experience is not to name, explain, or verify the existence of the sacred, the "singularly other," but to have a relationship with it. And our relationship with all that is singularly and absolutely other, Bakhtinism further contends, is dependent upon our ability to experience everything that seemingly is not. Thus the paradox of human existence, which from another perspective could as easily be construed as its miracle, is that the two presuppose each other; self and other are, to use Bakhtin's word, "transgredient." Otherness is not alien to consciousness but instrumental to its experience. Consciousness is not inimical to otherness but dialectically related to it and essential to its understanding. Experience thus needs no transempirical justification, as William James said; immanence is all. But if we no longer need to transcend the experience, Bakhtinism shows us how we can transcend the false oppositions between subject and object, self and other, presence and absence. It ultimately boils down to a question of the polyphony of our interpretations, our discourses, our critical practices. The function of the humanities, as interpretation, as discourse, as social practice, is to deepen understanding of the relationship between consciousness and alterity by creating critical forms in which their dialogical possibilities, both within cultures and across cultures, can be more fully enhanced.

7

American Studies
as Cultural Criticism

For Leo Marx

One way of gauging the health of any field is to determine the kinds of questions it begs. Judged by this rough standard, the field of American Studies—it would scarcely do to use the word *discipline* for something as variegated and disparate as the interdisciplinary study of what Henry Nash Smith once called "American civilization past and present, and as a whole"[1]—is in considerable trouble. Though there is no dearth of intellectual activity in the field and though this activity is encouraging expansion in the field in a variety of promising new directions, from racial, ethnic, regional, and gender studies to oral history, the examination of material culture, folklife as well as folklore, cliometrics, semiotics, the history of photography and film, and so forth, one finds abundant evidence as well of a decided indisposition to ask any longer certain questions having to do with what could simply be described as "the point of it all." In many cases, of course, it is perfectly possible to contribute in significant ways to the practice of a field or a discipline without being aware of a whole range of questions that bear upon its nature and function, but the particular field itself can only advance if one is able to measure the implications of particular contributions to its practice for an understanding of field's larger meaning and purpose.

Yet in American Studies such concerns have often been greeted with a certain measure of diffidence. The metacritical attempt to unearth the assumptions that support this kind of interdisciplinary study, in the hopes of determining why, as Hayden White once put it, "this type of inquiry has been designed to solve the problems it characteristically tries to solve,"[2] is frequently regarded either as intellectually precious or as methodologically self-defeating. This is not to suggest that proponents of such investigations necessarily assume that they will yield any consensus about the conception of the field itself, only that any field that fails to promote such investigations, they believe, will never discover those issues that are truly at stake in its practice.

It should be apparent, I hope, that I am not decrying the lack of theory in American Studies, though theory of a specific sort is certainly needed; nor am I issuing yet another call for increased methodological self-consciousness, though a more sophisticated grasp of the entanglements and entailments of method certainly wouldn't hurt. Rather, I am proposing that a field, no less than a discipline, defines itself—as, say, a subject area alone does not—chiefly in relation to the questions it asks, the problems it poses, the arguments it encourages; while none of these matters can be contemplated in isolation from actual research, the research that is actually produced within any field ultimately matters, in the sense of being susceptible to definition and assessment, only in relation to such things—only by virtue of the way it refines the questions, clarifies the problems, and deepens the argument.

1

The field of American Studies has not possessed this clear a sense of itself at least since the 1950s and early 1960s. This was the period of ascendancy of the so-called myth and symbol school, a fairly misleading, even possibly pejorative, designation for a group of studies beginning presumably with Henry Nash Smith's *Virgin Land* in 1950 and terminating, perhaps, with Alan Trachtenberg's *Brooklyn Bridge* in 1965. Before that time, the field itself was merely suggested in outline by a series of bold interpretive syntheses that still remained recognizable as one or another kind of conventional history, from V. L. Parrington's *Main Currents of American Thought* and Constance Rourke's *American Humor* to F. O. Matthiessen's *American Renaissance*, W. J. Cash's *The Mind of the South*, and Alfred Kazin's *On Native Grounds*.

After that period, the outline of the field quickly blurred and fragmented with the rapid development of competitive offshoots like Black Studies, Popular Culture Studies, Southern Studies, Asian-American Studies, Chicano studies, and so on, each claiming a significant measure of conceptual autonomy and all seeking some degree of methodological differentiation.

The results of this new diaspora have been mixed, but surely one of its effects has been to cast increasing suspicion on the work of the myth and symbol school. The charges brought against such representative titles as *Virgin Land* and *Brooklyn Bridge,* or R. W. B. Lewis's *The American Adam,* John William Ward's *Andrew Jackson,* and Leo Marx's *The Machine in the Garden,* have been varied and numerous: either they focus too exclusively on the acts and expressions of influential minorities and elites; or they employ too restricted and potentially dehistoricized a notion of image and myth; or they place excessive emphasis on the distinctiveness of American problems and solutions; or they treat ideas as though they possessed an existence independent of the people who think them; or they foster the impression that people in the past somehow meant their work to address problems in the present. In short, they have been held accountable variously for the sins of elitism, modernism, exceptionalism, Cartesianism, and presentism.

Yet virtually all of these critiques miss any appreciation of what lent these books, and others like them, their intellectual focus and cultural urgency, what it was that enabled them—for the first time but I trust not the last—to provide the fledgling field of American Studies with a shared and sharable sense of identity. The question that has not been asked by their critics, or in any event has rarely been addressed with sufficient rigor, has to do with the larger purposes served in these studies by their specific tactics of symbolic interpretation. And until such a question is confronted, the field of American Studies will not only remain confused about what these books actually accomplished but also fail to exploit the intellectual resources they still hold out to the field even in the present period of its new federalism. More specifically, it will be difficult to confront the kinds of challenges to which the field of American Studies will inevitably be submitted in an era when the myth of American exceptionalism, and the facts supporting it, has now been discredited and the field itself is currently under new pressure to situate its own investigations and findings in a more explicitly cross-cultural context.

As to this latter exigency, the salience of cross-cultural comparison in American Studies has always been obvious but is now essential for at least several reasons. The first is surely geopolitical and economic. The United States exists as an institutional and political formation in a network of relationships that bind it materially, if not physically, to virtually all the nations of the world. To take but one example of modern restructuring, the multinational corporation has so fundamentally revised the meaning of national boundaries, not to say social differences, that it has become essentially pointless to talk any longer about cultural purity or, in the contemporary disciplinary idiom, cultural uniqueness. The second reason that cross-cultural comparison thrusts itself upon the intellectual field of American Studies with new urgency is historical. The United States did not emerge as a social and cultural formation full blown out of the head of Zeus; rather, it developed from the transplantation of various European peoples and traditions, which were sometimes decisively supplemented with Amerindian, African, and Asian strains to create a mosaic of patterns that now define the collective figure we call "American." But this only underscores the fact that the figure in that carpet of commingled peoples and traditions which we now describe as "American" can only be perceived for what it is by understanding the disparate threads that in their comparative relations make it up. The third reason American Studies must become more comparative is cultural. If it is now mandatory to understand the United States geopolitically as a presence within many national traditions and historically as an extension beyond many national traditions, it is also necessary to understand the United States culturally as the expression of many national traditions, or at least as the expression of many variant and highly variable traditions that still coexist within a single but ever elusive and always changing system of possibilities. To put this more simply, we are now in a position to see that whatever we mean by the United States as a cultural formation, we mean nothing less than a configuration of comparable but often competing regional or sectional or otherwise minority traditions that were, and are, always seeking primacy over one another, or at least are seeking not to be displaced by one another.

The difficulty with placing the field of American Studies in these cross-cultural contexts is that for complex sociopolitical and spiritual reasons there were powerful forces at work in the development of the field during the late 1930s and 1940s that discouraged such recognitions. Those reasons derived from the new influence the United States had suddenly begun to enjoy throughout the world, particularly following World War II, and the consequent tendency among many academics and other individuals interested in the United States to look for an explanation of this new state of affairs to whatever could be defined within its own traditions and values that made the United States distinctive and somehow special. There thus arose during the postwar years, when the intellectual field known as American Studies was assuming its first visible shape, a powerful temptation to organize the study of the United States in terms of what set it apart from other countries and peoples and cultures, and in relation to those emerging patterns of consensus that, at the level of feeling and assumption as well as of belief and practice, might thus account for its new and somewhat unanticipated—though many would not think wholly undeserved—preeminence in the comity of nations.

It is scarcely necessary to add that the effects of yielding to this temptation were almost uniformly unfortunate. Not only did it give further support to the mischievous if venerable conviction that the United States is somehow elected to fulfill a special mission in history, but the myth of American uniqueness fostered by this conviction also produced a scholarship often guilty not only of blurring the real differences and variations in our past but also of glossing over its serious disparities, disjunctions, and dichotomies. Yet it must be acknowledged, and frankly, that the American Studies movement not only suffered from the effects of these tendencies but in many instances actively encouraged them. It was all too easy to turn the interdisciplinary study of what was distinctive about, or at least particular to, the civilization of the United States into a subtle interpretation of, even apology for, America's new political and economic dominion in the international sphere. And wherever concern for American uniqueness or exceptionalism was seen to wax, critical comprehension of its own inner divisions as well as its cultural complexity and contextual relations seemed to wane.

Still, it would be misleading to imply that the field of American Studies developed out of culturally apologetic motives or that it proposed for itself the definition of a kind of political theology that was intended to give warrant to contemporary public policies. However captive some scholarship in American Studies has been to official cultural nostrums, and however susceptible some of the rest of American Studies scholarship has been to intellectual and international insularity, the underlying and persistent development of the field, albeit slow, has all been in the other direction. As the interdisciplinary study of the United States developed in the period from just before World War II to the present, it moved toward an ever clearer conviction of its own critical function in relation to national pieties and was aided in this process by a realization of the necessity of resituating the study of American institutions and behavior in a more cross-grained cultural environment.

2

This becomes apparent if we break down the process of development into three phases. The first phase can be dated from the late 1920s and early 1930s when for the first time in the systematic study of American materials a disciplined attempt was made to integrate the study of literature with the study of history. The great challenge during this first phase of the American Studies movement was to bring them together without turning literature into a reflection of history or reducing history to a chronicle of mere taste. But this is precisely how literature and history were both typically regarded at the beginning of this period, where literature was assumed to represent the world of moral and aesthetic value, history the realm of social and institutional fact.

To be somewhat more specific, general historians of the United States, from Charles Beard and Arthur Schlesinger, Sr., to V. L. Parrington and Samuel Eliot Morison, often invoked imaginative material but chiefly for purposes of illustration, to suggest themes, ideas, events from beyond the world of literature. Far from being literary or aesthetic, their organizing categories were essentially social, political, or economic, their assumption being that literature could be subsumed within such categories by being reconceived as a mirror image of the realities they named. Thus Walt Whitman was viewed as a representative of American egalitarianism, Mark Twain taken to epitomize frontier humor and vernacular coarseness, Theodore Dreiser and Upton Sinclair to exemplify urban realism, Henry James to typify genteel refinement and abstraction, and Willa Cather and Sarah Orne Jewett to suggest, respectively, regional piety and local color. According to such formulations, literature was perceived primarily as a form of reflexive behavior that was valuable not for what it constituted in and of itself but rather for what it reflected outside of and independent of itself.

At the other extreme one found literary historians and cultural critics who for the most part possessed only the most rudimentary notion of society. Except in some of the early work of Van Wyck Brooks, or Randolph Bourne's essays on literary radicalism, together with some of the writing of T. K. Whipple, Stuart Sherman, and Lewis Mumford, society was nominally conceived as comprising the subject of certain kinds of literature and generally accepted as constituting the background of all literature. But society in this sense made itself felt in literature only as a kind of content to be expressed, never as a component to be reckoned with, never, except in the formulas of American Marxists like V. F. Calverton and Granville Hicks, as one of the shaping forces in the production of the work itself. And since the efforts to bridge the gap between literature and history, art and society, were, in works like *The Liberation of American Literature* and *The Great Tradition,* clumsy at best, it would be almost another decade before any American critics not directly associated with the emergent American Studies movement would achieve, in such texts as Edmund Wilson's *To the Finland Station* and Alfred Kazin's *On Native Grounds,* real success in integrating the figurative with the social or the imaginative with the historical.

The first institutional attempt to span these two poles—the historical, which viewed literature principally as a reflex of society, and the literary, which viewed society and history as merely one of the thematic ingredients in literature—occurred at Harvard University in the early 1930s and was chiefly the inspiration of two men: the literary historian and cultural critic F. O. Matthiessen and the intellectual and cultural historian Perry Miller. Miller, clearly the more theoretically self-conscious of the two, was eventually to write, in his famous studies of Puritan mentality entitled *The New England Mind,* two of the seminal works of American scholarship in the modern era; but it was no doubt Matthiessen, in his masterwork of 1941 entitled *American Renaissance,* who produced the most interesting result of their collaboration and the most representative example of this first phase of research in American Studies.

The problem with ascribing equally representative status to Miller's work, if problem it deserves to be called, derives from the particular construction he placed on the idea of the mind and the peculiar role he assumed mind to play in human, or at least in American, history. Or, rather, the problem is that Miller was apparently of two minds himself about the function of intellect in historical experience. He assumed not only that history is part of the life of the mind but also that the mind is the most important factor in the making of history. Both of these assumptions followed from what Miller took to be the major shortcomings of previous Puritan scholarship, in which historical movements so often seemed to be driven by everything but ideas and the historian strove to emulate the purported disinterestedness and objectivity of the natural scientist. To this Miller countered at length, and with enormous erudition, that the real matter of history has less to do with what is supposed to have happened in the past than with what people said and thought about it, and that the task of figuring this out often requires an ability to distinguish between a peoples' professed or proclaimed understanding of the facts and their actual experiential comprehension of them. In short, history was not only the product or result of mind, on Miller's account, but also one of the mind's greatest achievements, and this rendered history in effect an art, an expression of that process of divination whereby the historian is able to differentiate, like any artist, between appearance and reality.

The difficulty with this way of formulating Miller's central working principle—as became evident not only in the quite different conceptions of the two volumes of *The New England Mind,* where the first is organized synchronically, the second diachronically, but also in much of his other writing both occasional and more deliberate—is that it implied two different ways of writing history. According to the first conception, where the mind is regarded as the central factor in the making of history, the historian was obliged to undertake a scrupulous examination of all that was thought and felt in any given period, or by any given individual, and from that great mass of assembled data attempt to discern which patterns of recurrence or deviation seemed most decisive or characteristic, assuming all the while that such patterns bear some correspondent relation to events, much like responses to situations. This was mind looking for all the world like a mere reflection of society but behaving more like a motive force in its own right, or at least like a contributing and often crucial element in any historical equation. According to the second conception, where mind is that faculty in and with which history itself is constructed, the intellect operates on a level far below the plane of conscious thought and exhibits "continuities of experience," as Miller said in one of his more memorable expressions, that underlie and often outlive the succession of ideas in which they are articulated. Mind expressing itself on this level could only be grasped by a kind of intuitive intellectual archeology and could only be fully appreciated with the help of imaginative reconstruction, and so Miller concluded that the history of ideas requires not only "a fluency in the concepts themselves but an ability to get underneath them."[3]

In the one case, then, history was conceived as the record of mind attempting to respond to events and alter, or at least mitigate, their effects. In the other, it was conceived as the creation of mind as it penetrates beneath the thicket of ideas to discern the presence and effect of intellectual patterns of which its representatives are usually ignorant. Either way, Miller's methods, however magisterial their results, were difficult to follow and even more difficult to reconcile. In his studies of the Calvinist legacy in American thinking, Miller was able to bring history and ideas, art and society, into stunning new confrontations with one another, but often in ways that left numerous readers wondering where the one began and the other left off.

Matthiessen's *American Renaissance* presented no such problems. Ostensibly a literary study of the five preeminent writers of the mid–nineteenth century—Emerson, Thoreau, Whitman, Hawthorne, and Melville—*American Renaissance* sought on a deeper level to become a peculiar kind of cultural history, one committed to releasing some of what Matthiessen believed to be the still unspent potential locked in the narratives and metaphors of our first great literary age. At this distance it is a little difficult to recall that in 1941 Matthiessen's five writers were not regarded as the foremost representatives of their era. That title went instead to the Fireside group composed of James Russell Lowell, Oliver Wendell Holmes, Henry Wadsworth Longfellow, and John Greenleaf Whittier. Matthiessen was therefore arguing a case for what was then regarded as an adversary tradition, and he argued it on what, from the perspective of scholarly taste at the time, had to be considered adversary grounds. Emerson, Whitman, and the others deserved to displace the Brahmin poets as more signal instances of nineteenth-century experience in the United States because they had been able to explore and express some of the fundamental problems and latent, radical possibilities of American democracy. As Matthiessen put it in his preface, they had all "felt that it was incumbent upon their generation to give fulfillment to the potentialities freed by the American Revolution, to provide a culture commensurate with America's political opportunity." Only they did so, Matthiessen contended, less by making democracy their subject than by expressing its aspirations and contradictions within the tensions and resistance of their forms, even by developing a new form, the organic form, which constituted, in Thoreau's *Walden* no less than in Melville's *White-Jacket* or *Moby-Dick,* a realization of those democratic aspirations and contradictions. "Their tones," Matthiessen could therefore concede,

> were sometimes optimistic, sometimes blatantly, even dangerously expansive, sometimes disillusioned, even despairing, but what emerges from the total pattern of their achievement—if we will make the effort to repossess it—is literature for our democracy. In reading the lyric, heroic, and tragic expression of our first great age, we can feel the challenge of our still undiminished resources.[4]

Matthiessen could say this because he believed that in the work of these five writers American democracy had finally become critical of itself, had finally been comprehended in terms of its flaws as well as its virtues. Their writing therefore constituted a literature "for our democracy," as Matthiessen phrased it, not because it idealized democratic hopes and achievements but because it exposed so searchingly some of their major weaknesses and omissions.[5] Instead of providing American democracy with a more systematically philosophic or culturally urbane justification than any other comparable works, their writing, at its best, revealed the striking and often appalling discrepancies between American professions of democracy and the American practice of democracy.

This was a significant and not untimely subject for Matthiessen to take on. In one stroke he seemed to have reorganized the settled canon of nineteenth-century American classics and reconceptualized the grounds for making such assessments. In place of the older view that literature reflects the society that serves as its background, Matthiessen demonstrated, in a manner of which Herder would have approved, how literature could become again, as it once was, a social force in its own right by fusing in its forms as well as its fables energies that were both cultural and fictive, political and mythopoeic, metaphysical and vernacular.

But in addition to rearranging the topography of nineteenth-century American literature, *American Renaissance* spoke to a deeply felt political and moral need. It appeared at a n.oment when the culture of the West was experiencing a severe political threat from the rise of fascism, and the traditions of liberal thought and politics that should have provided a bulwark of ideological defense had proved not only vulnerable but impotent. The issue was not so much what to do in response to the spread of fascism—that question was resolved once and for all at Pearl Harbor—as how to repossess and renew the intellectual traditions that had been overwhelmed and discredited in the process. Matthiessen's book seemed to acknowledge the moral and spiritual complexity of this crisis and at the same time to formulate, if only indirectly, a meaningful response to it. On the one hand, *American Renaissance* traced the currents of democratic thinking back to the art and thought of the nineteenth century, where they received their first cultural expression in America, and thereby demonstrated that while democratic humanism, like constitutional democracy, was anything but a native growth, it had nonetheless achieved a quality and kind of expression in the New World that were singular and decisive.

On the other hand, *American Renaissance* explored countercurrents within that tradition where democratic humanism had been confronted with the more tragic facts of experience and had emerged from that encounter with a realism and sobriety wholly absent from official expressions either of democracy itself or of the whole liberal outlook.

The result of this double focus in *American Renaissance* was, by implication at least, a redefinition of democratic humanism and a revaluation of the potential of American democracy. What Matthiessen's book attempted to demonstrate is that American democracy is not concerned primarily with the more "smiling aspects of ife," as William Dean Howells's famous apothegm put it, and that democratic humanism carried within itself the sources of its own self-criticism.

Interestingly enough, the results of Miller's work came to roughly the same thing. In his various studies of American Puritanism, Miller managed to convert a religious creed that only two decades before had been associated with everything bloodless, restrictive, and unreal in American life into an intellectually and morally serious vision of human experience, and one that not only contained the seeds of dissent from its own theological certainties and social authoritarianism but also possessed, withal, an ethically realistic conception of man and a philosophically skeptical view of all forms of political and historical utopianism. Thus whether on Matthiessen's reading or on Miller's, American culture was not, as the saying goes, "wholly without resources," and these resources now took on such an enormous significance in this period of social turbulence and political upheaval because they indicated a capacity resident in American culture to place some of its most central affirmations under radical self-scrutiny.

The problem with Matthiessen's book is that it was even more of a personal testament than Miller's work. Both were out to recover the "usable past," but Miller's methods bore at least some resemblance to conventional notions of the historical, while Matthiessen's methods, albeit literary, possessed a look distinctly their own, which adroitly, to be sure, but in ways difficult to replicate, combined the psychological with the political, the aesthetic with the theological, the intellectual with the social. Clearly, if the study of aspects of culture and society in the United States were to advance from the landmark work of Matthiessen and Miller, it would have to furnish itself with a more conceptually coherent notion of the relation among what might be called, following Leo Marx, expressions of individual consciousness, forms of collective mentality, and the social and institutional structures of lived existence.[6]

3

This is precisely what was sought by the myth and symbol group, a loose designation that refers to a series of scholars including Henry Nash Smith, R. W. B. Lewis, John William Ward, Leo Marx, Charles Sanford, Alan Trachtenberg, Daniel Hoffman, Charles Feidelson, Roy Harvey Pearce, and a number of others. If it has by now become obvious that the members of this group were in no sense interested in establishing any sort of ideological approach to the study of American issues, it is still true that the field of American Studies in the United States achieved the closest thing to a communicable sense of identity under the influence of their work. This work was united less by a common set of methodological commitments than by a common set of methodological aversions. To the degree that their orientation was literary and aesthetic, they sought to challenge the tendency of so much critical study during the 1940s and 1950s to restrict the whole meaning of verbal texts to an analysis of their specific metaphorical or linguistic properties. Instead they remained convinced, and not without considerable warrant, that the "deepest meanings," as Leslie Fiedler called them, of even the most self-consciously composed verbal forms, "extend beyond the single work to a whole body of books, and [especially in the case of imaginative literature] are to be sought in the archetypal symbols to which succeeding writers compulsively turn."[7] To the extent that their orientation was more historical and social, they intended instead to resist the temptation to define ideas in isolation from the actual circumstances to which they are a response, without falling victim to the corollary notion that ideas are but the mere extension of such circumstances. Their intention, in other words, was to transcend the rather brittle distinctions then in use between social fact and aesthetic value by exploring, through what Henry Nash Smith called a method of "principled opportunism,"[8] ways of reintegrating them.

Smith himself was to furnish probably the best statement of their central assumption when he claimed, in the preface to the first edition of *Virgin Land,* that the terms *myth* and *symbol* describe "larger and smaller units of the same kind of thing, namely an intellectual construction that fuses concept and emotion into an image." Like most of these scholars, Smith was concerned with myths and symbols that were not the product of individual minds only but of collective thinking as well, and he was quick to add that he was in no sense disposed to view such collective representations merely as direct reflections of empirical fact. "They exist," Smith maintained, "on a different plane. But as I have tried to show, they sometimes exert a decided influence on practical affairs."[9]

In a subsequent review of Smith's book, Alan Trachtenberg shrewdly observed that Smith's formulation established too rigid a distinction between myth and symbol on the one hand and empirical realities on the other. The problem with this dualism, as Trachtenberg pointed out and Smith later conceded, is that the mind and the environment are always in what Smith was eventually to call "continuous dialectic interplay."[10] Furthermore, as Smith was to note in the second edition of *Virgin Land*, his original way of putting this distinction overlooked, or at least discounted, the way "our perceptions of objects and events are no less part of consciousness than are our fantasies."[11] The real issue, then, was not simply to differentiate those events that are mental from those that are not but to clarify the way imaginative constructions contribute to the formation of social behavior and social experience colors the nature of the communal as well as the individual life of the imagination.

This, in brief, is what Smith and others like him set out to accomplish: to overcome the split between fact and value by showing how symbolic constructions, in this case images and myths laden with value associations, impinge upon the world of empirical fact, or, as Smith put it, "exert a decided influence on practical affairs." They do so, Smith maintained, because myth and symbols are able to fuse into collective images both cognitive and affective cultural meanings that allow these images to operate simultaneously on different planes of existence, such as the public and the private, and to integrate different spheres of experience, such as the refined and the popular. The intellectual challenge of this approach was simply to explain how, within social and cultural forms, such interactions and integrations occur without reducing all social behavior to symbolic action or treating every cultural symbol as though it were a material substance.

Yet the excitement Smith's book and others were to generate derived less from the fact that they formulated a credible historical argument than from the fact that they also mounted a serious critical one. Their primary interest was not in isolating and defining, as it were for their own sake, cultural patterns that somehow succeed in unifying disparate levels of personal and social existence, but in determining what such patterns are good for interpretively, which is to say, experientially. Thus these books generally proceeded as though the intellectual purpose of the field should be perceived, not as it is now in so much American Studies scholarship, as a demonstration of the existence and scope of particular cultural patterns, but as an assessment of their relative degrees of blindness and insight, as an evaluation of their hermeneutic usefulness in relation to the social and political as well as existential circumstances of their significance.

This becomes immediately obvious as soon as one examines the actual structure of their arguments. Take *Virgin Land,* for example, where Henry Nash Smith was not content merely to trace the historical origins, development, and eventual collapse of the myth of the Garden of the World in various spheres of nineteenth-century life and thought, but attempted, in addition, to gauge the interpretive adequacy of this myth in relation to everything from the social history of the settlement of the West to the literary evolution of the genre of the Western. Or consider *The American Adam,* by R. W. B. Lewis, which was devoted to considerably more than the impact of the Adamic myth on the nineteenth-century debate about the possibilities for experience in the New World but went on to evaluate this myth of heroic innocence in relation to the discoveries about human nature and destiny in nine-teenth- and twentieth-century America that it both did, and did not, enable. Or, again, think of Leo Marx's *The Machine in the Garden,* which went well beyond an explanation of how the classic writers of the nineteenth century used pastoral conventions to mute the threat of industrialism to explore whether, in the present century, pastoralism is capable of serving any longer as a symbolic strategy for dealing with the social and economic situations represented by the world of late industrial capitalism. The question each of these studies posed was not "How does this pattern of collective experience conform to large con-figurations of American culture conceived as a whole?" but "What difference did it make, or may it have made, to various Americans at particular historical moments and in specific social situations that col-lective portions of their experience could be patterned in conformity with these larger symbolic and mythic configurations?"

Insofar as this was cultural study, then, its purpose was no less revisionary than historical. It assumed that the aim of American Studies was neither analytic merely (to examine the nature of cultural forms and define the historical linkages that permit them to be com-bined into larger systems of meaning) nor phenomenological (to de-lineate the experiential dimensions cultural forms acquire because of the qualitative character of their systematic relationships) but diagnos-tic and, in the largest sense, corrective: to explain what these forms do, and do not do, both to and for the people whose forms they are, and thus to help free those blessed with the opportunities of historical hindsight from at least some of what Hayden White once called "the burdens of history."[12] The purpose of the field—indeed to return to my earlier locution, "the point of it all," as the myth and symbol scholars understood it—was to increase comprehension of the historical potentialities and liabilities of different ways of construing the relationship between consciousness and society.

4

But Leo Marx was among the first of the myth and symbol critics to realize that the field of American Studies could not proceed with this work of intellectual assessment until it supplemented its generally adequate theories of individual and collective symbolic expression with a more rigorous and nuanced theory of society.[13] For if society is not simply to stand for what, to go back to Smith's 1969 preface to *Virgin Land,* is there described as "the [realm of] extramental historical reality discoverable by means of conventional scholarly procedures," then American Studies needs a more systematic and credible way of explaining the relationship between those institutional structures that organize social behavior and the cultural formations of meaning by which these same patterns of behavior are made sense of and lent significance. And such a concept of society is particularly necessary, Marx contends, if one believes that a fundamental task of this interdisciplinary form of historical and cultural study should be not merely to measure the difference that certain ways of interpreting make, or could make, to social behavior, but conversely, to determine the restrictions that socially sanctioned patterns of order and experience place upon the kinds of cultural interpretations that can be made of them, or, for that matter, of anything else.

Marx's recommendation was prophetic. By the later 1960s and early 1970s, particularly in the wake of a heightened national consciousness of everything from the rights of minorities, the differences between regions, and the diversity among ethnic, racial, and sexual groups to the United States' involvement in, if not interdependence with, countries as distant culturally as well as geographically as Vietnam, Saudi Arabia, and South Africa, the focus of this group of critics began to appear too selective. Though their scholarship had always exhibited a certain wariness toward all claims about the uniqueness of American cultural patterns, and though in the writings of Smith, Marx, Miller, Charles Sanford, and Howard Mumford Jones they had done their fair share of comparative study, their books had been published during the period when America's postwar ascendancy was undergoing its first set of serious challenges internationally, and it was perhaps inevitable, though in some sense regrettable as well, that their writing should have become tainted with the sense of exceptionalism that came then so sharply under attack. But the problems associated with the characteristic method of approach of these scholars had something to do as well with the extensiveness of their critical program and particularly with their ability to put their own methods, not to say their own insights, in question.

Not surprisingly, this charge was first brought against the myth and symbol school by those new inter- or cross-disciplinary forms of study cognate with American Studies that began to appear during the same period and that acquired much of their momentum from a reaction to the selective narrowness supposedly epitomized by the myth and symbol school itself. These new curricular and intellectual configurations, which were sometimes new only in the sense of their recent recognition, included Amerindian or Native American Studies, Afro-American Studies, Popular Culture Studies, Women's Studies, and a host of more specialized subfields from geographical designations such as Southern Studies, New England Studies, or Northwestern Studies to more discrete ethnic designations like Chicano Studies, Asian American Studies, or Eskimo Studies. It should be noted that this exfoliation of programs and fields cognate with American Studies occurred simultaneously with the development or refinement of a host of new methods in the human sciences generally, from topophilia, or the phenomenology of space, to semiotics, or the theory of signs. What is worth remarking is that so many of these newer methodologies, like so many of the newer forms or fields of study they helped spawn, either encouraged or, more likely, depended upon cross-cultural comparison, and virtually all of them exploited what could be called a hermeneutics of suspicion in relation to all monolithic claims about American culture and its uniqueness. For example, the title adopted by most black studies programs in the United States, Afro-American Studies, insisted upon the comparison and contrast of cultures and peoples from several different continents, and it would be hard to conceive of what something like Women's Studies could become if it did not promote the analysis and assessment of the experience of women both synchronically across cultures as well as diachronically within them.

This hospitality toward a more comparative and critical, even revisionist, approach to the study of peoples and their experience within culture and society, an approach that would begin to permeate the American Studies movement as these newer methods and cognate fields began to register their presence in the world of scholarship, would gain further impetus from research done simultaneously within American Studies itself in various regional specialties. The most spectacular results of these regionalist studies were probably achieved by scholars working on the history and culture of the South, where it became clear, as C. Vann Woodward was to put it in *The Burden of Southern History,* how regional studies might serve as an important check and balance, if not a remedy, for national studies. Southern Studies of necessity dealt with a subject that lent itself to comparison with other sectional experiences like those associated with the North and the West, but this is by no means all that Woodward intended to suggest. He also meant that detailed examination of the experience of particular geographical and cultural regions within the United States might prove a corrective for the myths that had been fostered about the United States as a whole. If, for example, it could be argued that the most conspicuous traits of our national character have been formed, as David Potter argued, by economic abundance, or instead as Arthur M. Schlesinger maintained, by our experience of success, or again as R. W. B. Lewis proposed, by our obsession with moral innocence, or yet again as Tocqueville speculated, by our free institutions, or, finally, as Thornton Wilder once suggested, by our lack of connection, our indifference to place, our rootless mobility and remoteness, then the experience of the South, Woodward reasoned, presented a sharp contrast. In contradistinction with the myths of American opulence, success, innocence, freedom, and abstraction, the South, at least in relation to its historical consciousness, presented an image of poverty, failure, moral culpability, semifeudal servitude, and veneration of the local, the concrete, and the provincial.

But if the work of Woodward and others was slow to push American Studies scholarship towards a realization of how the study of discrete elements within the national experience elicited a comparative perspective, then research on transnational institutions like slavery in the writings of David Brion Davis, or on imperialism in the work of Robin Winks, or on ideology and myth in books by Edmundo O'Gorman and Howard Mumford Jones, was to encourage American Studies scholars, still more slowly, to begin probing relations between the United States and other hemispheric, European, and even Third World countries and cultures, and in a way that might shed a more searching and more discerning light on official cultural nostrums and academically sanctioned traditions of understanding.[14]

It is scarcely necessary to add that American Studies scholarship still has an enormous distance to move in the direction of reconceiving itself as a field that is at once critical and comparative, cross-cultural and revaluative. American Studies has yet to contemplate how it might reorganize itself in behalf of an attempt to come to terms with, and lend due weight to, all the cultural, ethnic, and racial strains of meaning that make up the mosaic of experience within its own national borders. The field has an extraordinarily long way to go before it will be in a position to comprehend what it might mean to reconstitute itself in relation to the ligatures and strictures, not just historical and geopolitical but also ideational and sensible, that bind it to cultures and societies beyond its own borders. In order for that work to proceed conceptually and methodologically, that is, in order for the cross-cultural challenge to be met critically within American Studies, I believe that the field needs to develop a more sophisticated understanding of what cultures consist of and of how they change. For this understanding to emerge, I further believe that it will prove necessary to develop, as Leo Marx has suggested, a more complex model of the relationship between culture and society, and this will entail reformulating the central subject of inquiry in American Studies in terms that are at once more valuational and more political.

5

Social anthropologists like Clifford Geertz and social critics like Kenneth Burke have already made considerable headway in clarifying our notions about culture and its primary offices. For Geertz, as for Burke, culture consists of systems of symbolic meaning that serve an essential functional or heuristic purpose. Designed as they are instrumentally, these systems help us survive our contacts with the environment by interpreting them, that is, by translating them into construable signs so that we can not only better negotiate these relationships but also add the experience of other people to our own.

One point that has been noted about such systems by Geertz, Hayden White, and others is that they arrange their symbolic interpretations not only horizontally but also vertically, by assigning to each a somewhat different value or quality in the general scheme of things. Thus to experience the world or life in terms of the signs or symbol systems of which cultures are composed is, essentially, to experience the hierarchies of significance in relation to which they organize the various components of life or reality. A second point is that such systems often possess only a tangential relationship to the social patterns they are devised to comprehend and often to legitimate. Geertz explains this by saying that if culture and society are interdependent, they nonetheless remain independently variable. By this he means that if the systems of meanings that comprise culture are in continuous interaction with the patterns of action that compose society, culture and society still operate according to distinctive principles of organization and therefore exhibit a tendency to move in different, sometimes even opposed or contrary directions. Cultures are integrated in terms of logico-meaningful relations, societies organized in terms of causal-functional relations, and this explains for Geertz the frequent incidence of discontinuity and disjunction between them.

But this formulation seems to leave unanswered the question so often raised in cultural study: namely, how can culture and society so consistently influence one another even when they are moving in different, if not conflicting, directions? In fact, it tends to remove cultural meanings from the sphere of social influence altogether, and just at a time when, in the study of many contemporary cultural forms, we have come to realize how culture itself contributes to social processes, how, indeed, cultural meanings and values are often among the most important elements of social production itself.

Here is where the work of social theorists like Raymond Williams, Arnold Hauser, and Theodor Adorno has proved so helpful. What they have repudiated is the notion that cultural meanings can be studied in the abstract—either as belonging to a realm of absolute or universal values, or as related to a body of material in which human thought and experience have been specifically recorded, or in terms of the social patterns and institutional structures in which a particular way of life has been essentialized. Any adequate analysis of culture, they argue, requires detailed study not just of each of these various elements but of the active relationships among them; it will, in short, attempt to discover the nature of the organization "which is the complex of these relationships."[15] But Williams has been particularly insistent that cultural study should not be restricted solely to the nature or principle of the organization as such, but to the nature or principle of the organization *as experienced*—"the particular living result of all the elements in the general organization."[16] This "living result," according to Williams, will be expressed in what he calls "a structure of feeling," which is simply another term for "meanings and values as actually lived," or the "affective elements of consciousness and their relationships."[17]

For Williams and many other radical social and cultural theorists, from Antonio Gramsci to Frank Lentricchia, the single most important clue to the way these affective elements combine to furnish an experience of the interaction, even symbiosis, of culture and society is provided by the notion of hegemony. Hegemony simply refers to the lived system of meanings and values in any culture that become reciprocally confirming the more they are experienced as practices. Another way of putting this would be to say that hegemony projects a view of culture as the lived domination and subordination of particular concerns that are not always associated with, but never wholly dissociated from, the hierarchies of significant values that differentiate one class or group from another and often serve the interests of some at the expense of the interests of others. To introduce the concept of hegemony into cultural study is not, then, as certain of its detractors maintain, to reduce cultural study to another form of political science but rather to compel students of culture to raise new questions about what might be called its politics of organization. For what the concept of hegemony does is to remind us that cultural meanings, however protected their status in enclaves of inherited or acquired privilege, cannot be divorced from "the whole lived social process as practically organized by specific and dominant meanings and values."[18]

If cultures are thereby unified, or at any rate integrated, by "structures of feeling" that bind people together by furnishing them with meanings that permit them, and in many cases compel them, to reorganize their experience in relation to valuational gradients, such structures, and the practices they encourage or enforce, have little to do with whether the members of that society have thought or undergone the same thing. They have solely to do with the interpretive resources at the disposal of individual members of that society that help them make meaningful sense of such matters by redefining their relations with one another in relation to the hierarchies of significance such sense implies. But this would suggest that the subject of investigation in American Studies therefore needs to be reconstrued. The real subject of American Studies should be the structure of experience within culture by means of which certain relations of dominance and subordination are socially maintained in the name of meanings and values that are at least emotionally, if not cognitively, acknowledged as alternatives within a distinctive but always developing range of possibilities.

Understanding the American experience, then, like any cultural experience, requires something quite different from an analysis of its qualities and attributes and the way those qualities or attributes are related one to another on some horizontal spectrum. Understanding any cultural experience, including the American, involves an understanding of those qualities in the lived or felt context of their relations, that is, in terms of the whole implied system of hierarchically arranged, hegemonic modalities of which this or that expression or pattern of behavior is but one variant.

6

Among the many recent works in American Studies that seem to exemplify this new awareness—one thinks immediately of such texts as Sacvan Bercovitch's *The American Jeremiad,* Donald Mathews's *Religion in the Old South,* Eugene Genovese's *Roll, Jordan, Roll,* Richard Slotkin's *Regeneration through Violence*, and George Forgie's *Patricide in the House Divided*—Alan Trachtenberg's *The Incorporation of America* is particularly instructive. Trachtenberg's book carries the study of what the subtitle calls "Culture and Society in the Gilded Age" to a new plateau by showing how changes in the organization of society affected the constitution and ethos of culture. Trachtenberg generally means culture in the broad sense, as the way of life and of construing life in a whole society. The change with which he is most centrally concerned occurred in the reorganization of American economic existence, but its effects were to far transcend the restructuring of business practice and the extension of the market economy throughout the nation. This revolution in the life of industry and business was to alter perceptions of American society itself, and of many of its most dominant features, through the creation not only of new hierarchies of governance and esteem but also of new modes of conceiving and valuing them.

It was William Dean Howells who first realized that the institutional development of the modern corporation during the years following the Civil War had insinuated itself into the very forms of cultural perception in America, but no one before Trachtenberg, to my knowledge, has managed to demonstrate concretely, and in various spheres of social and cultural experience, how perceptions and feelings were thereby altered, and with what consequence. There have been numerous studies of the corporate form of business organization and its association with such related developments as the spread of industrialization, the rise of the metropolis, the revolution in transportation, the advances in communications, the growth of the applied sciences, the deepening of secularization, the restructuring of American family life, the transformation of the practice and purpose of politics, and so much more; but the impact on beliefs and values of incorporation itself has always been slighted.

The reasons for this oversight are not hard to locate. For one thing, the pressure exerted by the reorganization of American economic institutions on the mental and emotional life of most Americans took place far out of sight, in a region of sensibility and sentiment often masked to its participants and typically beyond the reach of many of the methods of historians. It was expressed not so much in words and deeds as in the tropes, metaphors, and images by which people struggled to understand and cope with such things. For another, the process of cultural incorporation proceded frequently by way of conflict and contradiction, as Trachtenberg points out. The spread of the corporate system in business, as in politics or education or even the realm of civic display, engendered opposition at the level of familiar values that was only slowly and subtly overcome, and the nature of what triumphed can only be fully gauged by measuring the style as well as the substance of the antagonism, by appreciating the quality as well as the content of the resistance.

Trachtenberg's topical approach to his subject is admirably suited to this kind of investigation. In each of his seven chapters he explores a different aspect of social life in the Gilded Age, from the close of the frontier and the mechanization of American industry to the development of "machine" politics and the rise of genteel culture. Within each chapter, he moves back and forth between the level of myth, of popular cultural perception, and the level of institutional change, where the creation of a new economic order altered the relationship between everything from capital and labor to creator and consumer. Just as each chapter opens with the way a set of images was fused into a relatively new and socially idealized concept—the West, the Machine, the Chautauqua Movement—so each chapter closes by looking closely at one or more cultural forms in which the conflict between idealized concept and new material and institutional rearrangements was refracted and in some sense played out.

In this light, The *Incorporation of America* may look like any other study associated with the myth and symbol school. Trachtenberg insists, for example, that the figurative material "by which people represent their perceptions of themselves and their worlds" is of fundamental historical importance not only because it functioned in this period as a primary vehicle of self-understanding but also because it constituted a historical force in its own right and operated like any other component of the public world, "often coloring perceptions in a certain way *even against all evidence*" (italics mine).[19] What sets Trachtenberg's book apart is that it shows how changes in other elements of the public world in the Gilded Age impinged upon and transformed figurative representations themselves. Incorporation fundamentally revised, in some cases even remodeled, American thinking and feeling in this era, and nowhere was that transformation more clearly visible than in the altered conception of America itself.

Incorporation as a cultural process changed the conception of America by raising new questions about who "owned" its symbolic as well as physical properties and thereby who possessed the right to define and control them. As Trachtenberg relates, the controversy that arose during this period over the meaning of the word *America* was expressed in everything from nineteenth-century historiography to the formation of urban policy. It could be seen in the conflict between the coalition of farmers, laborers, and radicals known as the Populists and the Republicans who were swept into office with McKinley in the election of 1896, no less than in the debates surrounding American industrialization and the cultural images that were attached to legendary inventors and entrepreneurs such as Thomas Edison. It could be detected in the discussion surrounding the new theory of American fiction known as realism and in the emergence of that new institutional expression of middle-class refinement and genteel learning known as the Chautauqua Movement. But it was perhaps most dramatically expressed in the subjects that constitute the first and last chapters of Trachtenberg's book. The first deals with how the American West, both as symbol and as material resource, was incorporated into the new reinterpretation of American history known as the "frontier thesis," but only as the West, as Trachtenberg notes, had been seized from the Indians through figurative as well as literal acts of violence. The second focuses on the World's Columbian Exposition of 1893 in Chicago and its famed White City, which Trachtenberg brilliantly interprets as an image of the America of the future now unified by and expressive of the trinity of property, money, and genteel culture.

These two chapters that frame the book are significantly related by the fact that Frederick Jackson Turner first expounded his thesis about the Western frontier at a meeting of the American Historical Association, which was held in conjunction with the Exposition. Still more important, the real intention of his address, even if it wasn't fully apparent to Turner himself, was to explain how the West could remain a source of the values that define America even after the territory it described had been officially closed. The question with which Turner was faced, according to Trachtenberg, was how to justify the importance of the frontier experience in the new world of the American metropolis when the advent of the latter was supposedly being heralded in the classical architectural arrangements of the White City. Turner's answer, at least implicitly, was that if the frontier no longer existed as a physical fact, it still endured as a symbolic one. The legacy of the frontier was still accessible in those American character traits that had already been symbolically associated with the world of westward adventure—rugged independence, pioneer fortitude, nervous energy, inventive genius, and so on—and these traits were precisely what Turner, as so many others, thought were needed to equip the visitors to the White City to meet the challenges of an urban future organized, defined, and controlled by corporate America. Representing the material as well as figurative alliance of business, politics, industry, and high culture, the White City merely domesticated these nineteenth-century pioneer character traits by providing an architectural occasion and forum for their coordinated interaction and civilized glorification.

In such terms as these, then, *The Incorporation of America* presents a fresh interpretation of the integration of culture and society in the Gilded Age. It effectively challenges the image of the era as the age of the robber baron, of individualism run rampant, by demonstrating that in fact the age yielded to an almost opposite—and much more modern—image of social and personal organization. And it thereby suggests that, far from culminating one historical period, the Gilded Age actually inaugurated another. But in relation to the contemporary challenges facing the field of American Studies itself, *The Incorporation of America* accomplishes considerably more. Where most other studies of the same type would have concentrated on determining the effect of cultural perceptions on social actions and institutional developments, Trachtenberg succeeds in suggesting how this procedure may be reversed: through an assessment of the consequences that new social and institutional formations have had, and continue to have, on cultural modes of thought and feeling.

Trachtenberg prefers to describe this kind of cultural criticism as "critical cultural history," referring not only to a historical consciousness that is oppositional but also to one that redefines the political task of criticism itself. Drawing upon the work of Adorno, Benjamin, and others, Trachtenberg asserts that "the task of criticism must not be so much to search for the particular interest-groups to which cultural phenomena are to be assigned, but rather to decipher the general social tendencies which are expressed in these phenomena and through which the most powerful interests realize themselves. Cultural criticism must become social physiognomy."[20]

The key term in this reformulation of the enterprise of cultural criticism is not *criticism* but *culture*. And culture is not merely an extension of the literary and aesthetic or a higher order of generality than the social. Culture refers to a different subject matter than the literary and defines a distinctive process within the social. Rather than expanding the literary, culture "effaces it"; instead of mirroring the social, culture particularizes, complicates, and deepens it. Culture is that putative totality of social experience which continually subverts our tendency to foreground and reify specific objects of perception by displacing "the immediately given fact with the profoundly mediated process" by which it comes to us, by replacing "the fact with its network of relations."[21] In effect, culture is that network which, as Trachtenberg remarks, though "always present in its totality," is "rarely apprehended except in its partiality."[22]

This view of culture in turn helps to clarify for Trachtenberg the meaning of the word *text*. Texts are never encountered, "except under those figurative laboratory conditions some of our literary criticisms have deceived themselves into believing they have approximated," independent of those relations that bind them "to other texts, other discourses, other practices."[23] All texts are mediated, or "translated," as Clifford Geertz describes it,[24] and such mediations occur not in the abstract but in that most concrete of relational networks which we refer to by the term *reading*. But a reading that is "cultural" is very different from a reading that is literal or even "literary." Not that culture itself can't be construed as a text, but only that the text of culture does something radical to the text "pure and simple":

> "Culture" distances the reader from the "text" pure and simple—and calls attention to what is absent, the missing mediation of the text's history, or as we might put it, the texture of transactions by and through which we know it as a cultural artifact. Thus does culture replace the familiar literary object with an unfamiliar reading, replacing a determinate fact with an indeterminate and continuing process, the aim of such a distanced reading being not to understand the presumed text in its presumed autonomy, but the network of relations into which the cultural text subsumes and reconstitutes the literary text.[25]

The text as a formalization of a set of determinate meanings is re-placed with the text as a historicization of a set of determinate read-ings. "Rather than sharing a subject matter with literary criticism," Trachtenberg concludes, "cultural criticism can be said to de-reify that subject matter, bursting through disciplinary boundaries in order to recover the text both as social experience and as social knowledge: as 'history' in the most concrete of senses."[26]

History in this sense is but another name for politics. However, the politics in question has little to do with parties and platforms and everything to do with sentiments and sensibilities. It is, in fine, the politics of culture, which, as Lionel Trilling noted nearly half a century ago, is the only kind of politics that interests us in the modern era— "the organization of human life toward some end or other, toward the modification of sentiments, which is to say the quality of human life."[27] The American Studies movement has shown that this is no longer a matter of power and privilege, as Trilling conceived it, but also of symbolism and semiotics, and when privilege and power become sym-bolism and semiotics, the cultural critic must practice what Clifford Geertz has described as "the wariest of wary reasonings on all sides of all divides, to get it right."[28]

8

Recent Criticism and
the Sediments of the Sacred

It could easily be argued that a chronicle of the relations between literature and religion, at least in the West, constitutes a history of spiritual
displacements. The first displacement occurred, as Erich Auerbach and
Northrop Frye have taught us, when the mythic structures that formed
the earliest content of Western literature gave rise to fictive forms that
undermined the religious authority of those structures by constituting a
kind of secular substitute for them.[1] The second took place when the
secular forms that had displaced sacred myth were themselves displaced
by fictive forms that sought to become an almost sacred alternative to
secular literature. And now it appears that literature, as it was once
conceived, may be on the verge of displacing itself in the direction of a
kind of critical writing, whether imaginative or discursive, that functions, as it were, seismographically to register these geological shifts
along the spiritual fault line of our culture and react to them.

It is, of course, quite difficult to pinpoint these displacements with
any accuracy, but it is generally conceded that the first occurred some-
time after the Middle Ages, with the humanization of such ancient
ritual forms as epic, tragedy, and comedy and the spectacular rise of

the novel; the second became evident when the personal lyric supplanted the public poem and the consciousness of the artist became
more important than the content of his art; and the third began to
appear when self-reflexivity, long having become an artistic end in
itself, proceeded to turn self-critical, even to turn itself inside out, in
an effort to discern whatever it is that such constructs of consciousness
both bring into focus and screen out from view.

The point to be noted is that wherever one enters this history of
displacements, one still finds traces of the sacred, and this deposit of
sacred traces has not failed to attract the attention of recent critics.
Indeed, if anything marks the difference between criticism of the fairly
recent past and criticism of the more distant past, it is not that the first
is less interested in religion than the second but rather that the first is
far more willing than the second to pursue this interest to extraordinary lengths. To confirm this, one need only consult a survey of recent
theoretical trends such as Frank Lentricchia's *After the New Criticism*.

Lentricchia begins his overview of the critical schools and approaches that have succeeded one another so rapidly in the postwar
period with Northrop Frye and his magisterial attempt to overcome the
subjectivism of the several variants of Anglo-American formalism by
reorganizing the study of literature in terms of what Frye defends as
the more scientific structure of myth and archetype. But when literature is defined, as in Frye's criticism, as displaced myth, myth can be
reinterpreted essentially as displaced belief, and then all the imaginative postulates of faith and commitment will seem to acquire their
origin, or to derive their justification, as they largely do for Frye, from
the Christian Bible, a text he tends to view as sacred and not secular
because, despite its immense complexity and diversity, he sees it as
unified anagogically by the single archetypal image of Jesus as the
Christ.

From Frye and myth criticism Lentricchia then quickly moves to
several versions of existentialism, where the category of religion reappears—in, for example, the conservative fictionalism of Frank Kermode's *The Sense of an Ending*—as the imaginative quest for an idea
of order, or Supreme Fiction, that can console us, at least for the time
being, in the present poverty of our experience as inhabitants of a
desacralized and open-ended world.

But almost before Kermode can flesh out all the new spiritual linea-
ments suggested by this Stevensesque religion of the imagination and its
explorations of "the intricate evasions of as," Lentricchia sees it being
supplanted by versions of phenomenology, in which the category of the

religious reappears in the guise of the unifying presence or consciousness of the artist, what we might call the creative cogito, that not only permeates all its expressive creations and makes of them a single act of sovereign intention but simultaneously compels their interpreter to undertake in response a quasi-religious act of self-effacement.

This version of phenomenology is most often associated with the work of Georges Poulet and also with the earlier writing of J. Hillis Miller, who brought Poulet's work, and that of the other Geneva critics, to the attention of many American readers. But it was Martin Heidegger and some of his followers who eventually pushed phenomenology much further. In Heidegger's work and that of his disciples, the category of religion is reintroduced into literary discussion in a way that very nearly swallows it: the work of art is reconceived as an act of revelation that accomplishes, through the presencing of the artist's own consciousness in his forms, a disclosure of the ethos, even the pathos, of Being itself.

But long before phenomenology in any of its several expressions could obtain a secure foothold in America, Lentricchia points out, it was seriously challenged and largely overthrown by a theoretical orientation known as structuralism. Structuralism simply repudiated the phenomenological obsession with the divine or human knower in favor of coming to terms with the deeper structures of experience, primarily semantic and semiotic, underlying it. The structuralists therefore relocated the religious in those elemental linguistic grammars or codes that we use to stabilize experience by inscribing it, that is to say, by textualizing it, and with the help of which we eventually make sense of such textually inscribed experience by, accordingly, learning how to read it, that is to say, to decipher it.

Yet the hegemony of structuralism could last only so long as critics and scholars failed to probe the stability either of the cultural texts so inscribed or of the codes and grammars in which they were written. But once it became clear that all cultural texts are relatively unstable, that all textual codes and grammars are comparatively indeterminate, then structuralism gave way to a more deconstructive concern, as it is usually defined, with what does, or just possibly doesn't, exist not only beneath the structures of consciousness but also beneath the structures that underlie them. Deconstructionists and poststructuralists alike speak of what opens out below such constructs, undermining the epistemological privilege they presuppose, as an abyss of meaning or meaninglessness that can only be reached through critical acts of de-centering, dismantling, demystification.

At this point, however, the category of "religion" or "the religious," albeit in negative form, slowly works its way back into criticism and begins to subsume all others. It does so through the operations of deconstructive criticism itself as they conspire to show how all categories, like all meanings, participate in the process of demolition and decreation within the text itself, a process that the critic merely joins rather than engenders and that moves in the direction of a seemingly ultimate emptiness, an infinite nothingless, an absolute undecipherability. Yet it is precisely here, in the adjectival modifiers that must almost of necessity be employed to characterize this negative ontological space—"ultimate," "infinite," "absolute"—that this contemporary critical mode, by all appearances most antipathetic to religious concerns, begins to swerve in another direction, a direction not unlike the movement Northrop Frye first detected in advanced modernism itself, the movement from an extreme irony back toward religious myth, the oneiric source.

Taken by themselves, these critical shifts and alternatives may attest to no more than the fickleness of modern critical fashion, or the uncertainty and nervousness that attend the practice of contemporary critical theory, but in the context of this discussion they point to something additional. Whatever is meant by the term, and however it comes into play and affects the outcome of such discourse, the category of religion is no mere superfluity in current critical controversy but one of its principal enablers and chief elements. Even in those most radical and revisionist reconceptions of the critical enterprise, there is an obsession with the problem and possibility to which religion attests: the existence of modalities of experience that remain ultimately unconditioned by what is now called either the privileges of perception or the predispositions of power. Yet there is more. The current fascination contemporary critics exhibit with sacred traces, which is often coupled with a complete indifference to the traditional inheritances of organized religion, represents a form of oblique but nonetheless dramatic testimony to the interrelations that have existed between literature and religion since the time of their earliest association, when literature took its rise from sacred myth and found some of its initial uses in religious rites. But their associations have remained intimate and intricate long after the period in which literature served as a medium of revealed truth or a component of religious ritual and have much to tell us about some of the more improbable ways that they have been brought into conjunction recently. Though the story of their relationship has been subject to frequent intellectual distortion and theological misinterpretation in the past, it nonetheless comprises an important chapter in the history not only of modern literary scholarship but also of contemporary critical discourse.

1

It could be easily demonstrated, I believe, that many literary genres and traditions, from medieval allegory and seventeenth-century metaphysical poetry to American transcendentalism, developed explicitly as outgrowths of religious traditions, and that forms of literature as various as Elizabethan tragedy, Romantic poetry, and the theater of the absurd continue to presuppose religious notions or to raise religious questions even when they make no obvious reference to inherited traditions of religious belief. Modern literary historians and critics have been particularly sensitive to the ways that various literary conventions, from the heroic couplet of the eighteenth century to the unreliable narrator of modern fiction, draw on, and consequently need to be interpreted by, religious conceptions; within the last several decades literary scholars have utilized a variety of critical methods, from the New Criticism to deconstruction, that either presuppose a theory of reality, or are presumed to yield insights, that can only be described as ontological as well as aesthetic. Thus while much contemporary literature exists at a considerable intellectual and emotional remove from orthodox religious tradition, and while most modern scholars have little interest in turning their criticism into a vehicle for theological discussion, still religious concerns and issues remain at the center of a surprising amount of critical discussion today.

It is therefore all the more curious that in contemporary critical forums this area of interest has so often been misunderstood or discounted, even by those who have contributed to it in important ways. Among many of its strongest advocates, for example, there exists the largely specious belief that the critical importance of the study of these interrelations is confined largely to the modern period and that the most significant work in this area of inquiry has been done almost exclusively by Anglo-American scholars drawing on the contemporary modest theological legacy of European existentialism. Among many of its most skeptical critics, on the other hand, there exists the no less dubious conviction that the study of literature and religion holds no real intellectual interest beyond the Jewish and Christian households of faith, where it exists primarily to permit those already committed to religion either to confirm their own beliefs or to repudiate the beliefs of others.

The difficulty on both sides has been provincialism. Those sympathetic to the study of literature and religion have often failed to realize that its scope extends far beyond the boundaries of apologetic theology to the theory of aesthetics and culture on the one hand and to literary history and the history of ideas on the other. Those suspicious of this field of inquiry have been largely insensitive to the important connection—which, though consequential, has not always been obvious—between the development of scholarly interest in the relations between literature and religion and the religious crisis of cultural modernism itself. Where proponents of this study have often lacked sophisticated understanding of those formal and structural properties of literature that legitimate its religious analysis in any age, critics of this area of study have frequently been insensible of those spiritual factors that, at least since the Renaissance, have lent particular urgency to the religious analysis of literature in the present age.

The relations between literature and religion thus tend to be far more varied and complex than is often imagined. Just as evidence of an interest in such relations can be found in almost every age of Western history, so the serious study of these relations has been pursued for a host of motives and has taken a diverse set of forms. Literature has been viewed by some, from Sir Philip Sidney to Leo Tolstoy and T. S. Eliot, as a way of confirming or at least of shoring up belief. It has been viewed by others, from Alexander Pope and Jonathan Swift to Miguel de Unamuno and Jean-Paul Sartre, as a way of challenging and even disconfirming belief. It has been conceived by still others, from Longinus to Percy Bysshe Shelley and Paul Valéry, as a way of preparing for or inducing belief. Literary classics as different as the *Gilgamesh* epic, *Beowulf, El Cid,* the classic tale from China known in English as *The Journey to the West,* Dante's *Divina commedia,* and the eighteenth-century Chinese novel *The Dream of the Red Chamber* have been variously interpreted as legitimating religious values and commitments, reconceptualizing them, repossessing them, relativizing them, defamiliarizing them, confounding them, and even, whether intentionally or not, undermining or supplanting them. And when one moves to texts whose cosmological and anthropological orientation is less overt but no less decisive, to texts like Giovanni Boccaccio's *Decameron,* Lady Murasaki's *The Tale of Genji,* the *Chanson de Roland,*

and Geoffrey Chaucer's *Troilus and Criseyde,* the relations between literature and belief become even more subtle and perplexed.

Equally manifold as the conceptions of literature's relation to belief have been the conceptions of belief itself, and religion's general relation to culture. By belief some critics and scholars have meant only those ultimate but most often subconscious commitments that find expression in individual works; still others have meant simply those largely unconscious or only half-conscious concerns that constitute the general worldview or metaphysical frame of mind that particular texts, like whole traditions, seem to reflect. The great majority of scholars have confined their understanding of belief to the body of insights contained in the great historic faiths, such as Judaism, Christianity, Islam, Buddhism, and Hinduism, but a sizable and influential minority have directed their attention instead to forms of belief that are theologically heterodox or metaphysically irregular, and not a few have been preoccupied chiefly with modalities of belief that lack any assured name, that seem to originate not from within institutions and dogmas as such but rather from within those unnameable experiences that lie somewhere back of them.

This diversity of conception and practice has raised numerous and still unanswered questions about exactly where the religious component is supposed to be found in literature and how it is to be defined. Should the religious factor in literature be associated strictly with traditional doctrine, or should it also be extended to encompass heretical desire? Are the most characteristic attributes of religion to be identified with specific ideas about God, man, and the cosmos that are expressed in works of literature, or with generic actions like penance, adoration, or rebirth that are represented by works of literature? And how is the religious component to be made accessible to critical scrutiny? Are we to understand it as being reflected in the themes of literature, dramatized by the motifs of literature, enacted in the structures of literature, inscribed in the forms of literature, or deposited in the languages of literature?

To these and other queries there are no certain or fully satisfactory answers; there is only the elaboration of further issues, which leads to continued debate. But the debate, at least among those who do not view this subject as ideologically privileged, has by now produced a measure of intellectual consensus, if not about those issues that have been finally resolved, at least concerning those issues that are worthy of more extensive discussion and refinement. These issues can be summarized as follows:

1. Literature and religion, at least at certain times and in certain ways, have been historically related in fact and conceptually related in theory. Hence to deny or overlook the nature and significance of their interrelations would be to cut oneself off from a portion of the meaning of each. To put this more emphatically, it is as misguided to suppose that one can understand, say, the literary heritage of the West dissociated from the variety of religious assumptions, doubts, and aspirations that underlie it as it is to presume that one can comprehend the manifold complexity of the Western religious experience without examining the literary as well as liturgical, doctrinal, and ecclesiastical forms in which that experience has been refracted.

2. While there is a certain propriety in raising theological questions about works of literature (so long as one does not assume that all works of literature provide answers to such questions or that all the questions works of literature raise are inherently theological), the discipline of theology does not provide any special methodological access to works of literature, and the religious meaning of works of literature cannot be reduced to a specific set of doctrines.

3. If literature and religion belong to the same universe of meaning, they nonetheless constitute and inhabit that universe in somewhat different ways. Literature, it might be said, employs meanings heuristically, to show where they lead by adumbrating the figurative or fictive if not actual consequences they possess; religion employs meanings more parabolically and paradigmatically, to show where they came from by clarifying the order of significance they entail.

4. If literature and religion are thus made of the same cultural material—namely, meanings—and serve the same experimental function—to help us understand and negotiate our relations with our environment through acts of symbolic intervention—then the study of both in conjuction, as of each individually, is a form of cultural studies that offers no immunity from the methodological demands and constraints placed on all other students of culture.

2

In the light of these several areas of agreement that now furnish the basis for further discussion among most scholars and critics who explore religious approaches to literature, it seems fair to conclude that literature and religion so often coexist in the same verbal space not only because we need them—we can scarcely manage our relations with the otherness of our surroundings without them—but also because in a certain sense they need each other. Religious institutions, ideas, and values may be said to provide us with those basic paradigms of experience by which we define the nature of that otherness of our circumstances and attempt to bring our lives into some measure of useful interaction if not of conformity with it. Works of literature then take upon themselves the role of exploring some of the latent as well as the manifest dimensions of those paradigms so that we can grasp their more disturbing, or at least more significant, potentials and eventually, perhaps, effect some mode of accommodation to them. And works of literature typically perform this function, which is at once mimetic and mithridatic, by organizing those dimensions into an encompassing structure whose essential purpose is to cast new light on what might be called their existential nature by clarifying the alternative kinds of imaginative response that can be made to such paradigms.

This means that the relation between literature and religion is in no sense merely additive or complementary but deeply symbiotic—literature is more than, as Charles Baudelaire once said, a metaphysics made sensible to the heart and expressed in images—but its operation is far more subtle and complex than is generally supposed. Religious paradigms function in actual experience only as a kind of "court of last resort," a court that, while essential to the structure and well-being of the entire judicial system, is rarely called into session until all appeals to lower courts dealing with less ultimate matters have been thoroughly exhausted. Therefore, we constantly need to confirm the operational status of these paradigms and to determine their range of control over the constantly changing, often confusing field of contemporary experience. This is one of the offices performed by works of art: their purpose is to help us know what we feel about these paradigms, and feel what we know, by illuminating the implications of what they conceal as well as disclose, of what they disguise as well as express. Another office performed by works of literature is to determine when these paradigms no longer make sense of the actual or possible shape of our experience and to propose, where necessary, through the imagination of altered images of order, how they might be changed. Still another office is to decide what it means when paradigms die, and if need persists for the kinds of consolations they once provided, to furnish us with alternative paradigmatic models— what Wallace Stevens once called "fresh spirituals"—to take their place.

3

If we confine ourself for the moment to the Western literary tradition, it is possible to argue that literature has been related to religion in at least three structurally distinctive ways and that these three ways tend roughly to parallel major shifts in the spiritual history of the Western imagination. From the time of classical antiquity to the Renaissance, literature in the West for the most part exhibited a complementary, if not deeply supportive, relation to inherited religious traditions. In some instances, such as medieval miracle plays like *Mystère d'Adam* or the Chester and Wakefield cycles, which grew out of liturgical drama and dealt with biblical stories and motifs, or later morality plays such as *The Castle of Perseverance* and *Everyman,* which deal with personified abstractions of virtues and vices who contend for man's soul, literature served directly as an allegorical representation of religious ideas and feelings that were explicitly Christian. In other instances, ranging from classical epics like the *Iliad,* the *Odyssey,* and the *Aeneid* to medieval and Renaissance romances like *Sir Gawain and the Green Knight* and Edmund Spenser's *The Faerie Queene,* literature provided a form for the exploration, articulation, and revivification of religious conceptions and sentiments by displaying their fusion with contemporary social, political, and aesthetic beliefs. In either case, however—and one could add examples ranging from Sophocles' *Oedipus at Colonus* through Sir Thomas Malory's Arthurian tales to late Renaissance works like John Bunyan's *Pilgrim's Progress* and John Milton's *Samson Agonistes*—literature served to valorize religious ideals and values, whether Christian or pagan, by replicating in its structures no less than its themes both the premises of religious faith and the forms of religious experience.

Toward the end of the Renaissance, however, a major shift of emphasis occurred. Where before works of literature had tended to defend and reify traditional systems of faith and experience, now they began to challenge and dispute them. One can see this shift as early as the late Middle Ages with the new emphasis on courtly love—the romances of the twelfth-century French writer Chrétien de Troyes epitomize the type—and the new spirit of humorous, secular impiety introduced into the literature of romance through the French tradition of the fabliau, which was so successfully exploited by Chaucer in *The Canterbury Tales.* But the new critical spirit toward conventional religious ideas and feeling also found its way into the mainstream of Western literature through such tributary routes as the tradition of

Renaissance prose, in such works as Erasmus's *Encomium Moriae*, Sir
Thomas More's *Utopia*, Michel Eyquem de Montaigne's *Essais*, and
Francis Bacon's *Advancement of Learning*, and also through the Renaissance translations of such modern and ancient classics as Baldas-
sare Castiglione's *Cortegiano*, Plutarch's *Lives*, and Livy's *Ab urbe
condita libri*. These influences, coupled with the expansion of knowledge precipitated by Renaissance voyages of exploration and discovery, were eventually to alter entirely the relation between imaginative
literature and traditional religious understanding, allowing some
writers to conceive of literature as a criticism of inherited orthodoxies
and paving the way for others to turn literature into an instrument for
subverting them. Works that criticize forms of religious orthodoxy run
from the comedies of Molière to the romances of Nathaniel Hawthorne, from Voltaire's *Candide* to Mark Twain's *The Adventures of
Huckleberry Finn*. Works that intend to undermine conventional religious ideas and feelings include texts as different as Denis Diderot's *Le
Neveu de Rameau* and Herman Melville's *The Confidence-Man*, Baudelaire's *Les Fleurs du mal* and the novels of Thomas Hardy.

The third great shift in the structure of relations between literature
and religion did not become perceptible until the end of the eighteenth
century. Where before these relations had been either complementary
or oppositional, the Romantic movement introduced in a massive way
the idea that literature might become an alternative to or substitute for
religion. This view gained adherents throughout the nineteenth century
among writers as different as Novalis and John Keats, or Shelley and
Friedrich Nietzsche, but it was not until the end of the century, in the
poetics of French symbolist writers like Stéphane Mallarmé and in the
criticism of Victorians like Thomas Carlyle and Matthew Arnold, that
the conception of literature as a kind of surrogate or displaced religion
began to achieve public acceptance. This is the view that characterizes
Gustave Flaubert's *Madame Bovary* no less than James Joyce's *Portrait
of the Artist as a Young Man*, Rainer Maria Rilke's *Duineser Elegien*
no less than Arthur Rimbaud's "Une Saison en enfer," Thomas
Mann's *Doktor Faustus* no less than the later poetry of Wallace Stevens. The act of writing becomes the search for what Stevens calls
"Supreme Fictions" that for the time being will suffice, and the satis-
factions these fictions afford seem ironically to increase the more we
are made aware of their purely imaginative as opposed to empirical
basis.

There are, of course, numerous historical exceptions to this classificatory scheme. Certain strains of literature have exhibited an adver-

sary relation to inherited religious traditions for at least as long as there have been literary modes like tragedy and comedy, and other strains of literature have sought to substitute for approved traditions of faith and sensibility ever since the advent of courtly romance in the late Middle Ages and the reappearance of utopias in the early Renaissance. Just as works as different as Aeschylus's *Agamemnon,* Aristophanes' *The Frogs,* Jean Baptiste Racine's *Phédre,* Pedro Calderón's *La vida es sueño,* Christopher Marlowe's *Tamburlaine,* Johann Wolfgang von Goethe's *Faust,* and Feodor Dostoevsky's *Crime and Punishment* all attest to the sense of a gap, and very often a chasm, between the way life is supposed to be legitimated by culture religiously and the way life is experienced by the individual existentially, so works of romance and fantasy as various as Ludovico Ariosto's *Orlando furioso,* Luis Vaz de Camoes's *Os Lusiadad,* Francis Bacon's *The New Atlantis,* William Morris's *News from Nowhere,* and Aldous Huxley's *Brave New World* all presume to bridge that gap by formulating idealized alternatives to the historic relations between humankind and nature, between society and civilization.

However, the more significant limitations of this typology come about not because there are notable exceptions to its tripartite structure but because most literary texts of any religious complexity at all will incorporate several of these structural tendencies simultaneously. An excellent example is afforded by the poetry of T. S. Eliot. According to this schema, one would expect Eliot's poetry, at least in its most experimental modes, to exhibit a tendency to displace conventional religious notions with heterodox conceptions of its own devising. Yet as most of its more astute critics have demonstrated, Eliot's poetry seems to do just the opposite. Instead of subverting and displacing inherited religious beliefs, Eliot has apparently found a way of repossessing them and thus of giving them a new valorization in the present. The difficulty with this view is that it fails to account for the great power of religious disturbance in Eliot's verse and for the fact that the poetry is most disturbing religiously precisely where it is more, rather than less, dependent on traditional religious imagery. The explanation for this paradox lies not in the nature of the traditional symbols Eliot uses but in the untraditional uses to which he puts them. His verse can appear theologically conservative to some and theologically innovative to others because his interest is neither in reviving certain religious symbols nor in displacing them but in getting beneath and behind them, in evoking a sense of what they once signified in experience before the strangeness and disruptive energy of their initial meanings became domesticated through incorporation in an inherited mythological or theological framework.

But this complexity of religious structure is not restricted to modern works like the poetry of T. S. Eliot or W. B. Yeats; it can also be found in texts of more ancient vintage that are assumed to be interpretively stable, like Cervantes's *Don Quijote.* The irony is that Cervantes's great novel is not stable at all. To the eighteenth century, for example, the novel represented a critique of all religious and idealistic enthusiasms and a defense of the world of fact and reason. To the nineteenth century, by contrast, it constituted a defense of imaginative and religious ideals and criticism of the world of prosaic fact. And now in the twentieth century the novel is read in both ways: as an attack on all human idealisms and also as an indictment of the mundane. But again something seems missing from these interpretations, namely, a satisfactory explanation for the strange and beautiful power of the novel's tensions, contradictions, and conflicts in all their combinatory force. Cervantes's genius, even his religious genius, seems to derive from his ability to hold in tension precisely what these various traditions of interpretation would split apart: a desire to valorize the place of religious and moral idealisms even as he ridicules the lengths to which they can be carried, and a concern to challenge the claims of all vulgar materialism while upholding the sacred integrity of the actual and the ordinary. The result is a novel in which a new and unquestionably unorthodox meaning is given to the Christian understanding of incarnate life, and even to the Christian doctrine of the Logos, or Word made Flesh, but in a form that radically resists all theological and moral reductionisms.

4

Modern study of the interrelations between literature and religion has not emerged in anything like a self-conscious, systematic fashion. The motives propelling such study, the forms it has assumed, the significance attributed to it—all have been too various to reveal much in the way of a consistent pattern of development. Any adequate historical survey would have to trace the subject's origins at least as far back as the second edition of Giambattista Vico's *Scienza nuova* (1744), where, for the first time, the imaginative, or what we would call the fictive, was conceived as a generic category of human consciousness, of which the ultimately true and the merely poetic were but species, and the way was cleared for the development of a sympathetic understanding of myth and fable as expressions of the lived experience of a people. It would need to account for the manner in which Johann Gottfried von Herder, especially in *Ideen zur Philosophie der Geschichte der Menschheit,* took up this challenge by arguing that poetry is the essential language of humanity and poets the most representative authors of any nation. It would be obliged to trace the enlarged role of the aesthetic in human spiritual affairs, from David Hume's "Of the Standards of Taste" and Immanuel Kant's *Kritik der Urteilskraft* to Friedrich Schiller's *Über die ästhetische Erziehung des Menschen,* Georg Hegel's *Phänomenologie des Geistes,* and Samuel Taylor Coleridge's *Biographia Literaria.* And it would necessarily have to come to terms with the way the intersections of the aesthetic and the religious took on new clarity and centrality in the major works of the great nineteenth-century historians from Jules Michelet and Alexis de Tocqueville to Jacob Burckhardt and Hippolyte Taine.

If we restrict our attention to the present century, we can discern some pattern in the rise and fall of various critical schools, emphases, and orientations. In the 1920s, for example, new humanists like Irving Babbitt and Paul Elmer More encouraged an interest in the religious dimensions of literature that was decidedly ethical, even moralistic. A nonsectarian species of moralistic platonism provided the basis of all sound literature and culture, they assumed, and this ethical monism expressed itself for Babbitt in his stress on the importance of classical restraint, for More in his emphasis on the realization of human imperfection. Less than twenty years later the American New Critics, following one side of T. S. Eliot, shifted discussion of the religious elements of literature from the moral plane to the aesthetic. The literary work comes closest to religion, they argued, in formal terms, by reenacting the Christian model of the Incarnation through the artist's sacrifice of him- or herself to the materials of his or her craft.

No more than ten years after, with the arrival of existential and phenomenological theories from the Continent, the religious dimensions of literature were being discussed in terms that were explicitly ontological rather than moral or aesthetic. Under the influence of Martin Heidegger, critics were talking about the work of art as a form of disclosure—actually an unveiling—of Being itself, the artist becoming a kind of sacred visionary or intermediary for the divine. More recently, with the ascendance of structuralist and poststructuralist theories of art, the religious dimensions of literature have been reinterpreted in semantic or semiotic terms. The religious element of individual works of literature, as of whole strains or traditions, are now to be found, if anywhere, either in the linguistic codes out of which all verbal statements are made or in relation to the larger system of signs that compose culture as a whole.

Where it has exhibited any modicum of critical self-awareness, modern study of the relations between literature and religion has developed in several overlapping stages, each expressing itself in a distinctive set of forms and each characterized by a set of methodological orientations. The first stage began in the late 1920s and reached its prominence just before World War II. Its achievements were in the main the work of clergy rather than academics, though their influence carried over from the cloister to the university and even to the wider provinces of literary life. During this initial stage, two kinds of concern dominated the study of literature's relation to religion. Where liberal theological tendencies predominated, the study of literature became important to religious understanding for pastoral or therapeutic reasons. Literature was examined for its diagnostic or educative merits, either to help Christians comprehend the existential dilemmas of the world around them or to prevent Christians from being taken in by some of the palliatives of their own doctrines. Where conservative tendencies were more powerful, literary study was of religious use for dogmatic or prescriptive reasons. Literature was studied for its evaluative or apodictic merits, either to dramatize the problems of a life without faith or to serve as a propaedeutic for life within faith.

The second stage in the modern study of religion and literature developed shortly after World War II and continued unabated well into the mid-sixties. During this stage, and owing in equal measure to the influence of existential philosophy on Protestant theology and the rediscovery or revival of older models of traditional historical scholarship, critical study became dominated by concerns that were either broadly apologetic and correlative or essentially historicist. The apologists valued literature for its ability to give concrete and enduring expression to the great themes and motifs of Western religion and thereby to lend fresh theological relevance to aspects of the Judeo-Christian heritage. The historicists tended to value literature as a repository of the manifold religious inheritance of the West and therefore attempted to restore individual works to those concrete historical traditions that constitute a portion of their contemporary meaning. Thus while the apologists appreciated literature chiefly for the religion in it, the historicists appreciated religion chiefly for the literature of it.

The last, or third, stage began in the middle or late 1960s, when still newer philosophical currents—phenomenology, structuralism, hermeneutics, post-structuralism—made themselves felt, first in Europe and then in America (English criticism still seems comparatively untouched by these movements). In this period study of the relations between literature and religion focused on issues that are either generic or, in the broad sense, anthropological. Among those concerned with generic issues, critical interest has centered on determining the nature of literature (and writing in general) as part of a larger system of meaning and thus on finding spiritual residues sedimented or inscribed in the very being of language. Among those whose orientation is more anthropological, critical interest has centered on the nature of the human animal as that creature which not only makes the literature it needs but needs the literature it makes. Where the generic critic has operated as a kind of cryptographer whose business is to break down complex linguistic codes into their cultural components, the anthropological critic has functioned as a kind of ethnographer looking for traces of the human in the strange behavior of verbal forms.

5

Modern scholarship devoted to the relations between literature and religion has taken a variety of forms and employed a galaxy of methods. If one separates the methods somewhat artificially, it is apparent that until quite recently they were largely dictated by the forms taken by scholarship itself, and these forms have in considerable measure mirrored the historical patterns of literature's relation to religion. Hence one can loosely differentiate modern critical studies that treat literature as a valorization of religion, modern studies that view literature as a criticism of religion, and modern studies that interpret literature as an alternative to or substitute for religion.

Modern studies of literature as a valorization of religion have been for the most part historical and formal in orientation, focusing on literary traditions where religious themes, feelings, and assumptions have been valorized, or on literary techniques and structures that have made such valorization possible, or on writers for whom such valorization has been of paramount concern. Modern studies of literature as a criticism of religion have been predominantly philosophical or theological. They have either focused on the epistemological and ontological factors responsible for literature's critical view of religion, or on ethical and theological issues that have been the target of such criticism, or on the consequences such criticism possesses for an understanding of religion and morality. Modern studies of literature as a displacement of religion have been either structural or broadly mythographic and metaphysical in orientation. Where structural interests have predominated, attention has been directed toward those new modes of expression in which such literary displacements or substitutions have occurred. Where mythographic or metaphysical interests have been stronger, emphasis has been placed on the deviant or irregular worldviews on which such displacements and substitutions have been based.

But again a caveat is in order. Describing the general critical orientation that characterizes these several ways of studying the relationship between literature and religion in modern scholarship is not the same as isolating and defining the specific methods that modern scholars have used in analyzing this relationship. Scholars working in this interdisciplinary area have included New Critics, neo-Aristotelians, myth critics, Freudians, Marxists, Croceans, Burkeans, historicists, philologists, linguists, and many other modern types, but their distinctive methodological commitments can perhaps best be delineated in relation to the theoretical coordinates of the mimetic, the expressive, the rhetorical, and the formal-semantic. Thus religious interpretations of literature that concentrate on the writer's vision of experience have drawn on expressive and mimetic critical theories and have accentuated those factors influencing the writer's beliefs, whether expressed or implied, that have enabled him or her to constitute the world according to certain specifiable metaphysical principles. Religious interpretations of literature that examine instead the meaning and import of individual texts or of whole traditions have employed critical theories that are mimetic and rhetorical, seeking to draw out the implications of assertions made within the work or tradition either for the personal realm of individual belief and conduct or for the more public realm of social thought and action. Religious interpretations that probe literature's nature and function in human experience tend to fall back on rhetorical and formal-semantic critical theories, attempting to connect the sorts of things literature is purported to be—whether a kind of statement, gesture, or event—with the effects it is presumed to have, either on the psychoreligious makeup of individual readers or on the socio- and politicoreligious organization of particular reading publics. Finally, religious interpretations of literature that study the genetic lineage or generic identity of particular texts or kinds of texts have relied on critical theories that are both formal-semantic and mimetic and have tended either to situate literature within an anatomy of other, similar kinds of objects, forms, and techniques or to define the ontology of its linguistic and grammatical components.

In recent years these classic theoretical designations have given way to newer methodological orientations. The structuralist approach, whether of the Prague School associated with Roman Jakobson, Jan Mukarovsky, and N. S. Trubetzkoy, the Russian formalist school associated with Boris Eikhenbaum, Mikhail Bakhtin, and Victor Shklovsky, or the French school associated with Claude Lévi-Strauss, Roland Barthes, and Gérard Genette among others, is now the new mode of the formal-semantic and mimetic orientation. The phenomenological approach, deriving from the philosophy of Edmund Husserl, Martin Heidegger, and Maurice Merleau-Ponty and associated with the work of Roman Ingarden, Georges Poulet, Jean Starobinski, and the early J. Hillis Miller, has become the new mode of the expressive and mimetic orientation. The hermeneutic approach and its subsequent development into the poetics of the imagination on the one side and the aesthetics of reception on the other, originating in the modern period in the work of Wilhelm Dilthey and Hans-Georg Gadamer and now associated in the theory of interpretation with the work of philosophers like Paul Ricoeur and Mikel Dufrenne and in the theory of reception with Constance critics like Wolfgang Iser and Hans Robert Jauss, has replaced the mimetic and rhetorical orientation. And the poststructural or deconstructive approach, strongly associated with the Paris group loosely organized around Jacques Derrida, Michel Foucault, and Jacques Lacan and represented in this country by critics like Paul de Man, Joseph N. Riddel, and J. Hillis Miller, is the new conflation of the formal-semantic and mimetic orientation.

6

If the greatest problem confronting this field of study in the past was its susceptibility to subversion from within, the greatest challenge confronting it in the future may arise from its vulnerability to subversion from without. The danger in the past came from the theologization of criticism and the dogmatization of religion. Literary study was turned into a branch of theology and literary experience reduced to a dramatization of doctrines and rituals. At its worst the assumption that theology could provide the categories of literary interpretation and that religious dogmas could define the structures of literary experience produced a serious confusion of categories. Writers as self-consciously agnostic, even atheistic, as Samuel Beckett, Albert Camus, and Franz Kafka were turned into crypto-Christians, while writers as religiously unorthodox as Gerard Manley Hopkins, Ignazio Silone, and Nathaniel

Hawthorne were converted into spokesmen for the church. Even at best this assumption created the false impression that the whole of literature's relation to the sacred could be comprehended in theological as opposed to ethical, aesthetic, or sociopolitical terms.

With this problem now widely acknowledged and generally overcome, this field of inquiry is currently endangered by the elevation of criticism itself into a new hierophantic mode. This possibility currently poses a serious threat to all the newer critical orientations, but it seems particularly dangerous among those who want to couple criticism's new visionary status with a wholesale attack on the literary and cultural inheritance of the West. This eschatological mood in criticism has produced mixed results. In its most extreme form, it has reduced all writing to the level of a hostile act and turned criticism in general into a kind of higher pathology whose mission is to diagnose and, if possible, to eradicate the disease called literature. In more moderate form, it has merely made scholars and critics more self-conscious about the cultural and the metaphysical entanglements of their own methods and has raised long-neglected and sometimes essential questions about the nature and effect of literacy, that is, about our simultaneous infatuation with and dependence on scriptable forms.

To be more specific, the new critical dispensation to which all the recent methodological developments have contributed has promoted a more searching examination of the prejudices and perspectives of methods themselves and has sometimes encouraged a new metacritical attempt to unearth the root principles on which methods depend and from which they spring. This metacritical impulse has had—or at least could have—the effect of establishing better communication among specialists in all branches of criticism by encouraging more systematic reflection on the foundations of their particular disciplines and orientations. In any event, such reflection has produced fresh understanding of the extent to which all our interactions with the environment are controlled by linguistic protocols, mediated by symbolic actions and objects, and governed by the cultural endowment. The crucial question yet to be resolved is whether, as some of the advocates of these new methodological orientations contend, all our relations with the environment are wholly determined by the cultural endowment, are absolutely confined to symbolic exchanges, are completely imprisoned within linguistic warrants and prescriptions. For students of the relations between literature and religion, the key issue has become whether or not literature can be viewed in formal terms as representing any sort of challenge to such conclusions: is it possible, in other words,

to reconceive the office of imaginative literature as an instrument capable of propelling us toward, perhaps even putting us in touch with,
larger and more inchoate, though just as real, fields of experience that
we can never subjugate to the forms of our speech, that we can never
subsume within the conventions of language, that we can never domes-
ticate or control through symbolic intervention?

Formulation of an adequate answer to this question will determine
much of the critical relevance of work in this field of inquiry for years
to come and will necessitate theoretical advances on a number of
fronts. Chief among them, perhaps, is greater clarity about the religious assumptions and moral implications of various critical perspectives themselves. Just as all critical orientations afford a certain epistemological privilege, so they also mask an inevitable ideological
prejudice. By what techniques, then, are we to determine their range
of analytic control and assess their measure of interpretive utility and
interest? How are we to guard against making any critical method
absolute without making all methods relative? Are there any criteria
by which we can balance the illumination particular methods afford
against the bias they project?

Increased sensitivity to the respective increments of perception or
distortion associated with specific critical theories will depend in no
small part on development and utilization of more sophisticated models of religion and morality in the interpretation of literature and on a
more refined understanding of the bearing of such related interdisciplinary fields of investigation as literature and myth, literature and
folklore, literature and philosophy, literature and politics, and literature and popular culture. In this regard, conceptual advances in the
humanities have not kept pace with—indeed, in certain instances have
fallen woefully behind—developments in the social and behavioral sciences. Thus while the structuralists and their semantic predecessors
have taught us something about the processes of linguistic encoding in
cultural forms, we know comparatively little about what, for example,
Durkheimian sociology might reveal concerning literature's hieratic
role in the constitution and maintenance of various cultural minorities
and elites. We still have much to learn from Weberian sociology about
the functions played by literary symbols in the process of cultural
world formation and individual self-governance. We have just begun to
absorb what semiotics can teach us about the relations between particular levels and kinds of experience that are integrated within cultural
and religious sign systems. And we lack awareness of the insights
post-Freudian psychology might bring to the relations among the cog-

nitive, the agentic, and the affective in human experience and also into the role of sublimation, transference, and repression in the realm of the aesthetic.

Still another issue awaiting full address is the place and play of theological formulations in religious and cultural traditions. Do theological conceptions operate on any other level of cultural and religious life than systematic discourse? Are they as directly influenced by cultural frames of reference as they claim to be able to influence such frames? When we speak of theological formulations, do we refer only to a certain species of ideas or to a distinctive range of questions? How, then, does theology actually function in various traditions: to verify the existence of certain objects with which its propositions are supposed to correspond, or to determine the implications that certain propositions possess for the reorganization and enhancement of human experience?

Few of those issues can be addressed in the abstract. Their further exploration depends on new historical discoveries by scholars and critics alike. In the future, however, because of what we have learned about both literature and religion, the historical study of their interrelations is not likely to remain intracultural and diachronic but will become more cross-cultural and synchronic, as evidenced in so many of the seminal studies in the area, from Albert Béguin's *L'Ame romantique et le rêve* and E. R. Curtius's *European Literature and the Latin Middle Ages* to Erich Auerbach's *Mimesis*, M. H. Abrams's *Natural Supernaturalism,* and Hans Robert Jauss's *Alterität und Modernität der mittelalterlichen Literatur.* In addition to the insights yielded by their comparative approach, such works as these also suggest that advances in this area are not likely to occur in a wholly logical or incremental fashion, with each new discovery building on those previous and all slowly adding to the sum of our knowledge, but are certain to be more haphazard and revisionary, with new discoveries often challenging the whole store of accumulated wisdom and thus requiring at least a partial reconstruction of the entire tradition of interpretation. But the goal of research in the humanities has always been deepened understanding as well as increased knowledge, and for this purpose fresh starts and new beginnings are often as instructive as final accountings.

7

To sum up, then, as this intellectual interest has moved from the far edges of theology, history, and criticism into the mainstream of literary scholarship, it has brought with it problems and concerns no different from those that confront scholars in any other field of interdisciplinary literary study. What are the forms in which this relationship has occurred in history? How have these forms expressed or reflected the experience of individuals as well as communities? What causes these forms to emerge at certain moments of history, undergo revision at others, and disappear at still others? What does contemporary interest in the evolution, anatomy, and effect of such forms reveal about our own cultural and religious situation? And how may we rescue such forms from historical oblivion and reclaim them as a permanent component of the human endowment?

Underlying each of these questions is an issue that now sits squarely at the center of critical debate both in Europe and in the United States. That issue has to do with the complex grammar of motives that compel what someone has whimsically called our "rage to interpret." Do we interpret to remythologize or to demythologize, to decipher or to deconstruct, to inter or to resurrect? Or do we rather interpret, say, to determine the limits of literacy or instead to absorb the lessons of literary experience?

The usual modern answer to these questions, as formulated by Karl Marx, Sigmund Freud, and Friedrich Nietzsche, is that we interpret in order not to be deceived. The alternative possibility, as stated more recently by philosophers like Martin Heidegger, Gabriel Marcel, Hans-Georg Gadamer, and Paul Ricoeur, is that we interpret in order to be replenished. Where the first has been described as a hermeneutics of suspicion, the second has been called a hermeneutics of restoration. If the former is chiefly concerned with complicating our methods of reading, the latter is more interested in refining our understanding of what is read and of how it can be applied. At the present moment it would appear that we need to supplement—I do not say replace—the diagnostic emphasis of a hermeneutics of suspicion with the heuristic emphasis of a hermeneutics of restoration. What we need, and what a new hermeneutics of restoration would provide, is a study of such colletive expressions of meaning as literature and religion in terms of the ecology rather than the pathology of their relations, that is, in light of the whole—though not necessarily wholly unified—cultural experience in relation to which they were originally construed, and can still be construed, to make sense, even to seem true.

As it happens, there is considerable evidence that these two hermeneutic orientations are at points beginning to converge, and one point where this growing convergence is most obvious is in the study of religion in relation to culture, or, rather, the study of the issue that religion in its relation to culture raises: namely, the existence of modalities of experience that resist complete conditioning, or at least total domination, by what is now called either the privileges of perception or the predispositions of power. As but one example, I cite Edward Said's moving and trenchant eulogy for Michel Foucault, who died, ironically, in the very same hospital that had once served both as source of and scene for his great study of the science of mental illness, which Foucault viewed as one of the chief regulatory and repressive institutions of modern society:

> At the heart of Foucault's work is . . . the variously embodied idea that always conveys the sentiment of otherness. For Foucault, otherness is both a force and a feeling *in itself,* something whose seemingly endless metamorphoses his work reflects and shapes. On a manifest level, . . . Foucault wrote about deviation and deviants in conflict with society. More interesting, however, was his fascination with everything excessive, all those things that stand over and above ideas, descriptions, imitation, or precedent. . . . What he was interested in was, he said in *The Archeology [of Knowledge]*, "the more" that can be discovered lurking in signs and discourses but which is irreducible to language and speech; "it is this 'more,' " he said, "that we must reveal and describe."[2]

Thus Said concludes by remarking of Foucault's prose—and the same could be noted about the prose of other recent theorists—that the "Dislocations, . . . the dizzying and physically powerful prose, the uncanny ability to invent whole field of investigations: these come from Foucault's everlasting effort to formulate otherness and heterodoxy without domesticating them or turning them into doctrine."[3]

By quoting this long passage on Foucault, I do not wish to be misunderstood as building a covert case for a kind of critical reflection about which, as should be abundantly clear from the rest of this book, I possess some very strong reservations; nor do I wish to be interpreted as implying that the future prospects for the study of the ecology of the relations between literature and religion depend upon following the lines of intellectual inquiry laid down by poststructuralism. What I do mean to suggest is that all the recent forms of critical inquiry, from archetypal criticisim to deconstruction, have shared a desire not simply to interpret otherness but, through their own hermeneutic strategies, to keep the sentiment or imagination of it alive. And they have done so, I would submit, because of a widely felt but deeply troubling apprehension, reflected alike in the most searching thought and most disturbing art of our time, that the idea of "the other," like the experience of "otherness," may be the most serious casualty of modern life itself.

This is not the place to attempt to defend such an assertion; here I can only pause long enough to consider some of its implications for my present topic. At the most obvious level of things, I am saying that theories, in this case of literature and criticism, participate in wider forums of experience, in deeper strata of feeling, of which they are sometimes only partially conscious but that they nonetheless work not only to refract but also to reinforce or to revise. On a less obvious level, I am suggesting that these wider forums of experience, these deeper strata of feeling, not only encompass much of what we usually mean by religion in its cultural expressions but actually comprise it. To argue this is not only to make the, by now, relatively innocuous observation that religion, however its priorities are defined, is but one cultural form among others; it is also to insist that, from a cultural perspective, religion is indistinguishable from the actual experience through which the forms of its priority are lived. On a level less obvious still and even closer to the heart of the matter, I am asserting that there is a strange convergence of outlook and approach in that art and thought of our time which move beyond the spiritual solutions of modernism toward not a new immediacy of experience so much as an intractable irreducibility of experience.

Modernism, it might be argued, attempted to save the sensibility of otherness by subsuming it, or, rather, as in the poetry of Wallace Stevens, by converting the experience of otherness into the act of determining the consolations it once provided. Postmodernism, or poststructuralism, or whatever we are to call our current cultural mindset, seeks to salvage the experience of otherness from the putative forms of its expression by submitting those forms to ever more searching scrutiny in the hope that, through the dislocations and deconstructions of inquiry itself, one may discover their element of indecipherability, of incorrigibility, of alterity. This may not be the only way to keep alive the sense and sensibility of otherness in our time, but the symbolic forms that have rendered such experience once again imaginatively plausible surely deserve to be thought of as instances of what John Dewey meant by "severe thought," and the critical attempt to fathom their figurations deserves to be construed as an essential way by which to encourage what he described as its "discipline." Future prospects for the literary and cultural study of religion, no less than for the religious study of literature and culture, depend to a great extent on how deeply this insight is acknowledged and realized.

Notes

Chapter 1

1. Alfred Kazin, *Contemporaries* (New York: Little, Brown, 1962), p. 497.

2. Ibid., p. 496.

3. Ibid.

4. Isaiah Berlin, *Vico and Herder* (London: Hogarth, 1976), p. xvii.

5. Ibic., p. xix.

6. Conor Cruise O'Brien, "The Nationalistic Trend," *Times Literary Supplement*, November 1, 1985, p. 1230.

7. Edmund Burke, *Reflections on the Revolution in France* (London: World Classics, 1950), p. 107.

8. Samuel Taylor Coleridge, *On the Constitution of Church and State*, 3rd ed. (London: William Pickering, 1839), p. 46.

9. John Stuart Mill, quoted in *Mill on Bentham and Coleridge*, ed. F. R. Leavis (1950; London: Chatto and Windus, 1967), p. 105.

10. Ibid., pp. 105–06.

11. Raymond Williams, *Culture and Society*, p. 52.

12. For much of this subsequent discussion I am indebted to M. H. Abrams, "What's the Use of Theorizing about the Arts?" *In Search of Theory*, ed. Morton W. Bloomfield (Ithaca: Cornell Univ. Press, 1972), pp. 44–47.

13. Baumgarten, *Meditationes philosophicae*, quoted in Abrams, p. 44.

14. Abrams, p. 45.

15. Immanuel Kant, *Critique of Judgment*, in *The Philosophy of Kant*, ed. Carl J. Friedrich (New York: Modern Library, 1949), p. 292.

16. Ibid., p. 300.

17. Ibid., p. 301.

Chapter 2

1. Clifford Geertz, "Blurred Genres: The Refiguration of Social Thought," *American Scholar*, 49, No. 2 (Spring 1980), 165–79.

2. John Dewey, *Art as Experience* (New York: Putnam's, 1934, 1958), p. 346.

3. Lionel Trilling, *Beyond Culture* (New York: Viking, 1965). p. xii.

4. Edmund Wilson, Dedication, *Axel's Castle* (New York: Scribner's, 1931).

5. Lionel Trilling, *Sincerity and Authenticity* (Cambridge: Harvard Univ. Press, 1972), p. 1.

6. Lionel Trilling, *The Liberal Imagination* (Garden City: N.Y.: Double-day-Anchor, 1957), p. 89.

7. Ibid., p. ix.

8. Denis Donoghue, "The Zeal of a Man of Letters," *New York Times Book Review*, Sept. 18, 1983, p. 1.

9. Jacques Barzun, "The Imagination of the Real, or Ideas and Their Environment," in *Art, Politics, and Will*, ed. Quentin Anderson, Stephen Donadio, Steven Marcus (New York: Basic Books, 1977), p. 5.

10. *Axel's Castle*, p. 289.

11. Edmund Wilson, *To the Finland Station* (Garden City, N.Y.: Double-day-Anchor, 1953), p. 34.

12. Ibid., p. 317.

13. Ibid., p. 467.

14. *Beyond Culture*, p. 115.

15. *The Liberal Imagination*, p. 54.

16. Ibid., p. 50.

17. *Beyond Culture*, p. 113.

18. Quoted in *The Liberal Imagination*, p. 190.

19. Quoted, ibid., p. 191.

20. Ibid.

21. Ibid.

22. Ibid., p. 258.

23. Quoted, ibid., p. 259.

24. Ibid., p. 260.

25. Ibid.

26. Ibid.

27. Lionel Trilling, *The Last Decade* (New York: Harcourt Brace Jovanovich), p. 157.

28. Ibid.

29. *The Liberal Imagination,* p. 215.

Chapter 3

1. Jacques Derrida, "The Conflict of Faculties," quoted in Jonathan Culler, *On Deconstruction* (Ithaca: Cornell Univ. Press, 1982), p. 156.

2. Walter Benn Michaels, "Walden's False Bottoms," *Glyph,* 1 (Spring 1977), pp. 132–49.

3. Jacques Derrida, *Writing and Difference,* trans. Alan Bass (Chicago: Univ. of Chicago Press, 1978), p. 95.

4. Jacques Derrida, *Of Grammatology,* trans. Gayatri Spivak (Baltimore: Johns Hopkins Univ. Press, 1976), pp. 13–14.

5. Ibid., p. 13.

6. Ibid., p. 14.

7. Jacques Derrida, *Writing and Difference,* pp. 95–96.

8. Ibid., p. 95.

9. Ibid.

10. Ibid., p. 96.

11. Ibid.

12. Ibid.

13. Ibid., p. 95.

14. Ibid.

15. Ibid.

16. Gerald Graff, *Literature against Itself* (Chicago: Univ. of Chicago Press, 1979), pp. 202–04.

17. Hayden White, *Tropics of Discourse* (Baltimore: Johns Hopkins Univ. Press, 1978), p. 98.

18. Ibid.

19. Ibid., p. 91.

20. Ibid., p. 99.

21. John Dewey, *The Quest for Certainty* (1929; New York: Capricorn, 1960), p. 262.

22. Immanuel Kant, quoted in Hannah Arendt, *Between Past and Future* (London: Faber and Faber, 1961), p. 220.

23. Arendt, p. 220.

24. Immanuel Kant, quoted in Arendt, p. 222.

25. In *Power/Knowledge: Selected Interviews and Other Writings, 1972–1977* (New York: Pantheon, 1980), pp. 109–33, Michel Foucault talks as though the institutions productive of truth can, and should, be changed to constitute a new "politics of truth." Of this possibility he writes, "It's not a matter of emancipating truth from every system of power (which would be a chimera, for truth

is already power) but of detaching the power of truth from the forms of hegemony, social, economic, and culture, within which it operates at the present time" (p. 133).

26. See M. M. Bakhtin, *The Dialogic Imagination,* ed. Michael Holquist, trans. Caryl Emerson and Michael Holquist (Austin: Univ. of Texas Press, 1981), pp. 50ff.

27. Suresh Raval, *Metacriticism* (Athens: Univ. of Georgia Press, 1981), pp. 227–34.

28. Gayatri Spivak, trans. and foreward, "Draupadi," by Mahasveta Devi, *Critical Inquiry,* 8 (1981), 382–83.

Chapter 4

1. See Vincent Descombes, *Modern French Philosophy* (Cambridge: Cambridge Univ. Press, 1980), pp. 186–90.

2. William James, *Pragmatism* and *The Meaning of Truth* (Cambridge: Harvard Univ. Press, 1978), p. 34.

3. Ibid., p. 29.

4. Ibid.

5. Michael Oakeshott, *The Voice of Poetry in the Conversation of Mankind* (London: Bowes and Bowes, 1959), pp. 10–11.

6. Ibid., p. 14.

7. Richard Rotry, *Philosophy and the Mirror of Nature* (Princeton: Princeton Univ. Press, 1979), p. 360.

8. Geoffrey Hartman, *Criticism in the Wilderness* (New Haven: Yale Univ. Press, 1980), p. 14.

9. Ibid., p. 41.

10. Ibid., p. 246.

11. See Richard Rorty, *Consequences of Pragmatism* (Minneapolis: Univ. of Minnesota Press, 1982), p. 143.

12. See Barbara Herrnstein Smith, *On the Margins of Discourse* (Chicago: Univ of Chicago Press, 1978), pp. 79–106.

13. John Searle, "The Word Turned Upside Down," *New York Review of Books,* October 27, 1983, p. 78.

14. John Dewey, *Experience and Nature* (LaSalle, Ill.: Open Court, 1929), p. 35.

15. Ibid.

16. Ibid.

17. John Dewey, *Reconstruction in Philosophy* (New York: Holt, 1920), p. 186.

18. John Dewey, *Democracy and Education* (New York: Free Press, 1966), p. 87.

19. Rorty, *Philosophy and the Mirror of Nature,* p. 377.

20. Hartman, *Criticism in the Wilderness,* p. 8.

21. Kenneth Burke, *Counter-Statement* (Berkeley: Univ. of California Press, 1968), p. vii.

22. Frank Lentricchia, *Criticism and Social Change* (Chicago: Univ. of Chicago Press, 1983), p. 51. Lentricchia actually means to argue that all deconstruction is conservative: "Politically, deconstruction translates into that passive kind of conservatism called quietism; it thereby plays into the hands of established power" (ibid.).

23. See in particular *Criticism and Social Change,* pp. 15–19.

24. Ibid., p. 12.

26. Marshall Sahlins, *Culture and Practical Reason* (Chicago: Univ of Chicago Press, 1976), pp. 205–21.

26. Sahlins, p. 221.

27. Kenneth Burke, *The Philosophy of Literary Form,* 3rd ed. (Berkeley: Univ. of California Press, 1973), p. 1.

28. Ibid., p. 304.

29. Ibid., p. 303.

30. Kenneth Burke, *Language as Symbolic Action* (Berkeley: Univ of California Press, 1966), pp. 44–62.

31. The term *grammatological* is here meant in Burke's sense, not Derrida's. Burke's reference is to "the basic forms of thought which, in accordance with the nature of the world as all men necessarily experience it, are exemplified in the attributing of motives." Those forms have to do with some act that occurred physically or mentally, the situation of its occurrence, the individual or individuals responsible for it, the means by which it was performed, and the assumed purpose it was meant to fulfill, and they reduce to Burke's pentad of terms—Act, Scene, Agent, Agency, Purpose.

32. Kenneth Burke, *Terms for Order,* ed. Stanley Edgar Hyman (Bloomington: Indiana Univ. Press, 1964), p. 63.

33. Kenneth Burke, *Attitudes toward History* (Los Altos, Calif.: Hermes, 1959), p. 210.

34. *Terms for Order,* p. 51.

35. Ibid.

36. *Counter-Statement,* p. 183.

37. Ibid., p. 48.

38. Ibid., p. 51.

39. Quoted in Stanley Edgar Hyman, *The Armed Vision* (New York: Vintage, 1955), p. 380.

40. Kenneth Burke, *Permanence and Change* (Los Altos, Calif.: Hermes, 1935), p. 5.

41. *Counter-Statement,* p. 183.

42. Ibid., p. 110–11.

43. *The Philosophy of Literary Form,* p. 302.

44. Ibid., p. 304.

45. Quoted in Hyman, *The Armed Vision,* p. 381.

46. *Attitudes toward History,* p. 344.

47. *Terms for Order,* p. 86.

48. Ibid.

49. *The Philosophy of Literary Form,* p. 65.

50. Kenneth Burke, *Towards a Better Life* (Berkeley: Univ. of California Press, 1966), p. 208.

51. *The Philosophy of Literary Form,* p. 295.

52. Kenneth Burke, "Rhetoric—Old and New," *Journal of General Education,* 5 (April 1951), 202.

53. Kenneth Burke, "Linguistic Approach to Problems of Education," *Modern Philosophies and Education,* ed. Nelson B. Henry (Chicago: Univ. of Chicago Press, 1955), p. 271.

54. Ibid., p. 300.

55. Kenneth Burke, "Freedom and Authority in the Realm of the Poetic Imagination," *Freedom and Authority in Our Time,* ed. Lyman Bryson et al. (New York: Harper, 1953), p. 373.

56. Ibid.

57. "Linguistic Approach to Problems of Education," p. 293.

58. Michael Foucault, *Power/Knowledge,* p. 133.

59. William H. Rueckert, *Kenneth Burke and the Drama of Human Relations* (1963; Berkeley: Univ. of California Press, 1982), p. 161.

60. Ibid., p. 162.

Chapter 5

1. "Why We Read Jane Austen," *Times Literary Supplement,* March 5, 1976, pp. 250–52.

2. Geertz's response was initially prepared for delivery at the Lionel Trilling Memorial Seminar held at Columbia University on February 17, 1977. It was subsequently published as "Found in Translation: On the Social History of the Moral Imagination," *Georgia Review,* 31 (Winter 1977), 788–810.

3. Ibid., p. 799.

4. "Why We Read Jane Austen," p. 251.

5. Clifford Geertz, "On the Nature of Anthropological Understanding," *American Scientist,* Jan.–Feb. 1975, p. 14. In the form in which Trilling encountered it, this essay appeared under the slightly more interesting title "From the Native's Point of View: On the Nature of Anthropological Understanding," *Bulletin of the American Academy of Arts and Sciences,* 28, No. 1, and is reprinted in Clifford Geertz, *Local Knowledge* (New York: Basic, 1984), pp. 55–70.

6. Geertz, "Found in Translation," p. 796.

7. Ibid., pp. 803–04.

8. Clifford Geertz, *The Interpretation of Cultures* (New York: Basic Books, 1973), p. 5.

9. Ibid., p. 91.

10. Ibid., p. 45.

11. Ibid., p. 52.

12. Ibid., p. 218.

13. Ibid., p. 52.

14. Quoted, ibid., p. 77.

15. Quoted, ibid., p. 230.

16. Quoted, ibid., p. 450.

17. Ibid., p. 450.

18. Clifford Geertz, "Art as a Cultural System," *Modern Language Notes*, 91 (Dec. 1976), 1499.

19. Geertz, *The Interpretation of Cultures*, pp. 443–44.

20. Ibid., p. 444.

21. In his brilliant essay entitled "The Symbolic Inference; or, Kenneth Burke and Ideological Analysis," *Critical Inquiry*, 4 (Spring 1978), 507–23, Fredric R. Jameson points to a related but not identical phenomenon when he notes that Burke's dramatistic conception of art as a form of symbolic action helps explain the illusion that every work of art seems to be a response to a context that it has created itself. Stated differently, every text seems to be a response to a subtext of its own invention. Jameson here is doing more than pointing to the ontological priority of context over text; he is suggesting that any cultural object viewed as a text, as a symbolic mode of responding to a situation, brings into being as though for the first time, "that situation to which it is also, at one and the same time, a reaction. It articulates its own situation and textualizes it, encouraging the illusion that the very situation itself did not exist before it, that there is nothing but a text, that there never was an extra- or contextual reality before the text itself generated it" (p. 512). Yet against those who tend to accentuate the dominance of the text over its own subtext in order, presumably, to argue that the text's referent, the situation that provoked it, never existed in the first place, Jameson wants to argue that the situations are in fact real, no matter how much they may be "textualized" by the initial symbolic act, which, as Jameson points out, can't help measuring them in terms "of its own active project" (p. 512).

22. See Eliseo Vivas, *Creation and Discovery*, Gateway Ed. (Chicago: Regnery, 1955, 1965), pp. 109–244.

23. Geertz, *The Interpretation of Cultures*, p. 451.

24. Geertz, "Art as a Cultural System," p. 1478.

25. Ibid.

26. Ibid., p. 1483.

27. Quoted, ibid.

28. Ibid., p. 1488.

29. Ibid., p. 1477.

30. Ibid., p. 1498.

31. Ibid., p. 1499.

32. Ibid.

33. See Jameson, "They Symbolic Inference," pp. 507–23.

34. Geertz, "Found in Translation," p. 803.

35. Ibid., p. 799.

36. Ibid., p. 810.

37. Geertz, "On the Nature of Anthropological Understanding," p. 14.

38. Paul Ricoeur, *Interpretation Theory: Discourse and the Surplus of Meaning* (Fort Worth: Texas Christian Univ. Press, 1976), p. 92.

39. Geertz, "Art as a Cultural System," p. 1499.

40. Clifford Geertz, "The Way We Think Now: Toward an Ethnography of Modern Thought," in his *Local Knowledge,* p. 161.

41. Ibid.

42. Erich Heller, *In the Age of Prose* (Cambridge: Cambridge Univ. Press, 1984), p. 185.

Chapter 6

1. Edward Said, *The World, the Text, and the Critic* (Cambridge: Harvard Univ. Press, 1983), p. 21.

2. Ibid., pp. 21–23.

3. For this discussion I have drawn in part from Raymond William, *Keywords* (New York: Oxford Univ. Press, 1976), pp. 122–23.

4. Matthew Arnold, *Culture and Anarchy* (New York: Macmillan, 1906), p. xi.

5. Ibid.

6. Matthew Arnold, "The Popular Education of France," in *Democratic Education,* ed. R. H. Super (Ann Arbor: Univ. of Michigan Press, 1962), p. 22.

7. Ibid.

8. See John Dewey, *Art as Experience,* pp. 346–49.

9. *Keywords,* p. 76.

10. Ibid.

11. John Dewey, *Experience and Nature,* 2nd ed. (LaSalle, Ill.: Open Court, 1929), p. 326.

12. Barbara Herrnstein Smith, *On the Margins of Discourse* (Chicago: Univ. of Chicago Press, 1978), p. 145.

13. Ibid.

14. Ibid., p. 146.

15. Paul Ricoeur, "The Symbol Gives Rise to Thought," in *Literature and Religion,* ed. Giles Gunn (New York: Harper, 1971), p. 215.

16. William James, *The Varieties of Religious Experience* (New York: Modern Library, 1949), p. 499.

17. The philosopher Henry B. Bugbee makes a similar point in an essay that is oriented more phenomenologically than this chapter. See "Education and the Style of Our Lives," *Profiles* 6, No. 4 (May 1974).

18. Mikhail Bakhtin, *Problems of Dostoevsky's Poetics,* ed. and trans. Caryl Emerson (Minneapolis: Univ. of Minnesota Press, 1984), pp. 6–7.

19. Ibid., p. 7.

20. Ibid., p. 49.

21. Ibid., p. 58.

22. Wayne C. Booth, Intod. to Bakhtin, *Problems of Dostoevsky's Poetics,* p. xxi.

23. Quoted in Tzvetan Todorov, *Mikhail Bakhtin: The Dialogical Principle* (Minneapolis: Univ. of Minnesota Press, 1984), p. 107.

24. Quoted, ibid.

25. Quoted, ibid., p. 94.

26. Ibid., p. 95.

27. Quoted, ibid., p. 96.

28. Ibid., p. 106.

29. Quoted, ibid., p. 108.

30. Quoted, ibid., pp. 109–10.

31. Quoted, ibid., p. 110.

32. See Robert Scholes's chapter entitled "The Structuralist Imagination" in his *Structuralism in Literature* (New Haven: Yale Univ. Press, 1974), particularly pp. 168ff.

33. See Erich Heller, *The Disinherited Mind,* 4th ed. (London: Bowes and Bowes, 1975), pp. 80–88, 296–300.

34. Paul Ricoeur, *Interpretation Theory: Discourse and the Surplus of Meaning* (Fort Worth: Texas Christian Univ. Press, 1976), p. 93.

35. M. M. Bakhtin, *The Dialogic Imagination,* trans. Caryl Emerson and Michael Holquist (Austin: Univ. of Texas Press, 1981), p. 292.

Chapter 7

1. Henry Nash Smith, "Can American Studies Develop a Method?" *American Quarterly,* 9, Pt. 2 (Summer 1957), 297.

2. Hayden White, *Tropics of Discourse* (Baltimore: Johns Hopkins Univ. Press, 1978), p. 81.

3. Perry Miller, *Errand into the Wilderness* (New York: Harper, 1964), p. 185.

4. F. O. Matthiessen, *American Renaissance* (New York: Oxford Univ. Press, 1941), p. xv.

5. Ibid.

6. Leo Marx, "American Studies—A Defense of an Unscientific Method," *New Literary History,* 1, No. 1 (1969), 77.

7. Leslie Fielder, "American Literature," *Contemporary Literary Scholarship,* ed. Lewis Leary (New York: Appleton-Century-Crofts, 1958), p. 170.

8. Smith, "Can American Studies Develop a Method?" p. 207.

9. Henry Nash Smith, *Virgin Land* (New York: Vintage, 1950), p. v.

10. Henry Nash Smith, Preface to the Twentieth Anniversary Printing, *Virgin Land* (Cambridge: Harvard Univ. Press, 1970), p. viii.

11. Ibid.

12. White, pp. 27–50.

13. Leo Marx, "Comment" on "The Aging of America," by C. Vann Woodward, *American Historical Review,* 82 (June 1977), 597. Marx's challenge to the field of American Studies to develop more sophisticated conceptions of "the interaction between cultural formations and the structure of wealth, status, and power" that constitute society is one to which I have attempted to respond in this chapter, and precisely on the grounds elucidated by Marx that if the field "does not commit itself to a concept of social reality distinct from the putative mythologizing of collective consciousness, it is in danger of falling victim to the myths whose illusory character it would expose to view" (p. 599).

14. David Brion Davis, *The Problem of Slavery in Western Culture* (Ithaca: Cornell Univ. Press, 1966); *The Problem of Slavery in the Age of Revolution* (Ithaca: Cornell Univ. Press, 1975); Howard Mumford Jones, *O Strange New World* (New York: Viking, 1964); Edmundo O'Gorman, *The Invention of America* (Bloomington: Indiana Univ. Press, 1961); Robin Winks, *Canada and the United States: The Civil War Years* (Montreal: Harvest House, 1971).

15. Raymond Williams, *The Long Revolution* (New York: Harper, 1966), p. 46.

16. Ibid., p. 48.

17. Raymond Williams, "Literature and Society," *Contemporary Approaches to English Studies,* ed. Hilda Schiff (New York: Barnes and Noble, 1977), p. 34.

18. Raymond Williams, *Marxism and Literature* (New York: Oxford Univ. Press, 1977), p. 109.

19. Alan Trachtenberg, *The Incorporation of America* (New York: Hill and Wang, 1982), p. 8.

20. Alan Trachtenberg, "Comments on Evan Watkins' 'Cultural Criticism and the Literary Intellectual,' " *Works and Days*, 3, No. 1 (Spring 1985), 37.

21. Ibid., p. 36.

22. Ibid.

23. Ibid.

24. Clifford Geertz, "Found in Translation: On the Social History of the Moral Imagination," *Georgia Review* 31 (Winter 1977), p. 788–810.

25. Trachtenberg, "Comments on Evan Watkins' 'Cultural Criticism and the Literary Intellect,' " ibid., p. 37.

26. Ibid.

27. Lionel Trilling, *The Liberal Imagination,* p. ix.

28. Geertz, "Blurred Genres: The Refiguration of Social Thought," *The American Scholar,* 49 (Spring 1980), p. 179.

Chapter 8

1. Northrop Frye's fullest description of this process is probably found in his essay entitled "Myth, Fiction, and Displacement" in *Fables of Identity: Studies in Poetic Mythology* (New York: Harcourt, Brace & World, 1963), pp. 21–38, though the whole of his "Third Essay" on "Archetypal Criticism: Theory of Myths" is devoted to it as well in Frye's *Anatomy of Criticism* (Princeton: Princeton University Press, 1957), pp. 131–239. Erich Auerbach's views on this subject are best represented by *Mimesis: The Representation of Reality in Western Literature* (Princeton: Princeton University Press, 1953).

2. Edward W. Said, "Michel Foucault, 1927–1984," *Raritan Review,* 2, No. 4 (Winter 1985), 5.

3. Ibid., pp. 5–6.

Index